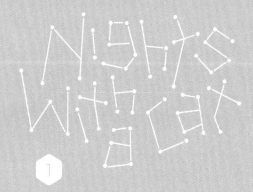

NIGHTS WITH A CAT

1

KYURYU Z

CONTENTS

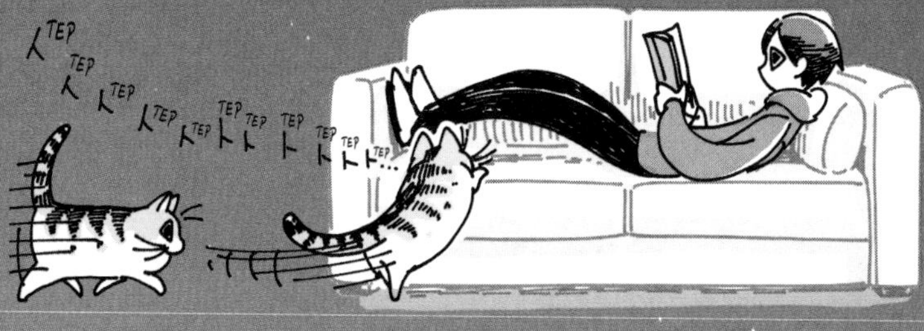
TEP TEP TEP TEP TEP TEP TEP TEP TEP TEP TEP...

The First Three Days with a Cat

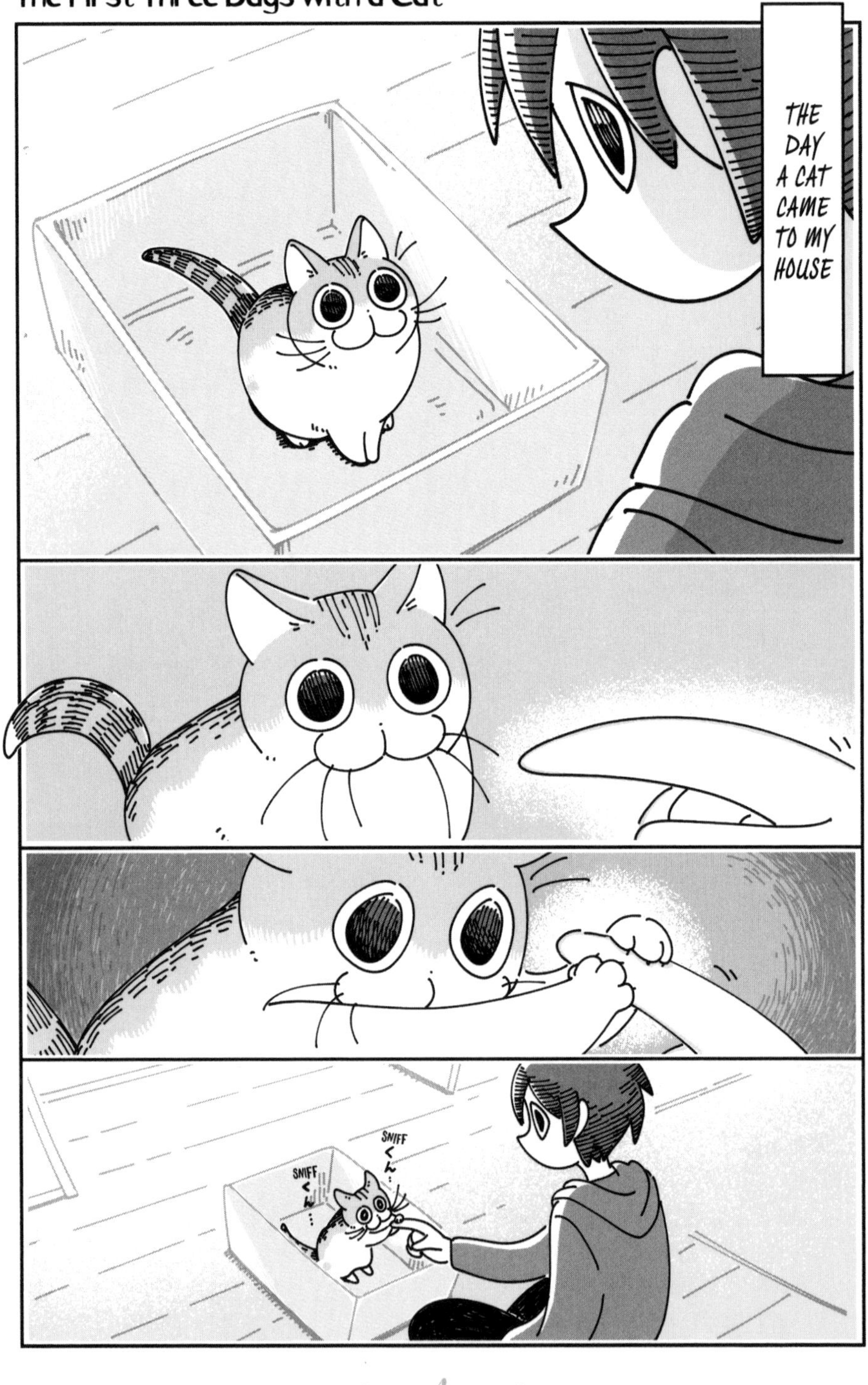
THE DAY A CAT CAME TO MY HOUSE
SNIFF くん…
SNIFF くん…

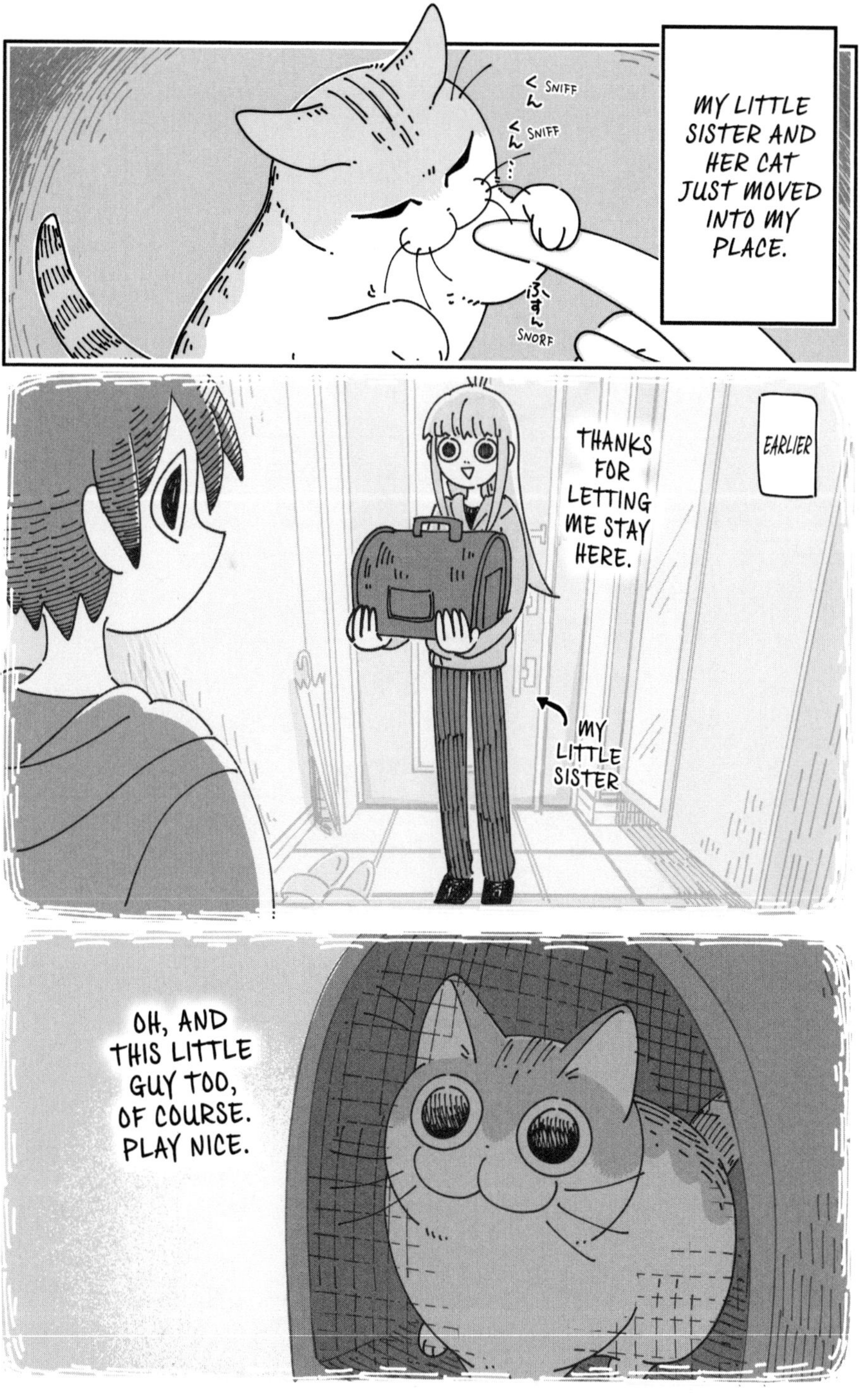
MY LITTLE SISTER AND HER CAT JUST MOVED INTO MY PLACE.
くん SNIFF
くん SNIFF
ふすん SNORF
EARLIER
THANKS FOR LETTING ME STAY HERE.
MY LITTLE SISTER
OH, AND THIS LITTLE GUY TOO, OF COURSE. PLAY NICE.

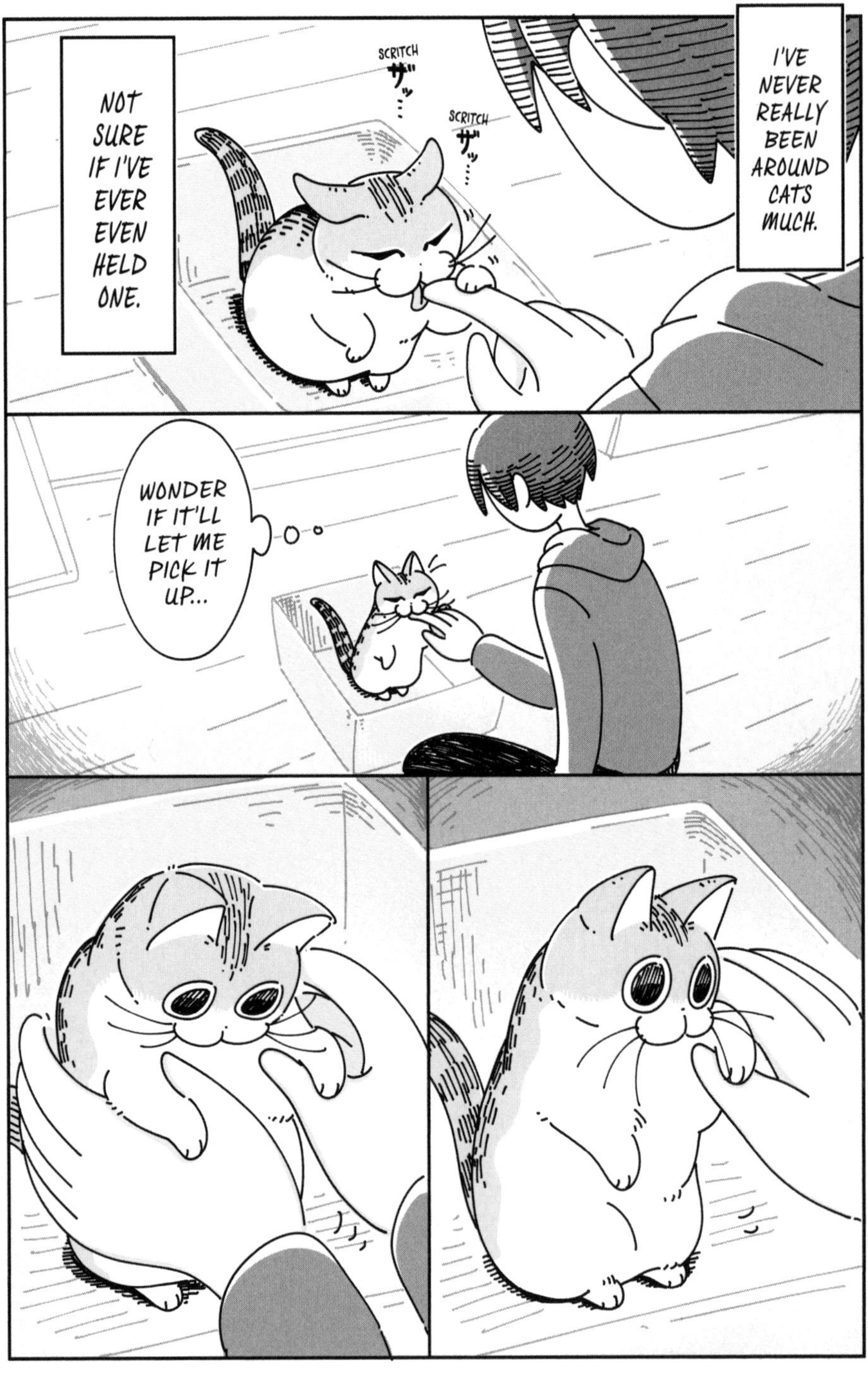
I'VE NEVER REALLY BEEN AROUND CATS MUCH.
SCRITCH
ザッ…
SCRITCH
ザッ…
NOT SURE IF I'VE EVER EVEN HELD ONE.
WONDER IF IT'LL LET ME PICK IT UP...

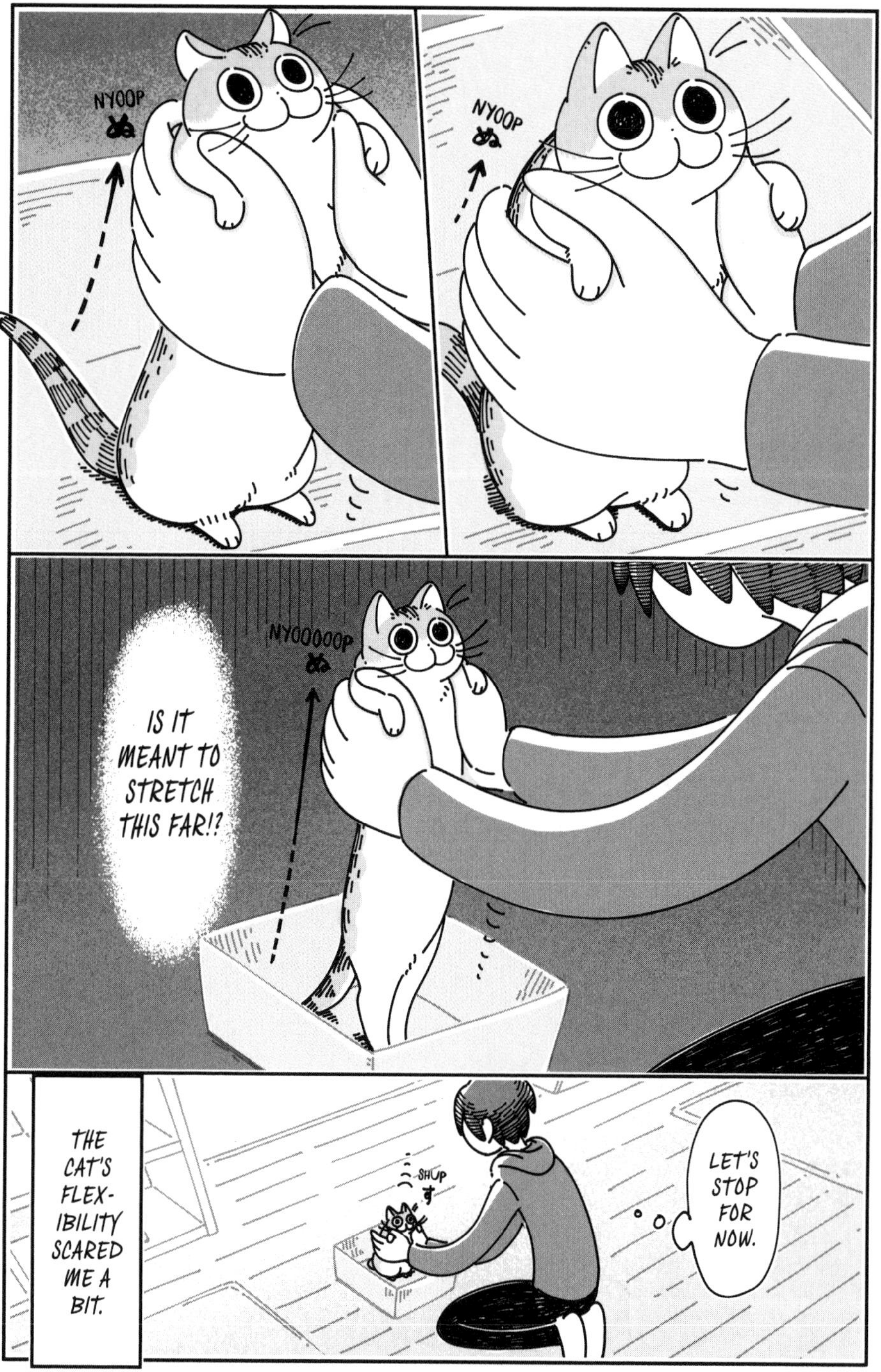
NYOOP
ぬ
NYOOP
ぬ
NYOOOOOP
ぬ
IS IT MEANT TO STRETCH THIS FAR!?
LET'S STOP FOR NOW.
SHUP
す
THE CAT'S FLEX-IBILITY SCARED ME A BIT.

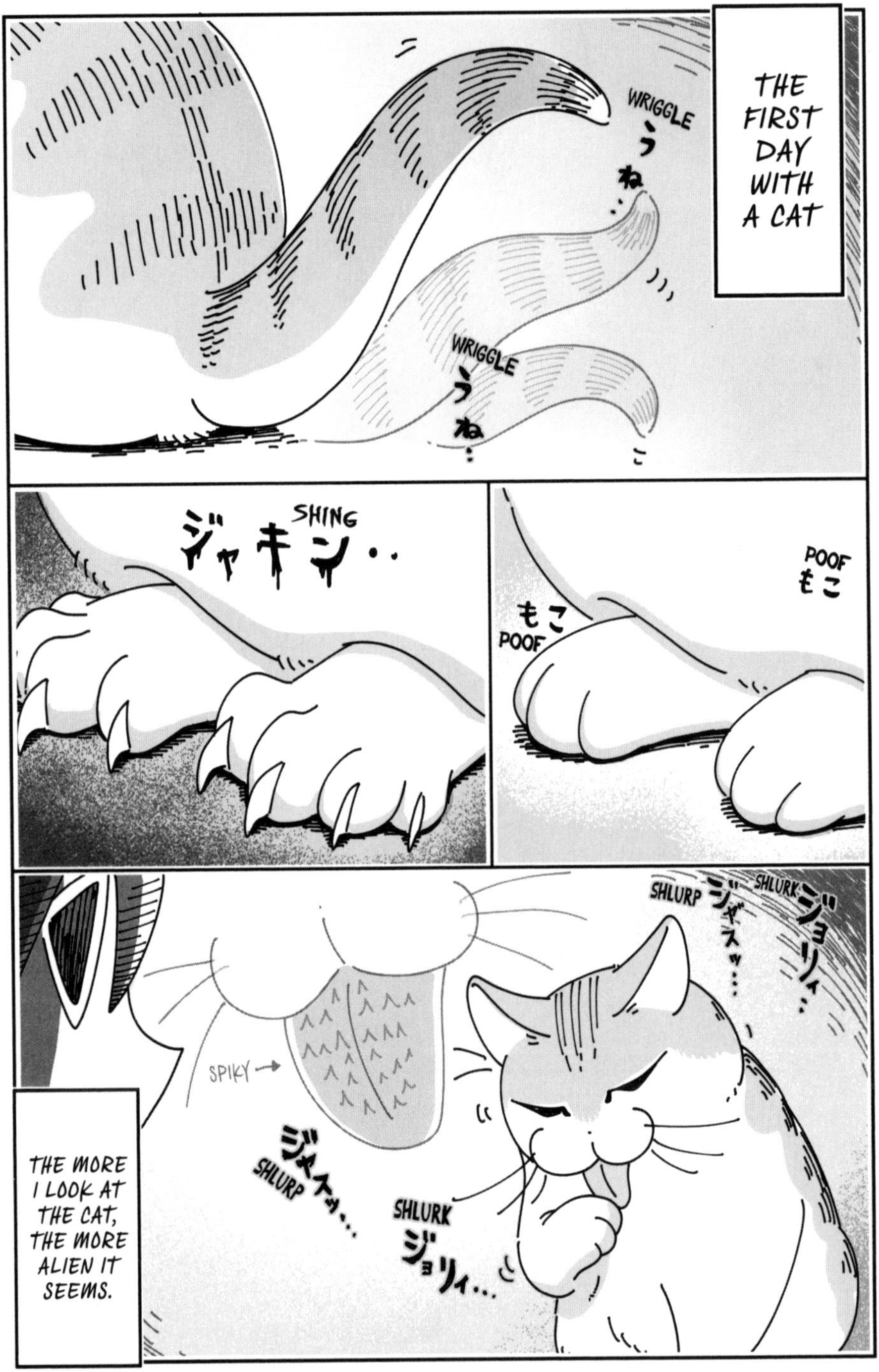
THE FIRST DAY WITH A CAT
WRIGGLE
うね…
WRIGGLE
うね…
POOF
もこ
もこ
POOF
SHING
ジャキン・・
SHLURK
ジョリィ…
SHLURP
ジャスッ…
SPIKY
SHLURK
ジョリィ…
SHLURP
ジャスッ…
THE MORE I LOOK AT THE CAT, THE MORE ALIEN IT SEEMS.

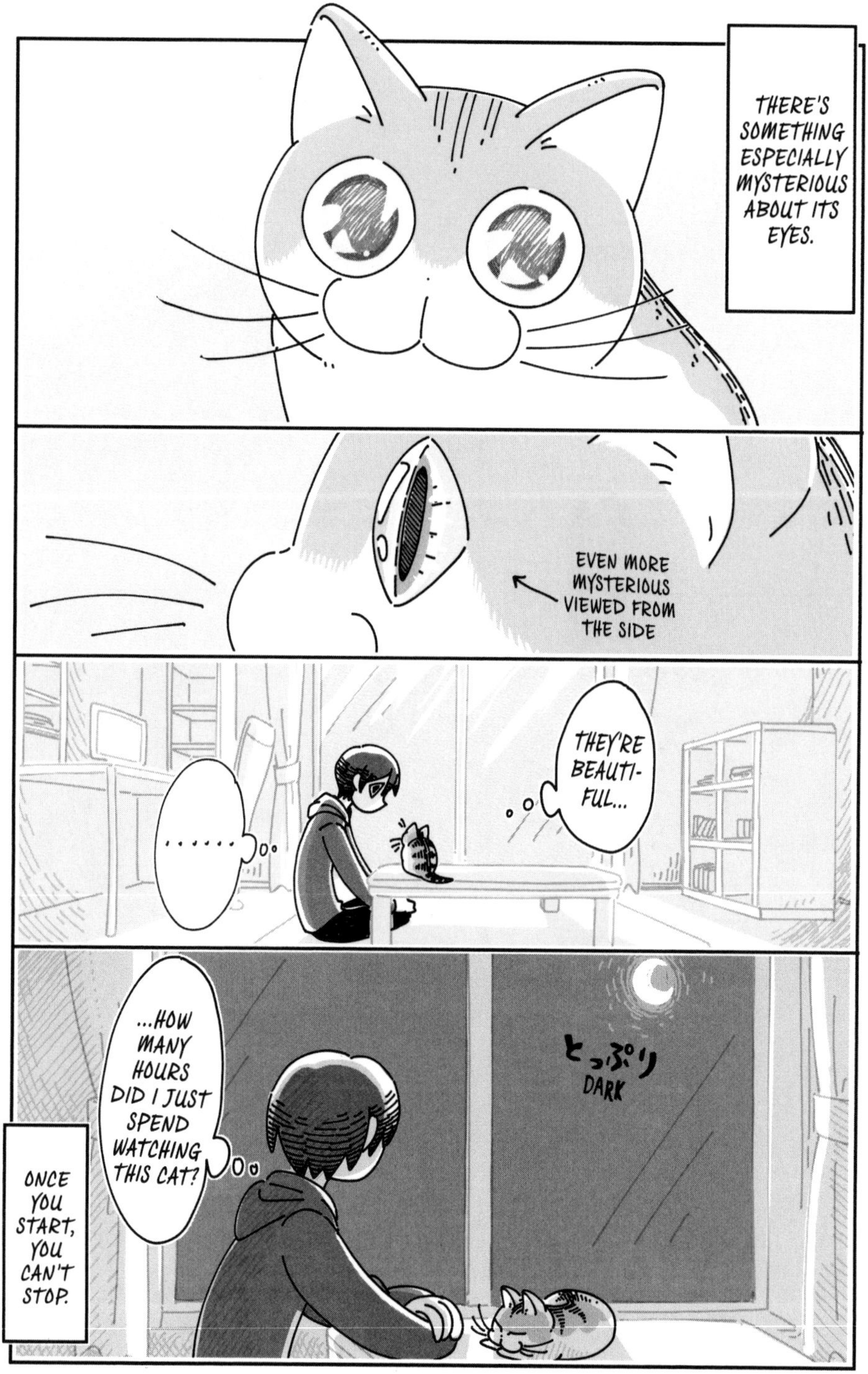
THERE'S SOMETHING ESPECIALLY MYSTERIOUS ABOUT ITS EYES.
EVEN MORE MYSTERIOUS VIEWED FROM THE SIDE
THEY'RE BEAUTIFUL...
......
...HOW MANY HOURS DID I JUST SPEND WATCHING THIS CAT?
とっぷり
DARK
ONCE YOU START, YOU CAN'T STOP.

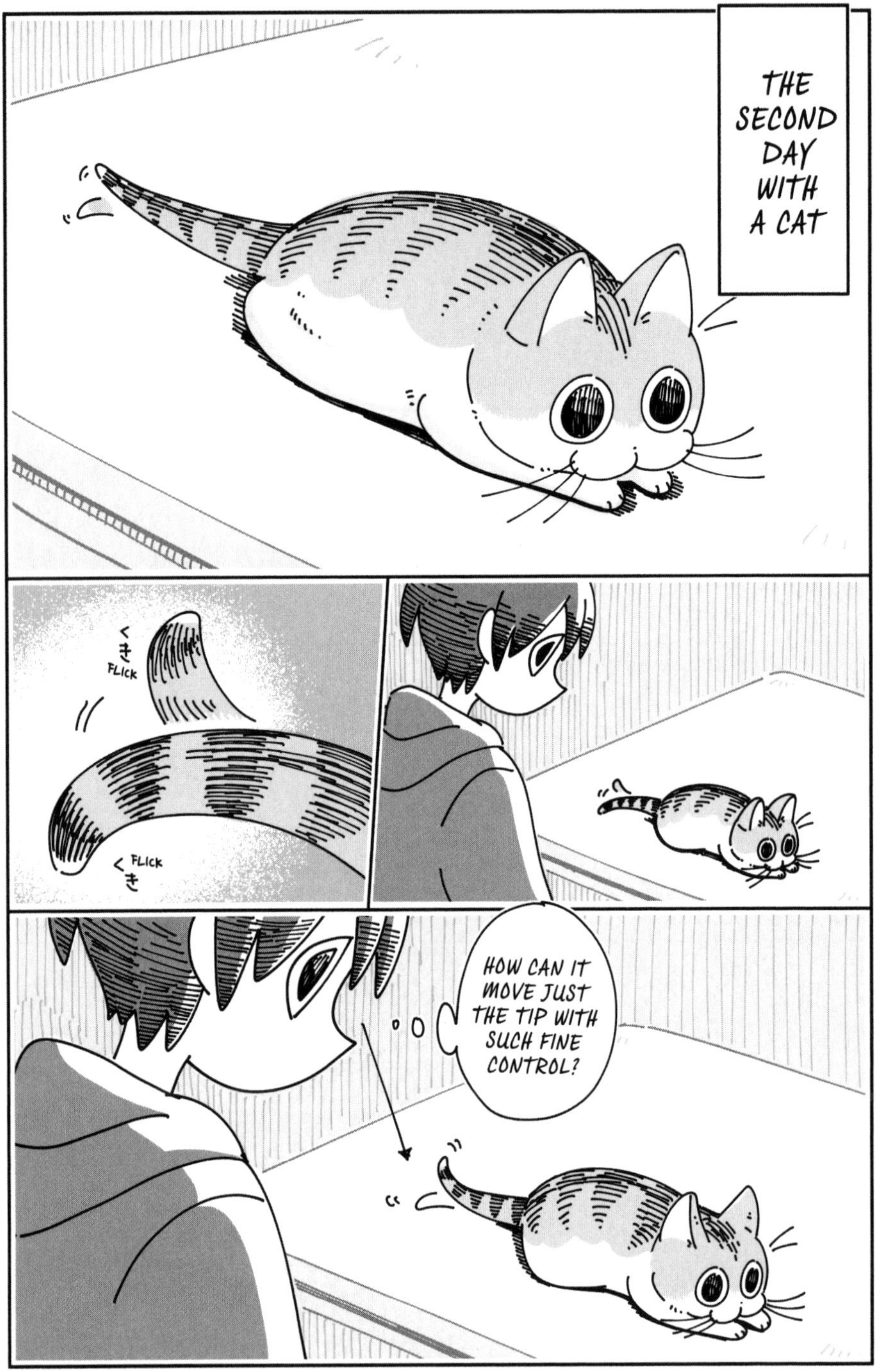
THE SECOND DAY WITH A CAT
くき
FLICK
くき
FLICK
HOW CAN IT MOVE JUST THE TIP WITH SUCH FINE CONTROL?

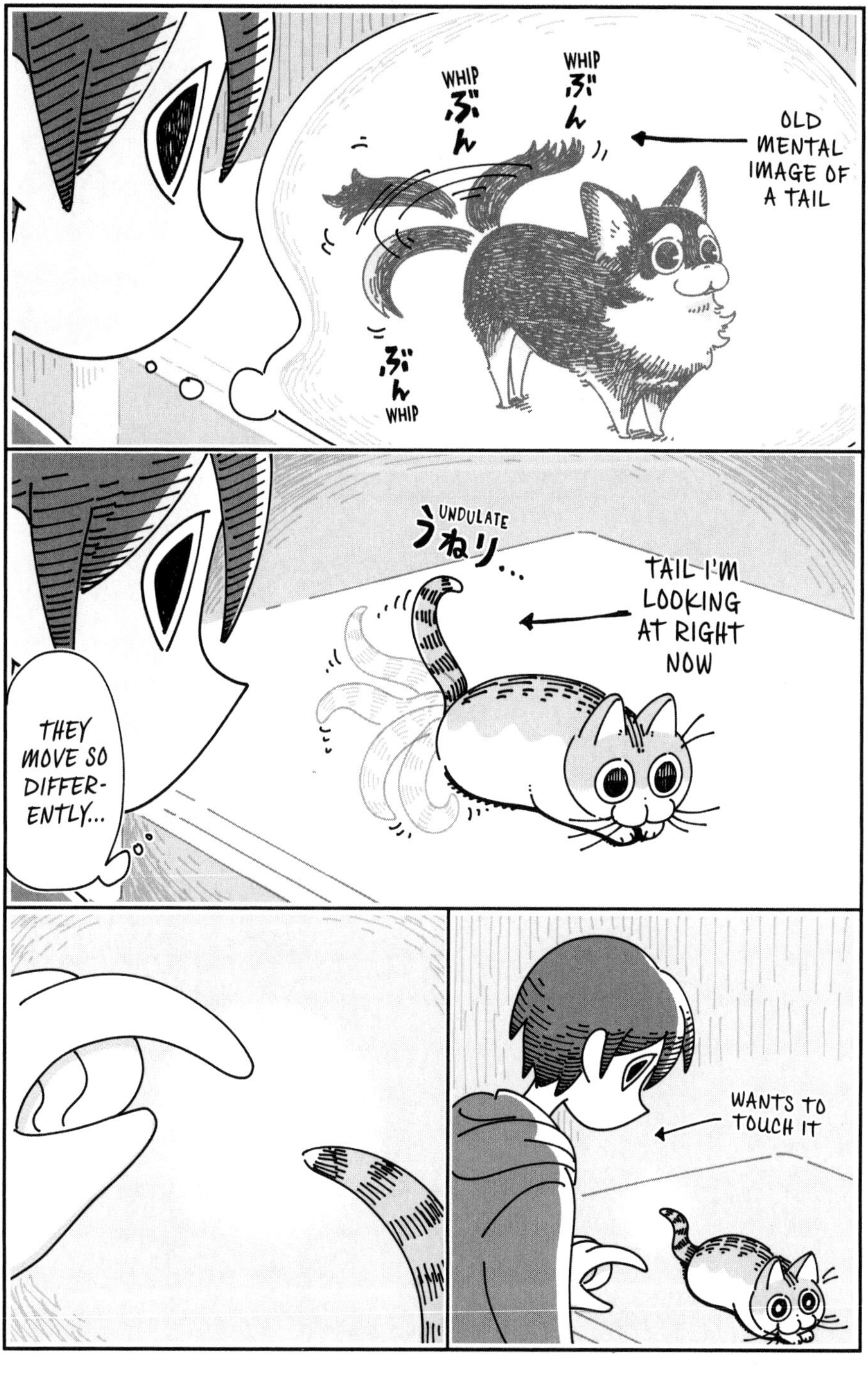
OLD MENTAL IMAGE OF A TAIL
WHIP ぶん
WHIP ぶん
ぶん WHIP
UNDULATE うねり…
TAIL I'M LOOKING AT RIGHT NOW
THEY MOVE SO DIFFER-ENTLY...
WANTS TO TOUCH IT

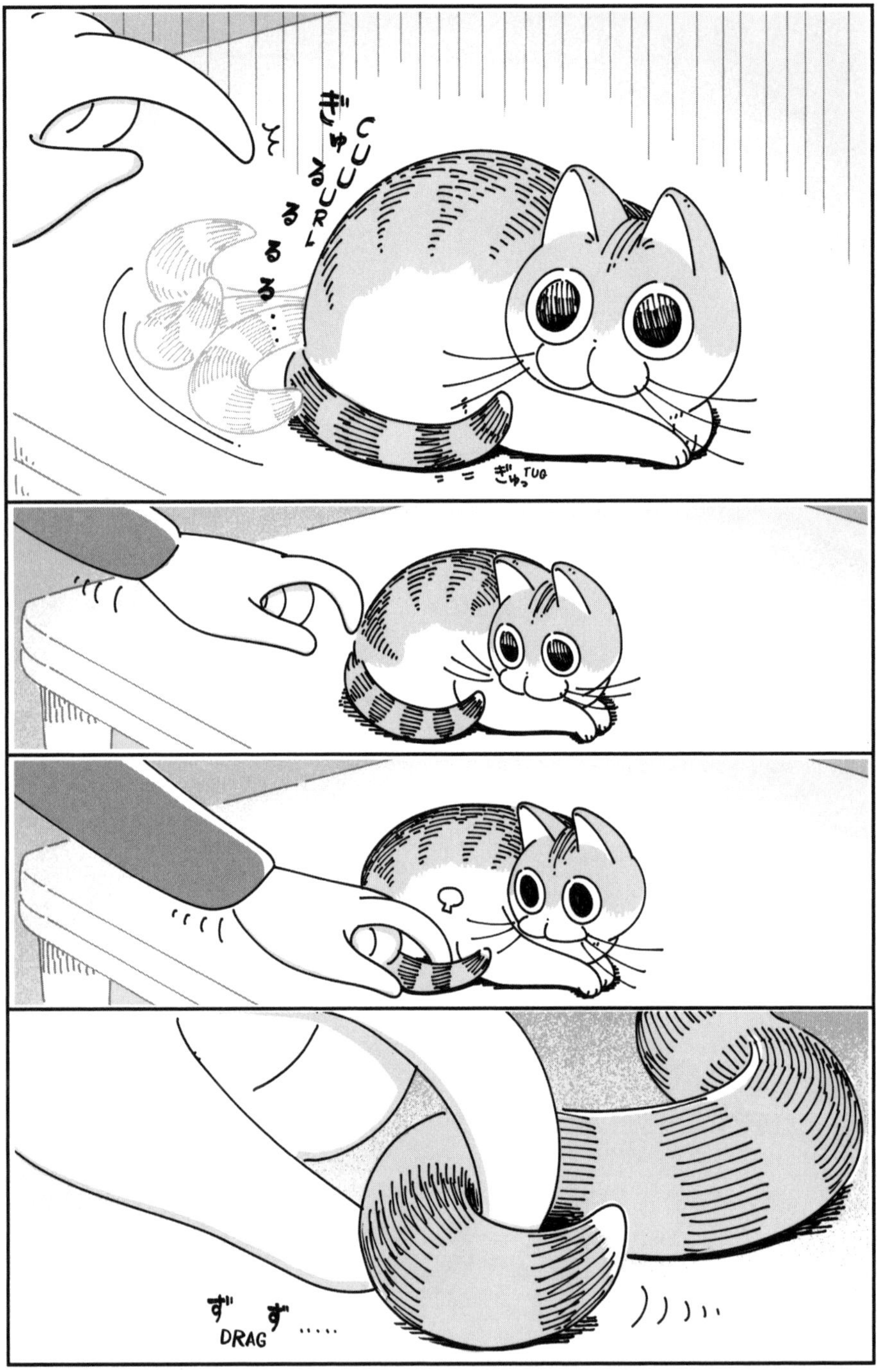
ぎゅるるるる…
CUUURL
ぎゅっ
TUG
ずず……
DRAG

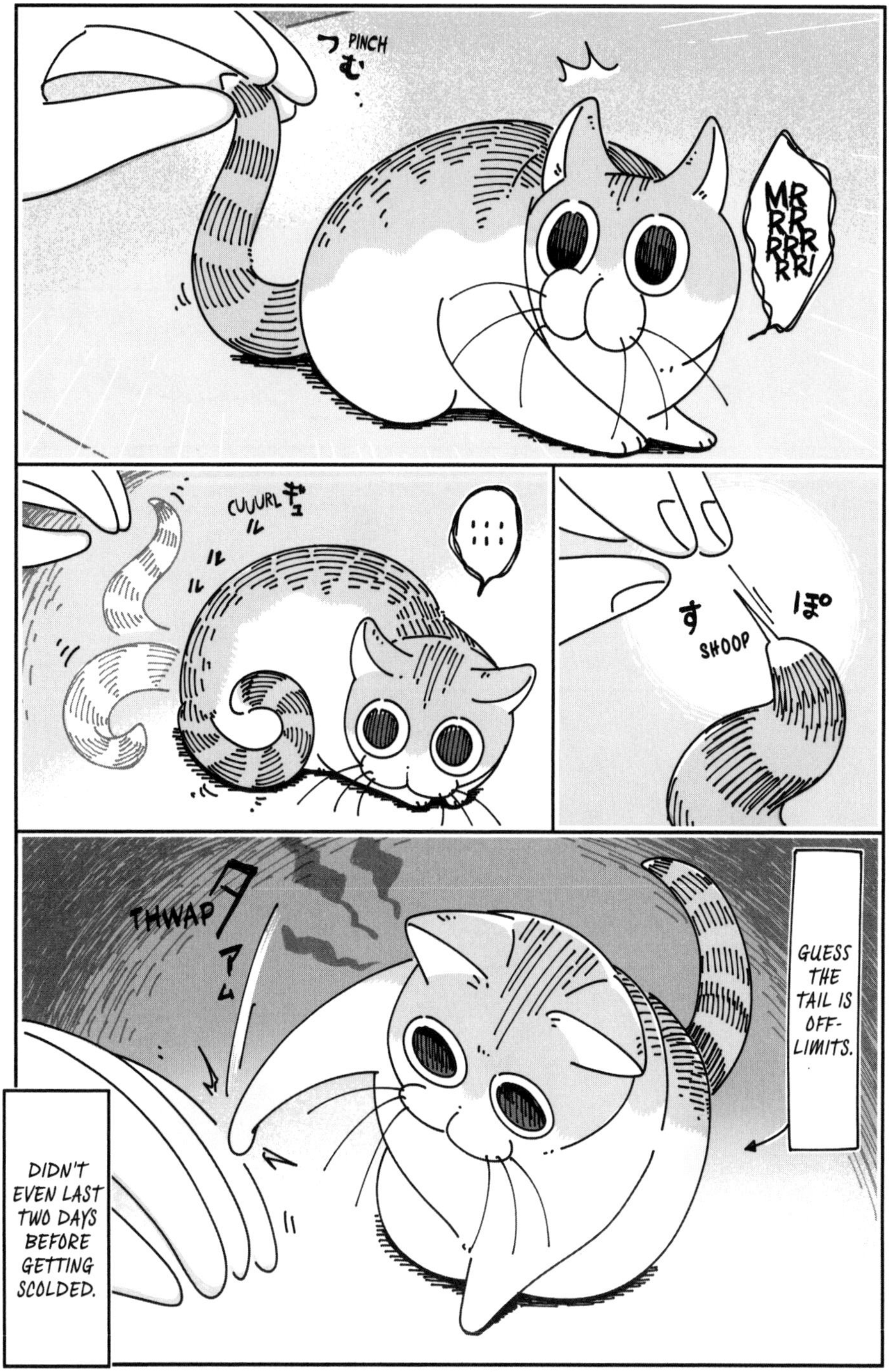

つむ
PINCH
MRRRRRRRR!
すぽ
SHOOP
ギュルル
CUUURL
......
GUESS THE TAIL IS OFF-LIMITS.
タアム
THWAP
DIDN'T EVEN LAST TWO DAYS BEFORE GETTING SCOLDED.

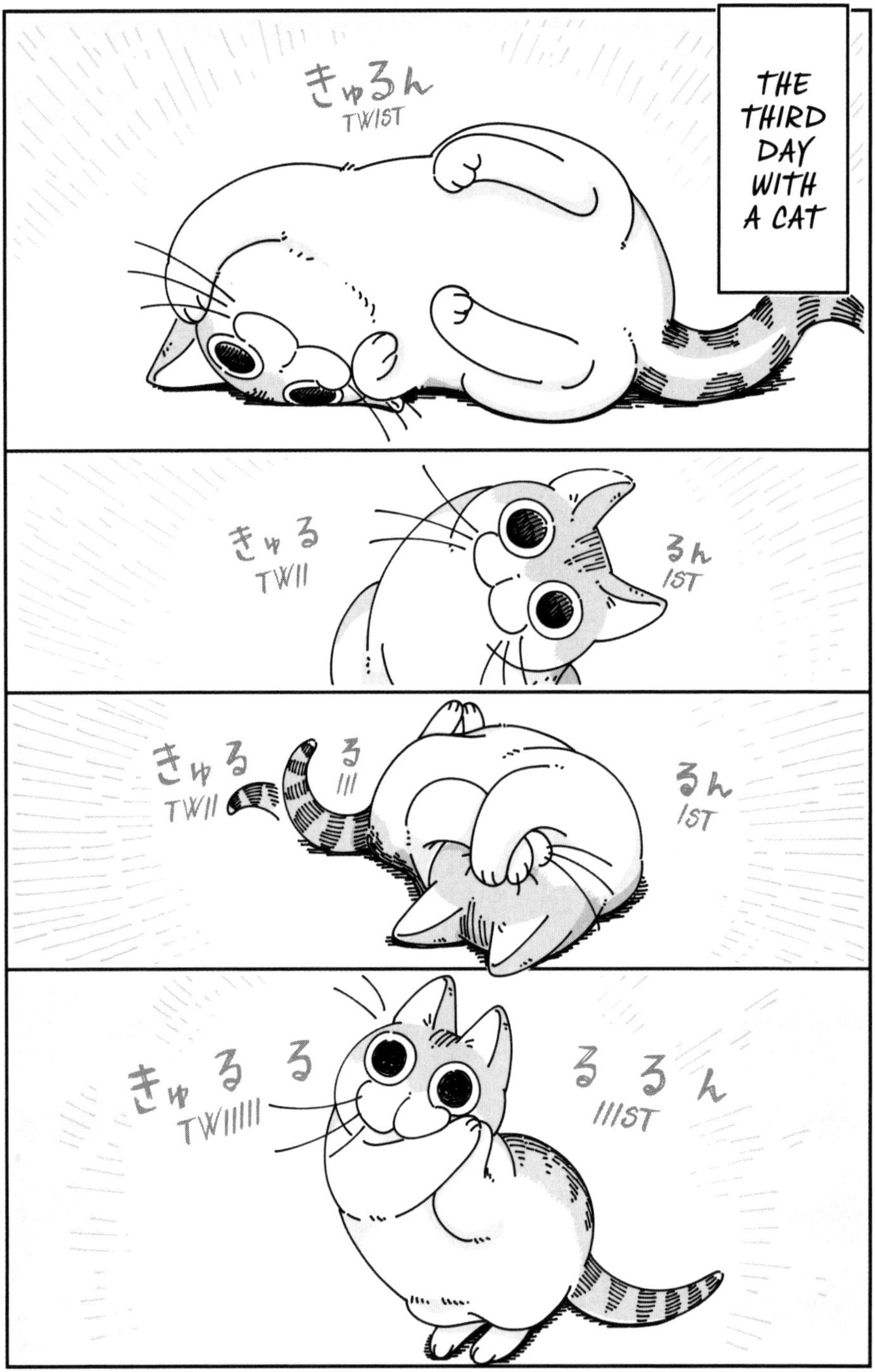
THE THIRD DAY WITH A CAT
きゅるん
TWIST
きゅる
TWII
るん
IST
きゅる
TWII
る
III
るん
IST
きゅる る
TWIIIII
る るん
IIIST

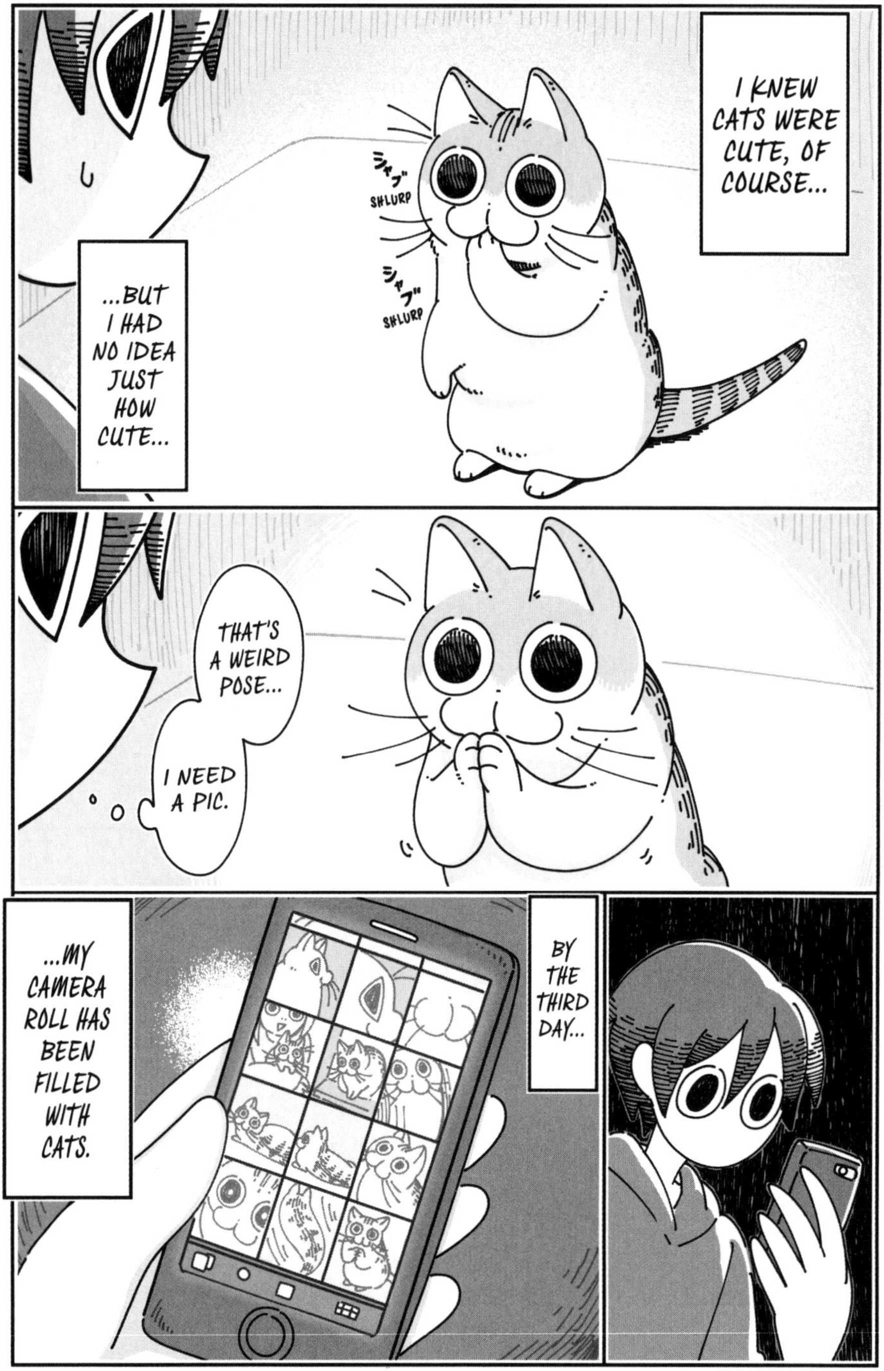
I KNEW CATS WERE CUTE, OF COURSE...
シャブ SHLURP
シャブ SHLURP
...BUT I HAD NO IDEA JUST HOW CUTE...
THAT'S A WEIRD POSE...
I NEED A PIC.
BY THE THIRD DAY...
...MY CAMERA ROLL HAS BEEN FILLED WITH CATS.

You Can't Just Swing It

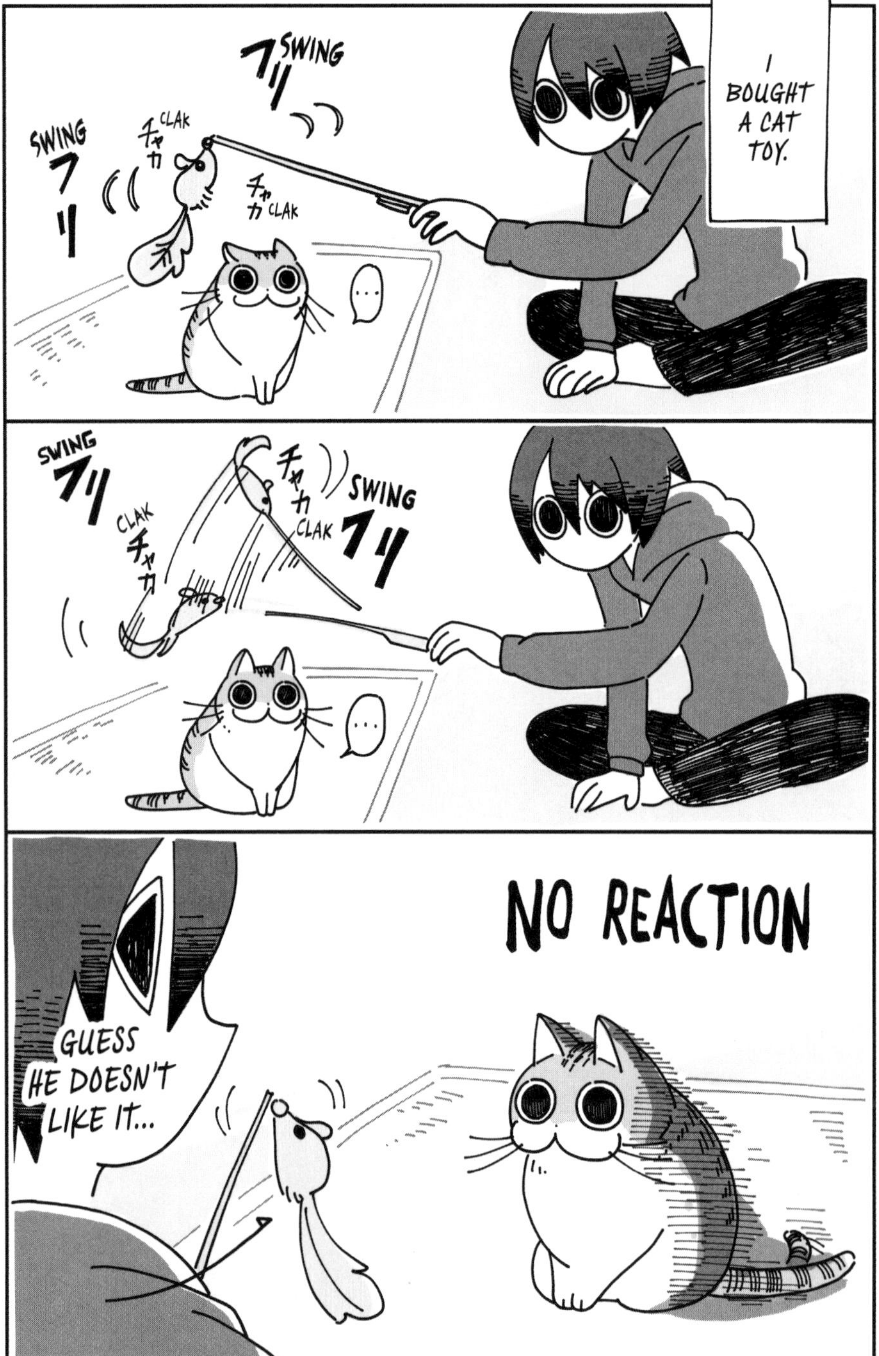
I BOUGHT A CAT TOY.
フリ SWING
チャカ CLAK
チャカ CLAK
SWING フリ
…
フリ SWING
チャカ CLAK
CLAK チャカ
SWING フリ
…
NO REACTION
GUESS HE DOESN'T LIKE IT...

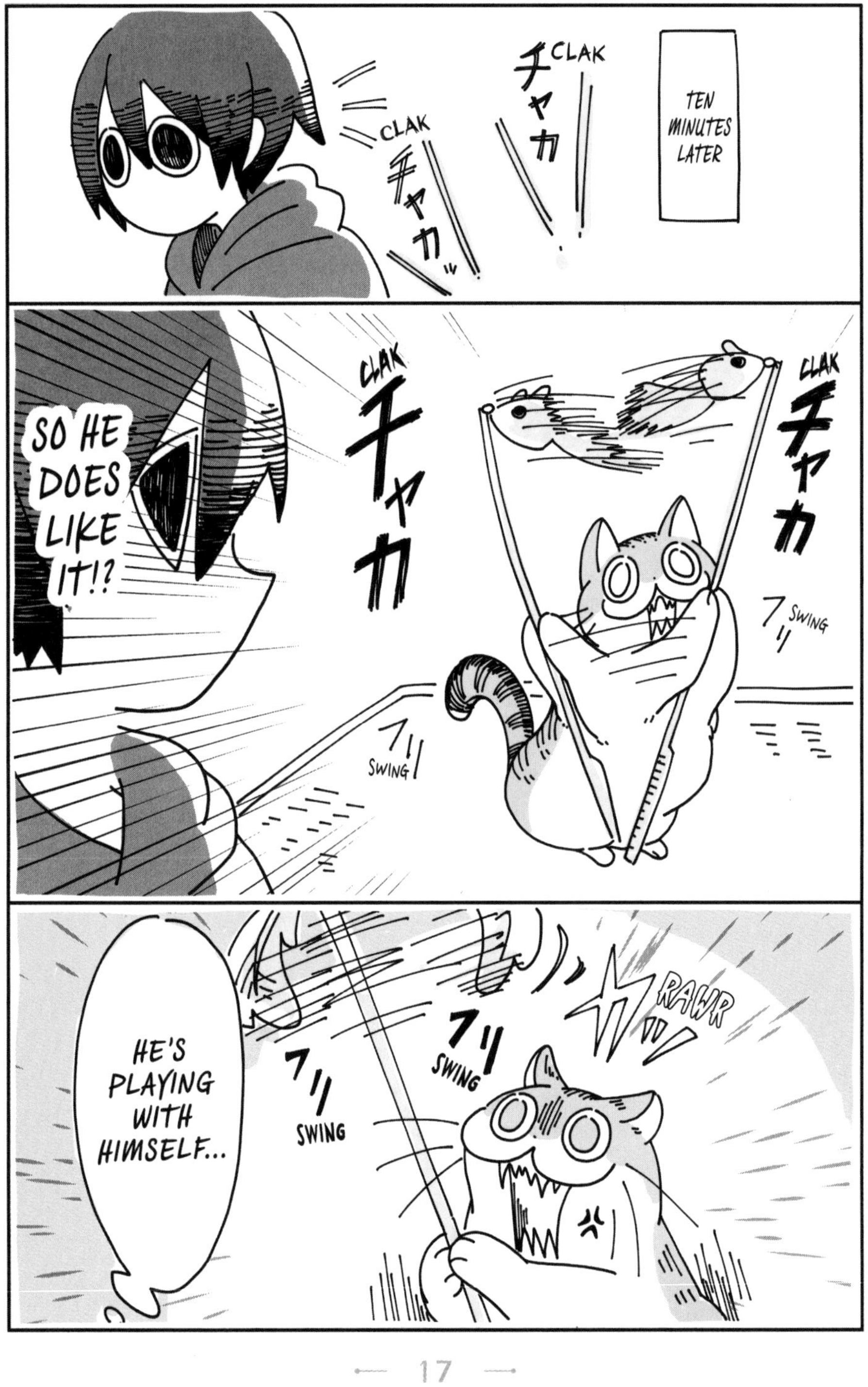
TEN MINUTES LATER
チャカ CLAK
チャカッ CLAK
チャカ CLAK
フリ SWING
チャカ CLAK
SO HE DOES LIKE IT!?
フリ SWING
RAWR
フリ SWING
フリ SWING
HE'S PLAYING WITH HIMSELF...

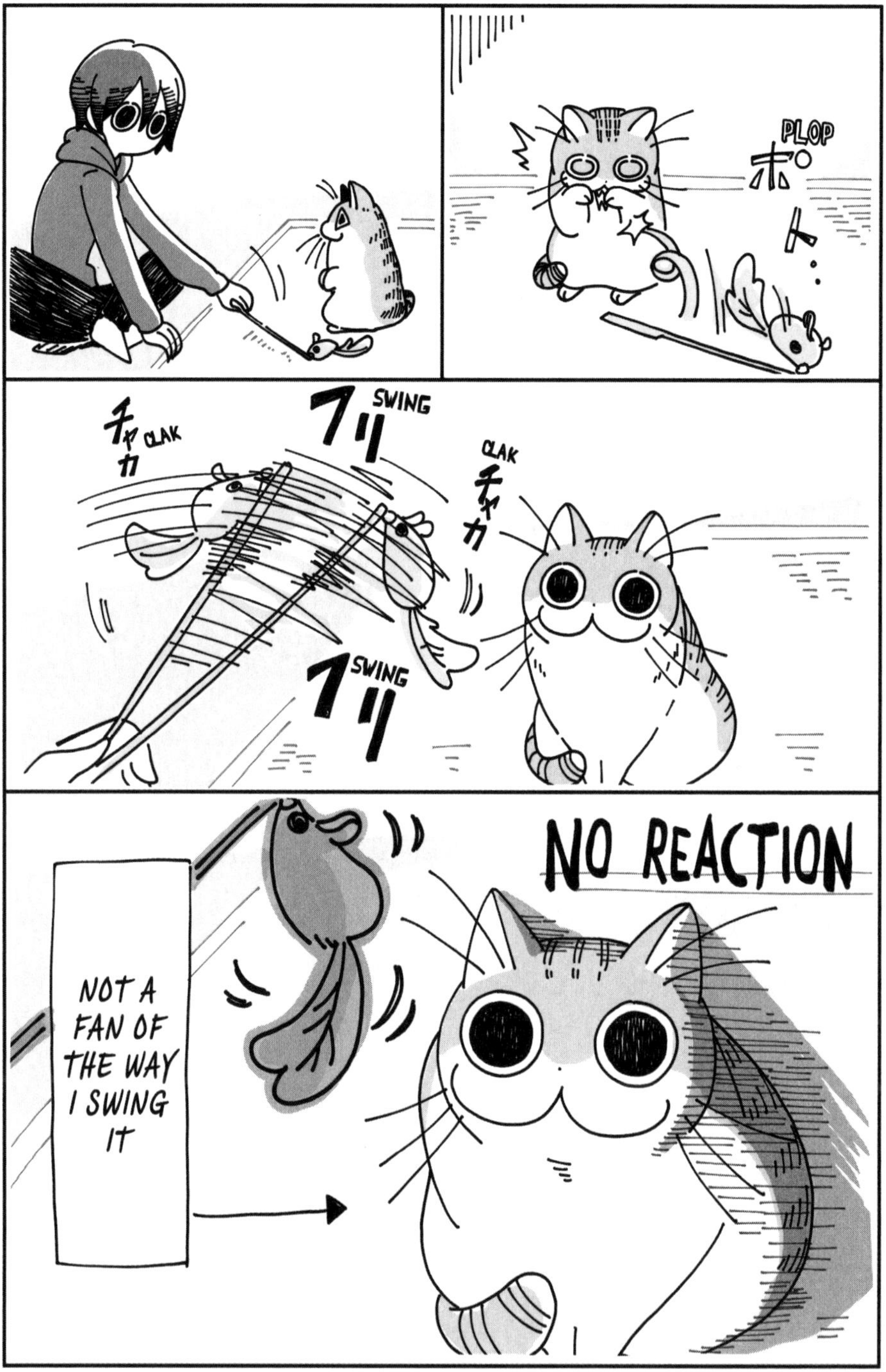
PLOP
ポト
CLAK
チャカ
SWING
フリ
チャカ
CLAK
SWING
フリ
NO REACTION
NOT A FAN OF THE WAY I SWING IT

Barcode Cat

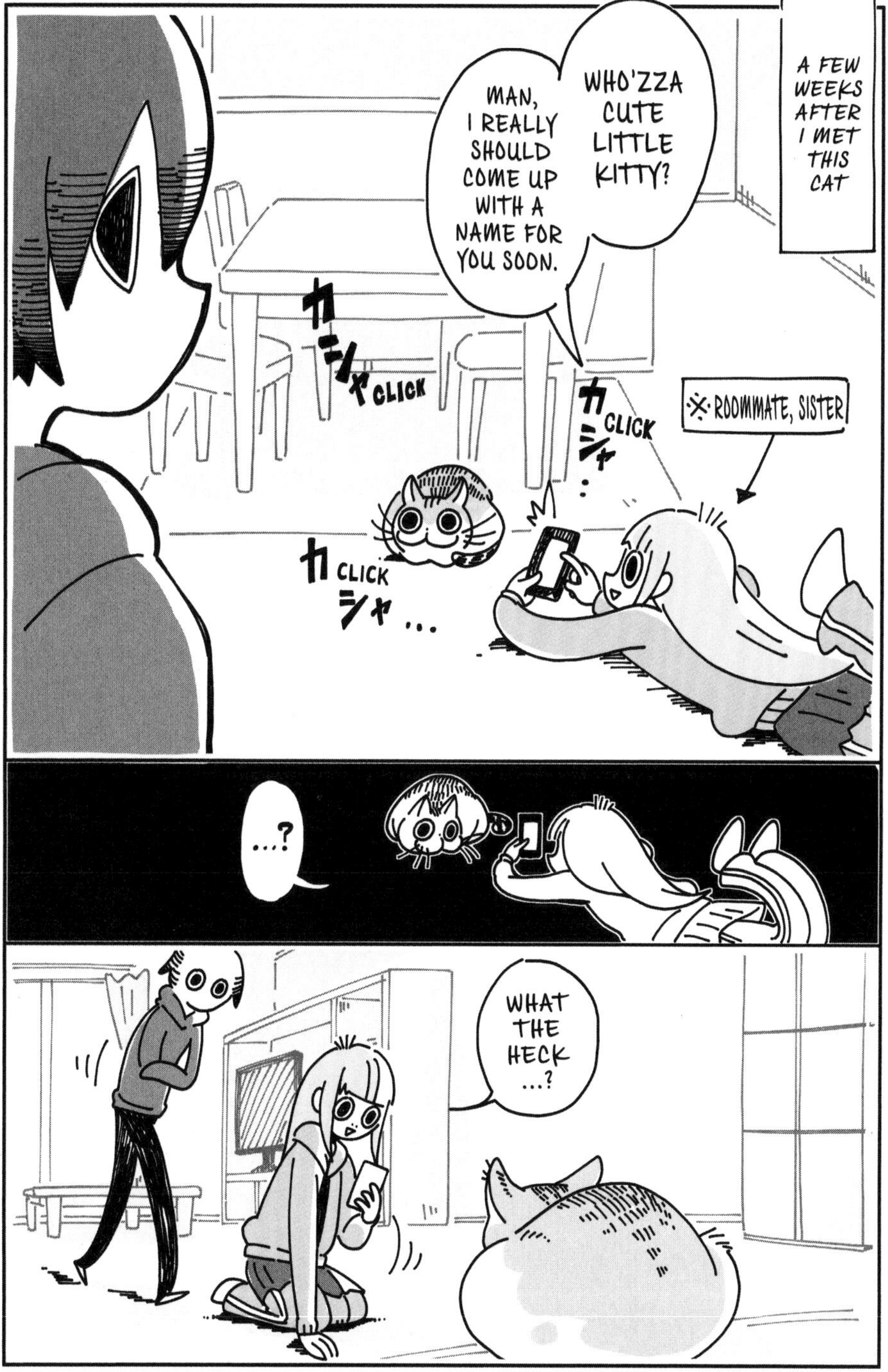
A FEW WEEKS AFTER I MET THIS CAT
WHO'ZZA CUTE LITTLE KITTY?
MAN, I REALLY SHOULD COME UP WITH A NAME FOR YOU SOON.
※: ROOMMATE, SISTER
カシャ CLICK
カシャ CLICK
カシャ CLICK
...?
WHAT THE HECK ...?

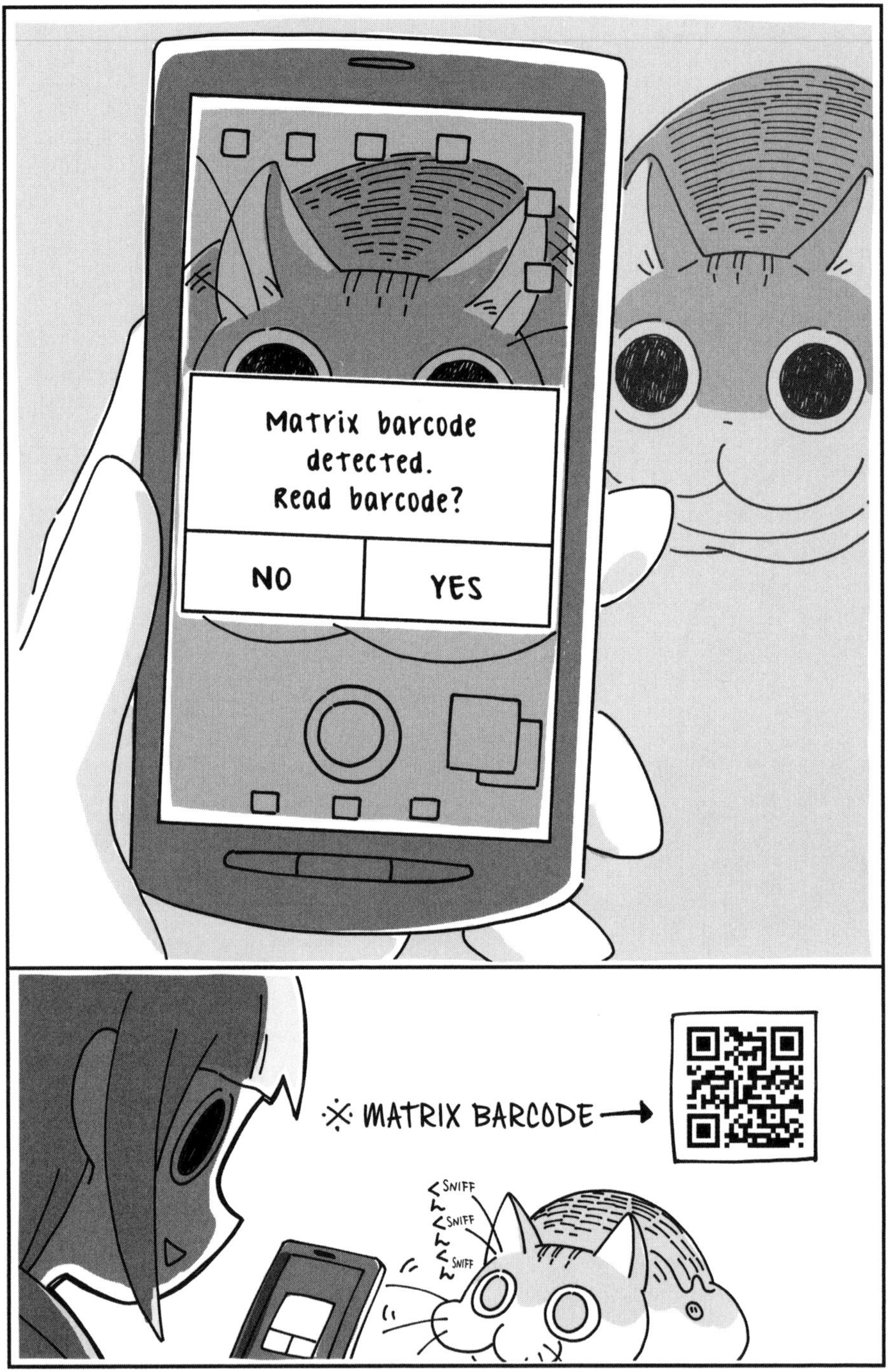
Matrix barcode detected. Read barcode?
NO
YES
※ MATRIX BARCODE
SNIFF
SNIFF
SNIFF

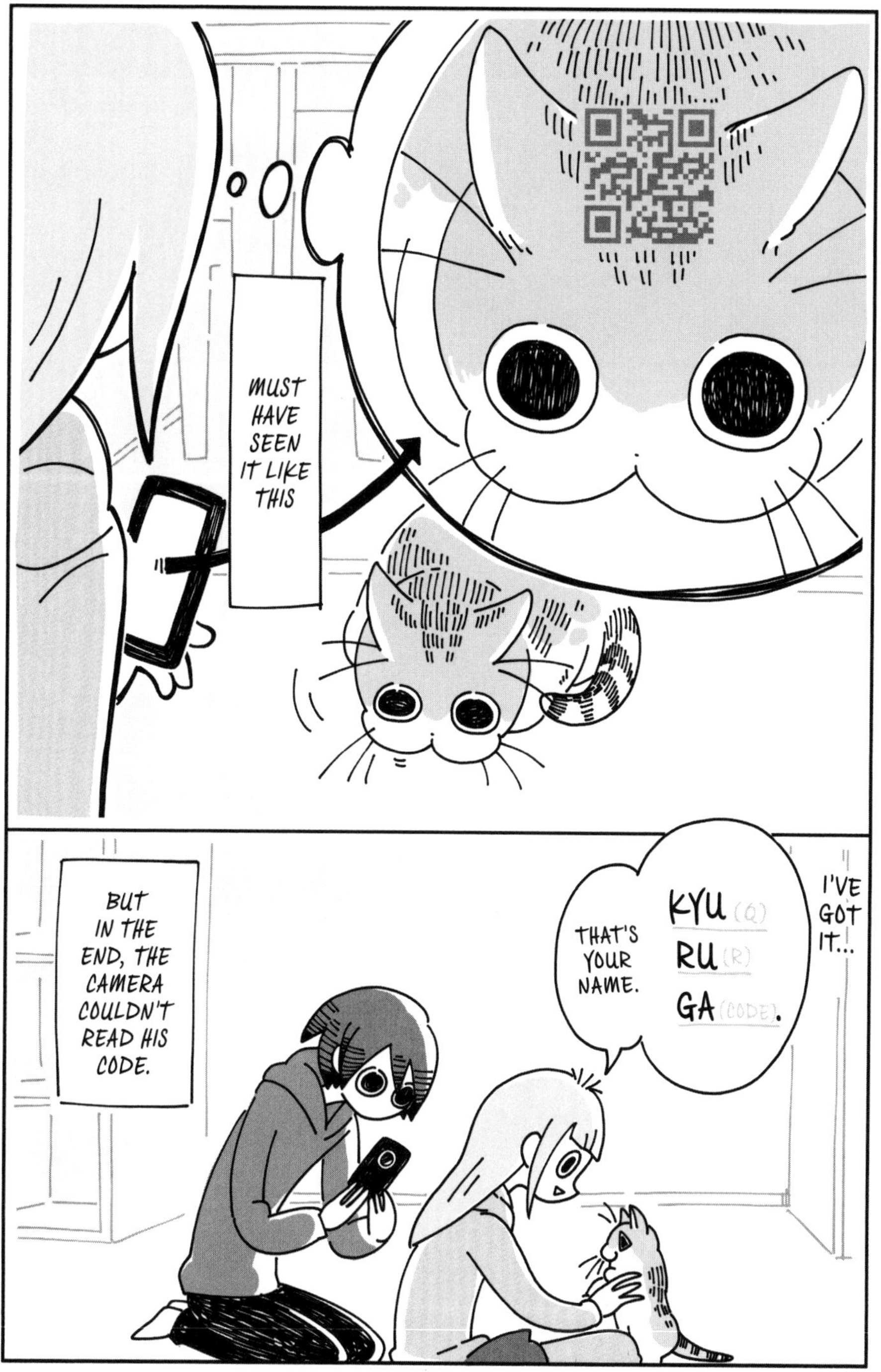
MUST HAVE SEEN IT LIKE THIS
I'VE GOT IT...
KYU (Q) RU (R) GA (CODE).
THAT'S YOUR NAME.
BUT IN THE END, THE CAMERA COULDN'T READ HIS CODE.

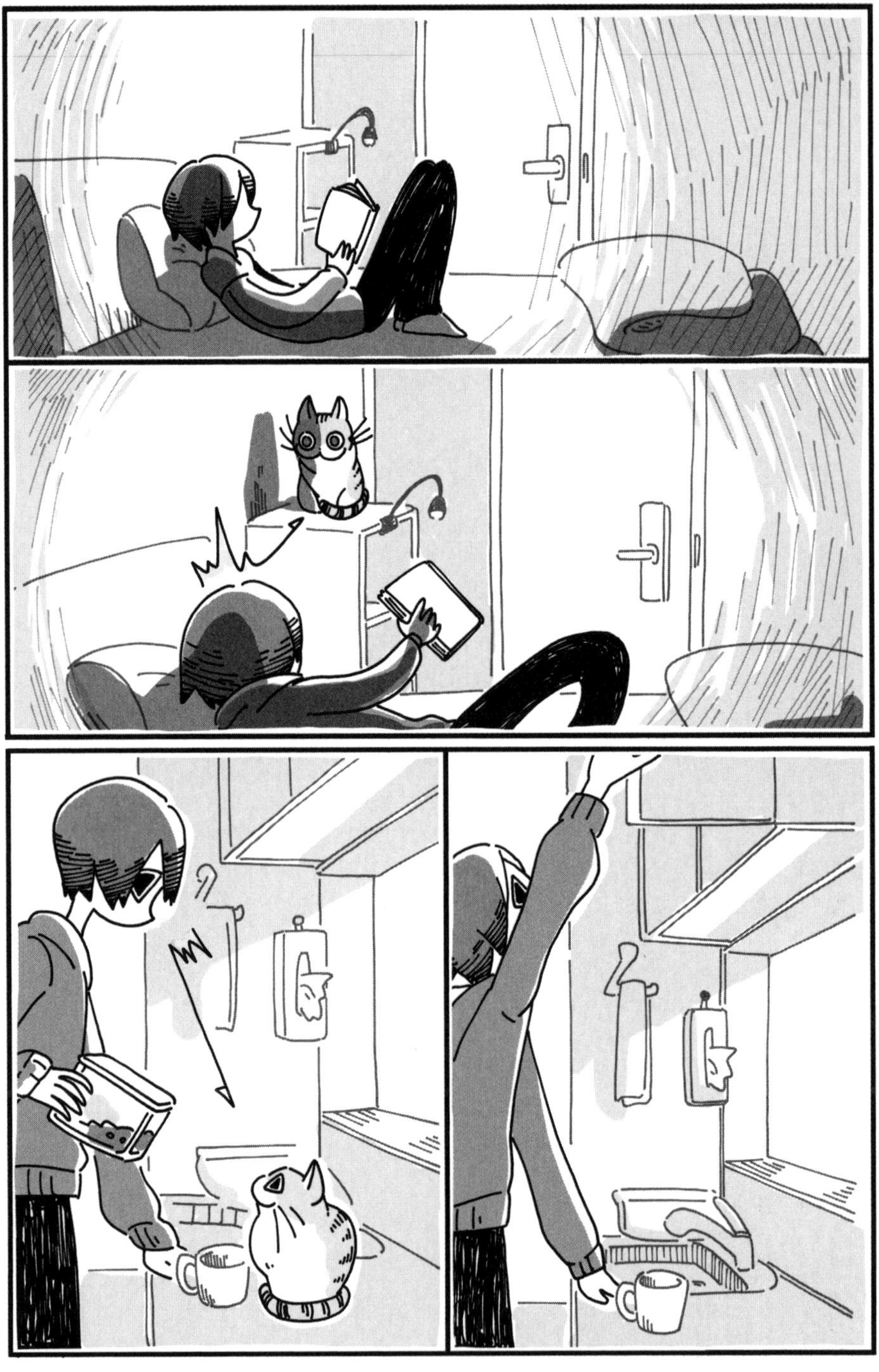

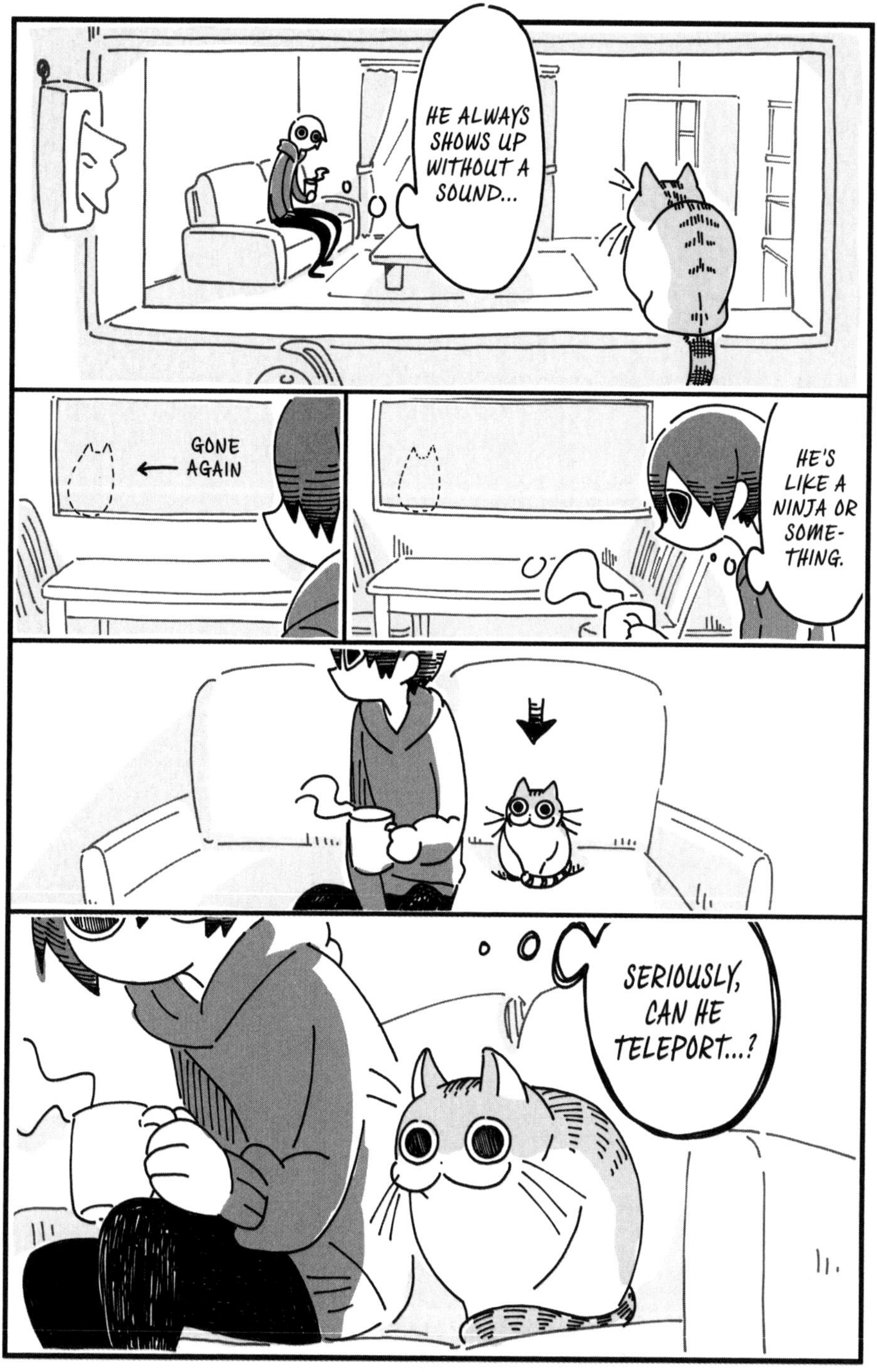
HE ALWAYS SHOWS UP WITHOUT A SOUND...
HE'S LIKE A NINJA OR SOME-THING.
GONE AGAIN
SERIOUSLY, CAN HE TELEPORT...?

He Only Speaks Words I Didn't Teach Him

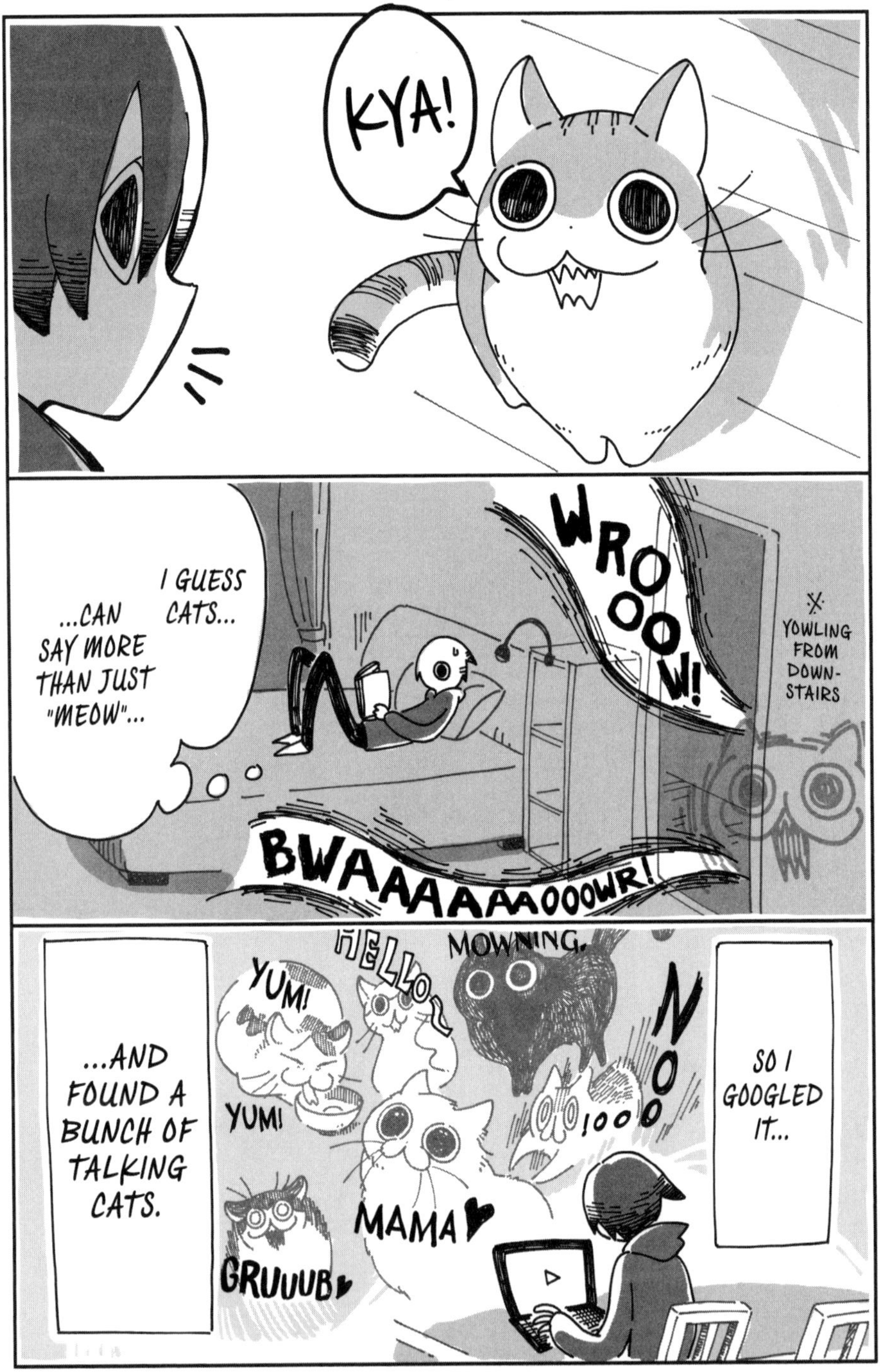
KYA!
※ YOWLING FROM DOWNSTAIRS
WROOOOW!
I GUESS CATS...
...CAN SAY MORE THAN JUST "MEOW"...
BWAAAAAAOOOWR!
SO I GOOGLED IT...
MOWNING.
NOOOO
HELLO~
YUM!
YUM!
MAMA♥
GRUUUB♥
...AND FOUND A BUNCH OF TALKING CATS.

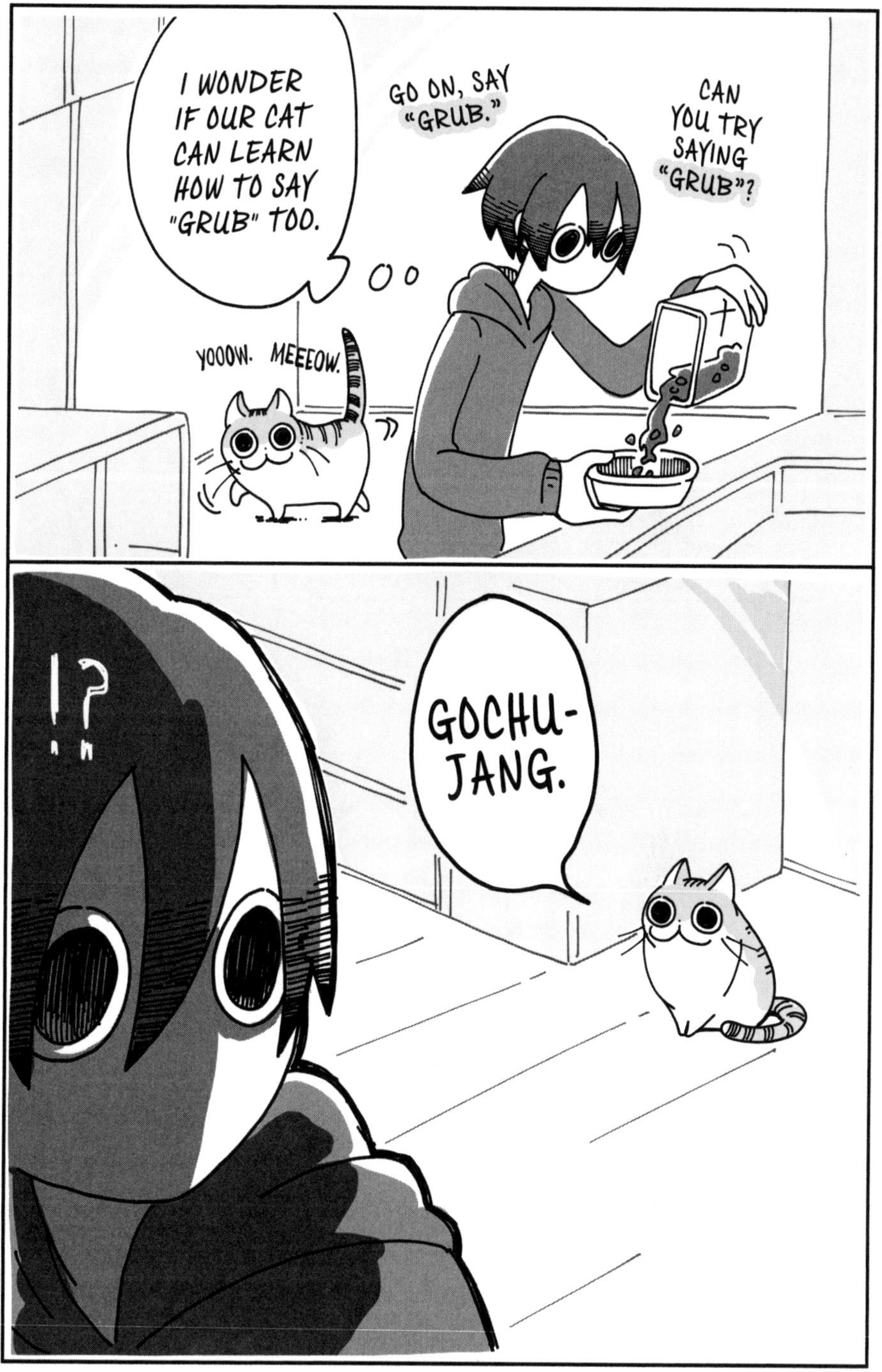
CAN YOU TRY SAYING "GRUB"?
GO ON, SAY "GRUB."
I WONDER IF OUR CAT CAN LEARN HOW TO SAY "GRUB" TOO.
YOOOW. MEEEOW.
GOCHU-JANG.
!?

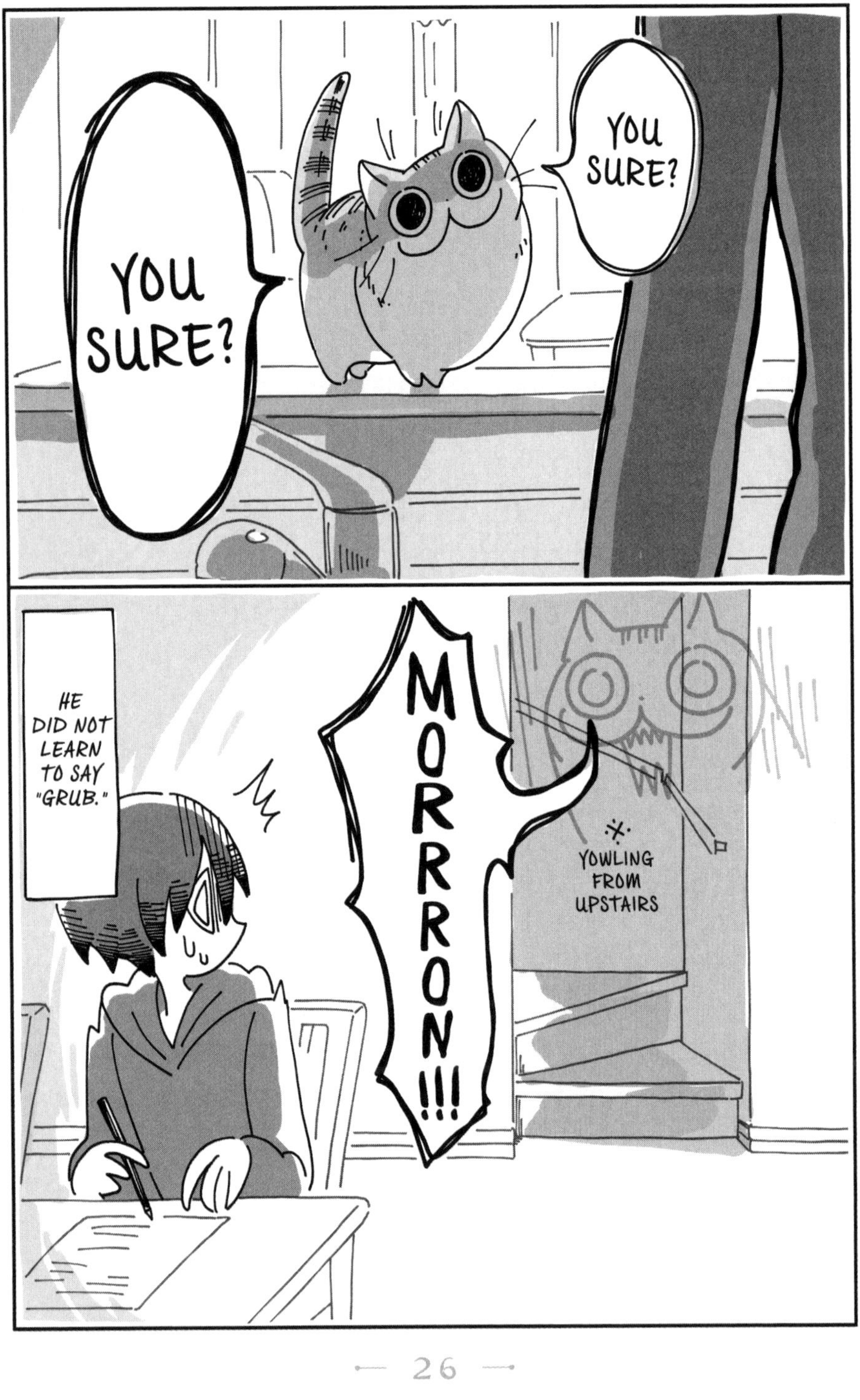
YOU SURE?
YOU SURE?
MORRRON!!!
※ YOWLING FROM UPSTAIRS
HE DID NOT LEARN TO SAY "GRUB."

Close Call Clementine

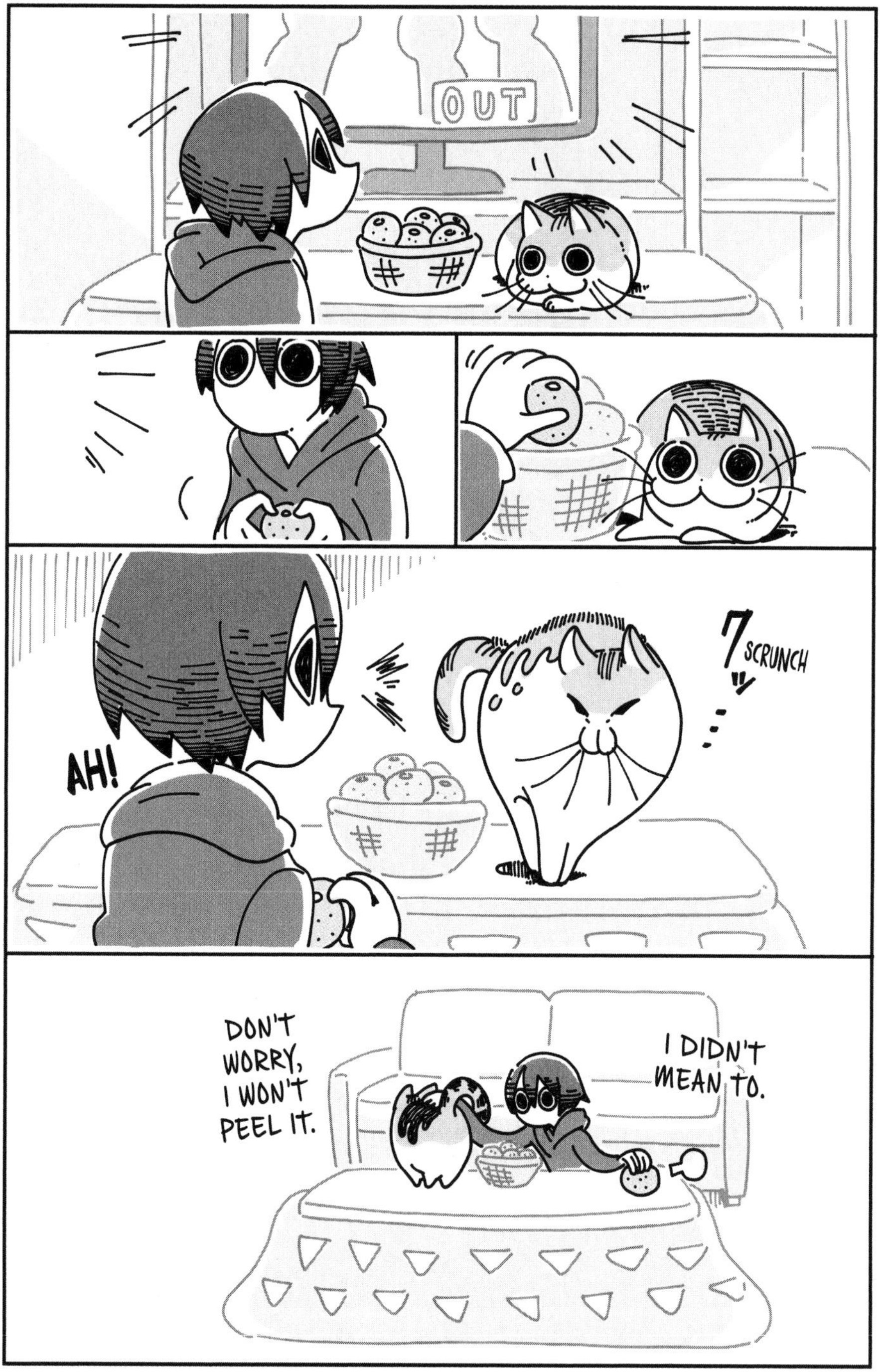
OUT
SCRUNCH
AH!
I DIDN'T MEAN TO.
DON'T WORRY, I WON'T PEEL IT.

Catlish for "Look at Me"

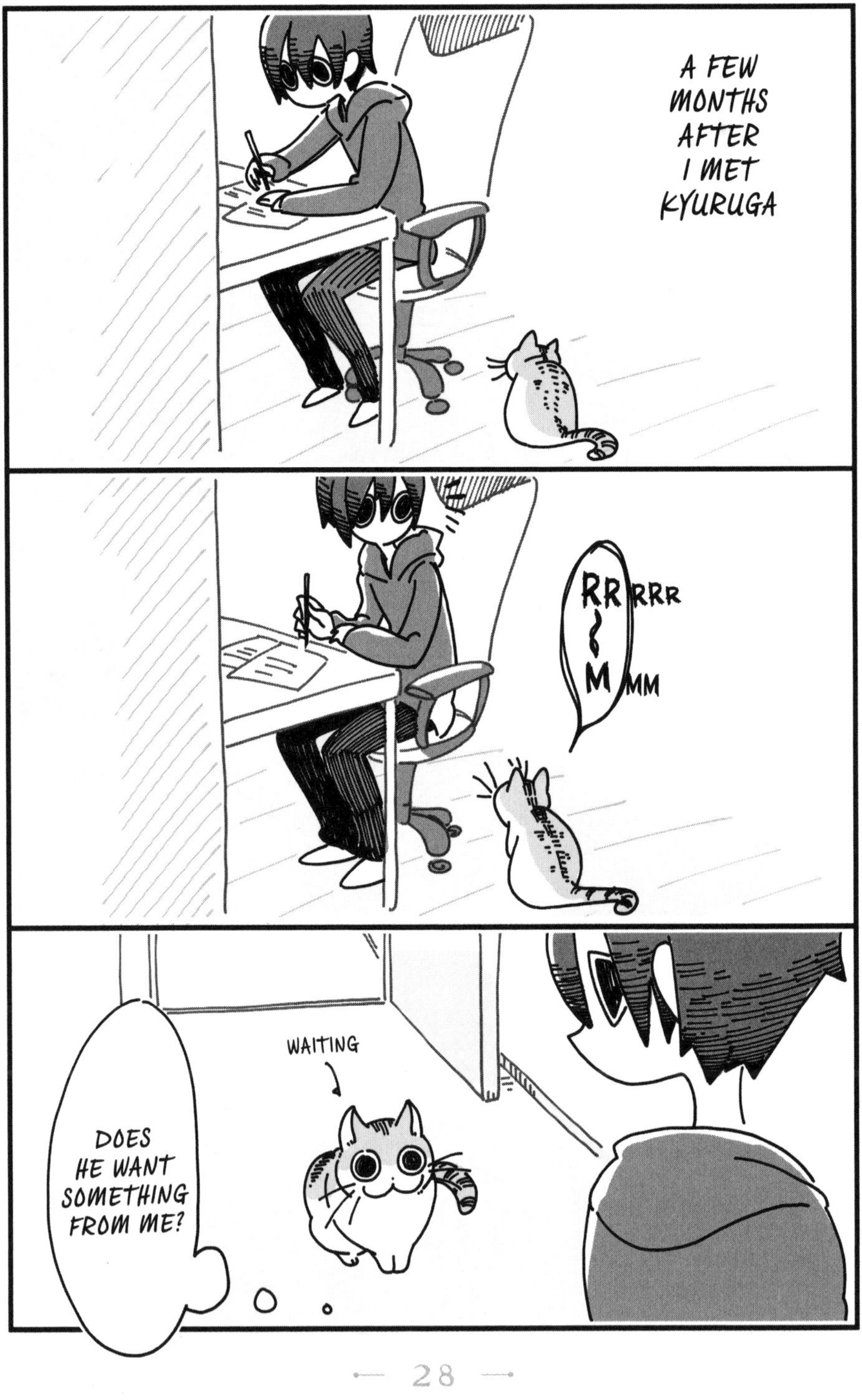
A FEW MONTHS AFTER I MET KYURUGA
RRrrr~Mmm
WAITING
DOES HE WANT SOMETHING FROM ME?

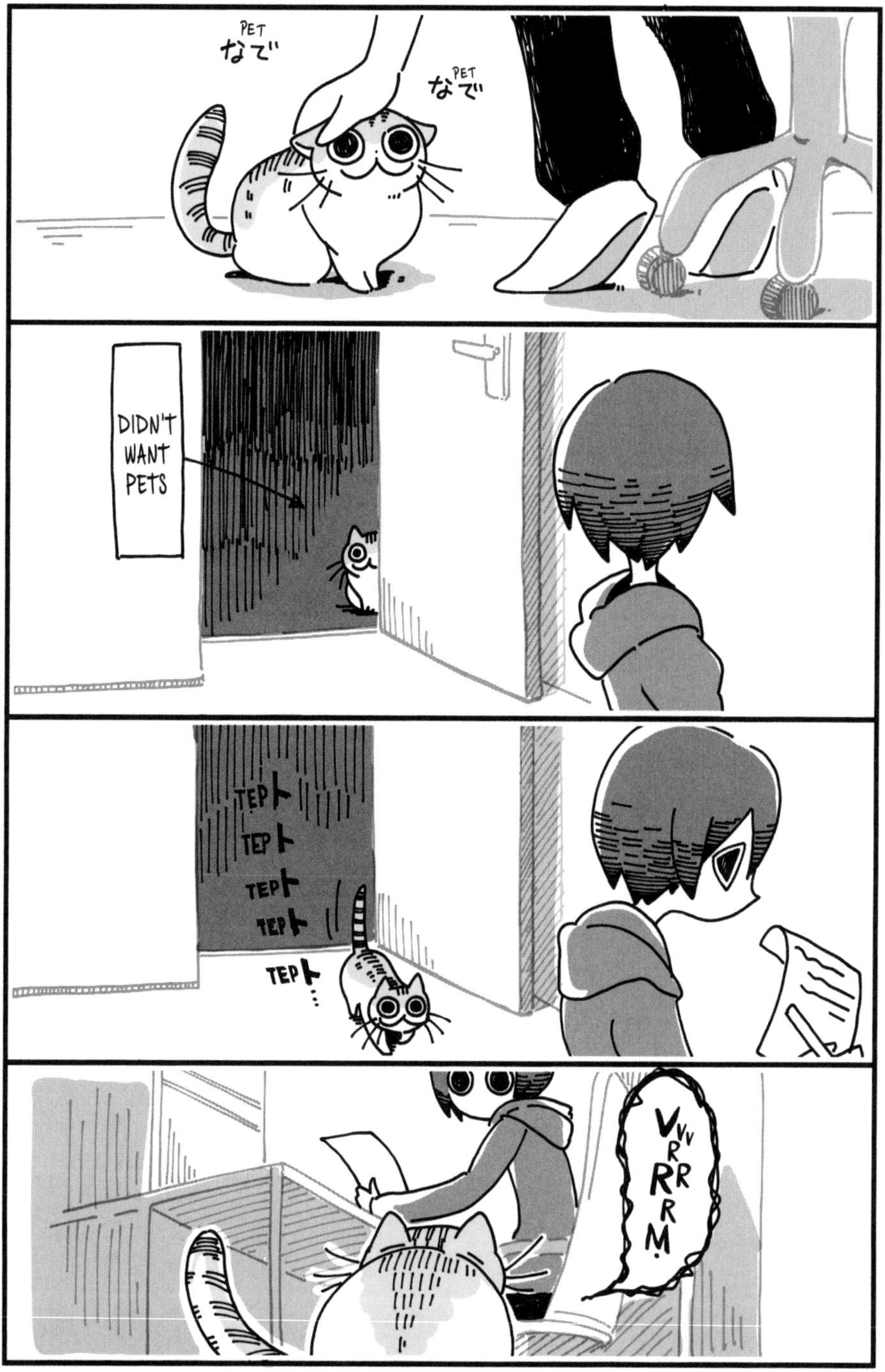
PET
なで
PET
なで
DIDN'T WANT PETS
TEP ト
TEP ト
TEP ト
TEP ト
TEP ト...
VVVV RRR RRM!

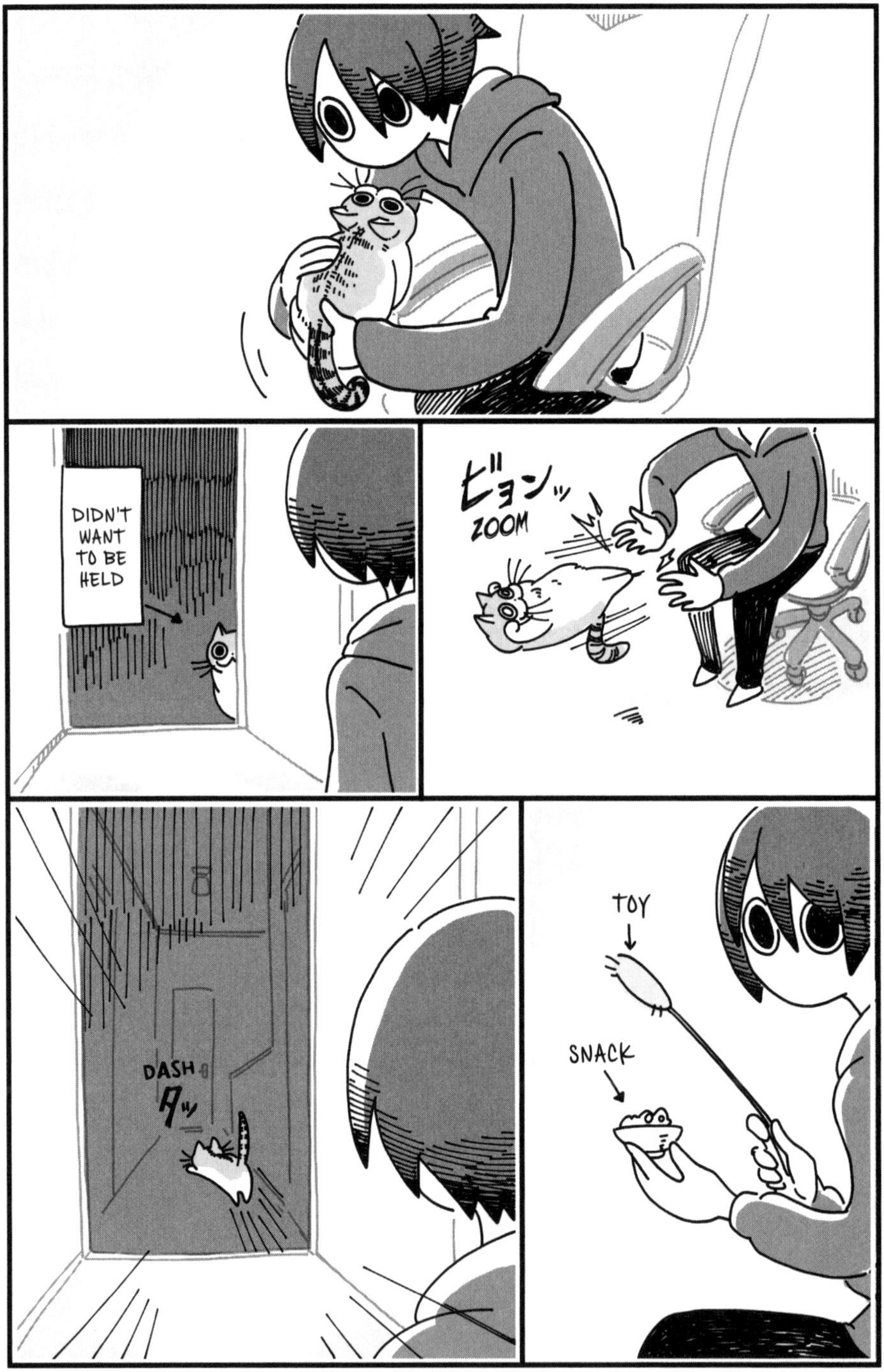
ビョンッ
ZOOM
DIDN'T WANT TO BE HELD
TOY
SNACK
DASH
タッ

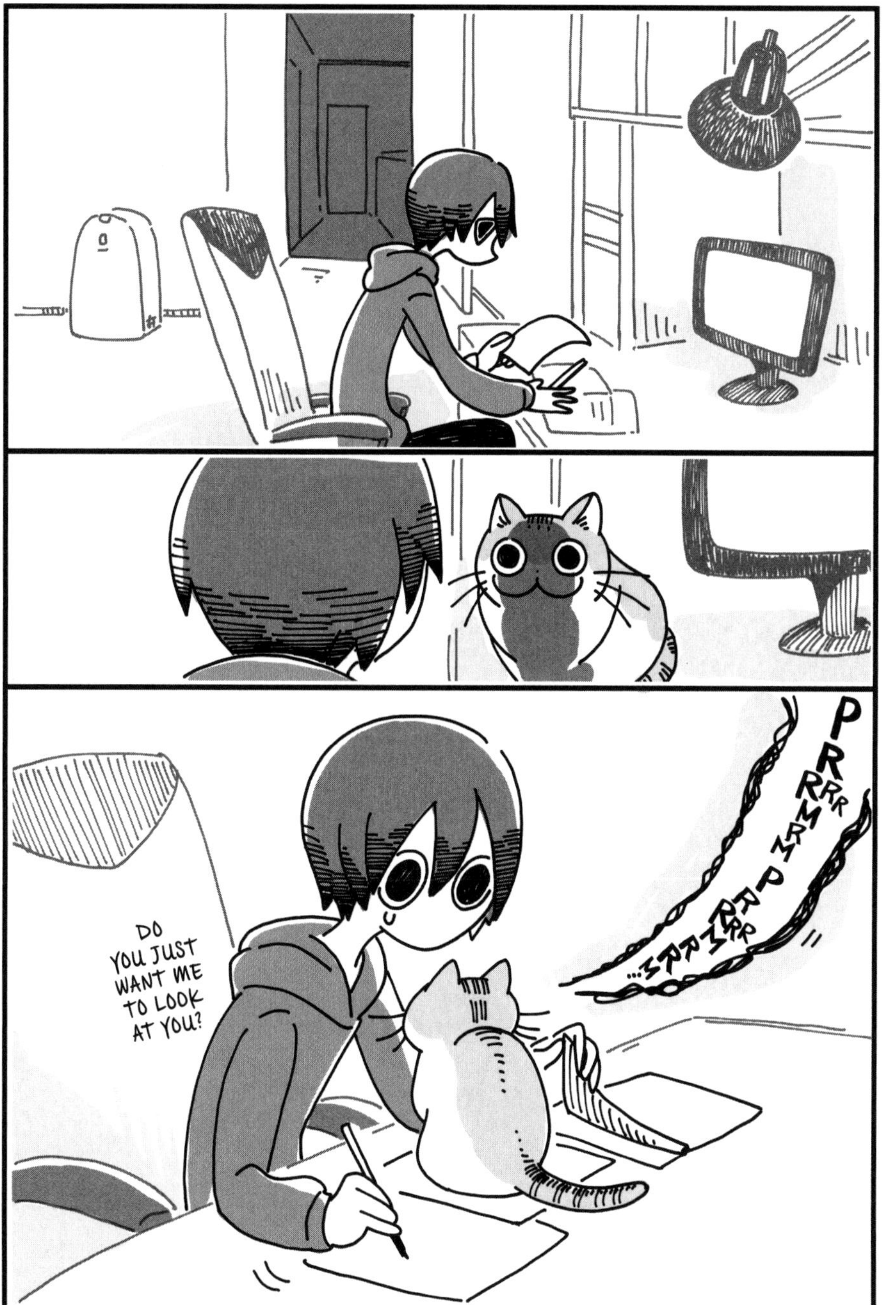
PRRRRMRM
PRRRRMRM...
DO YOU JUST WANT ME TO LOOK AT YOU?

Max Dilation

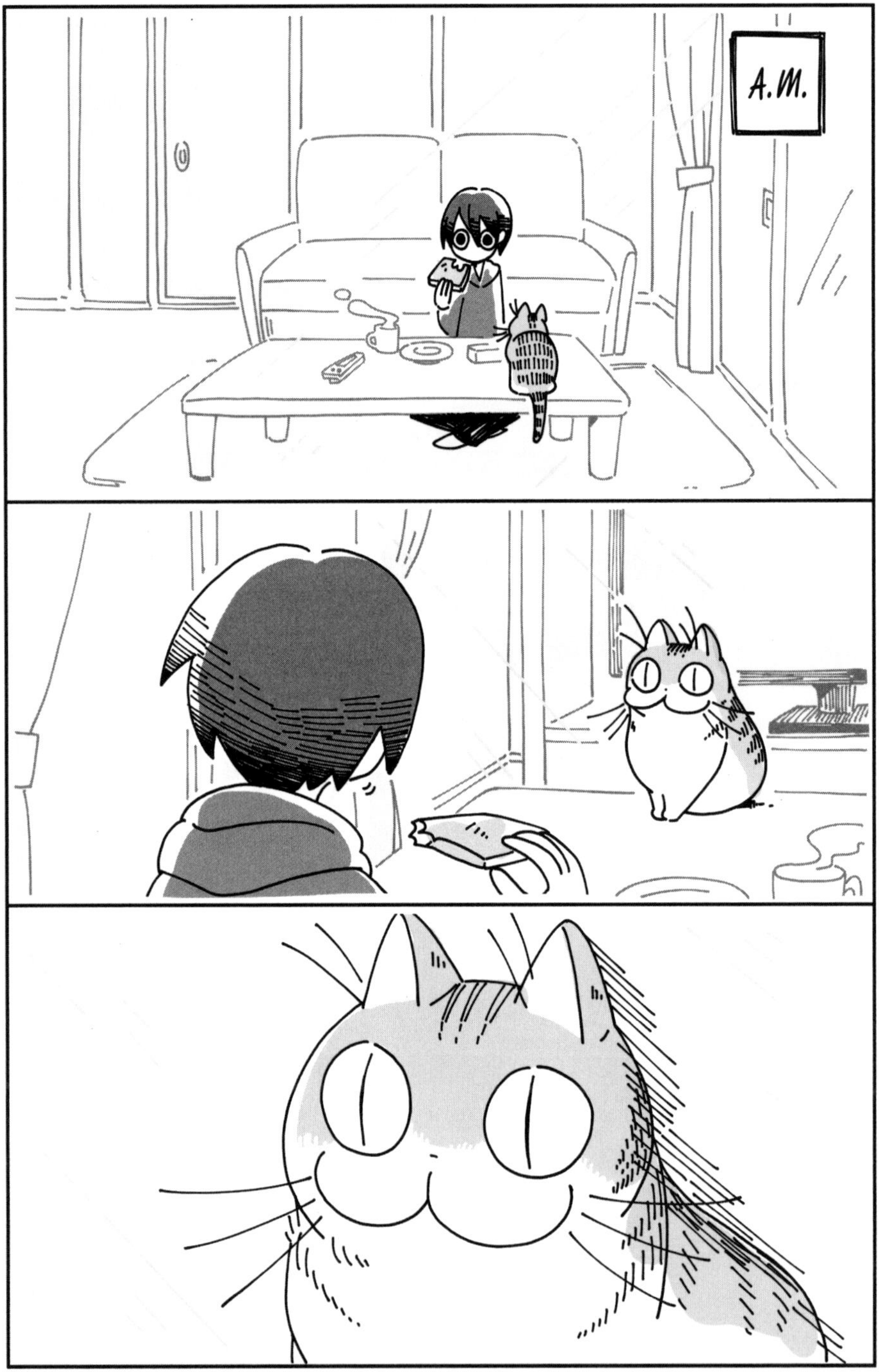
A.M.

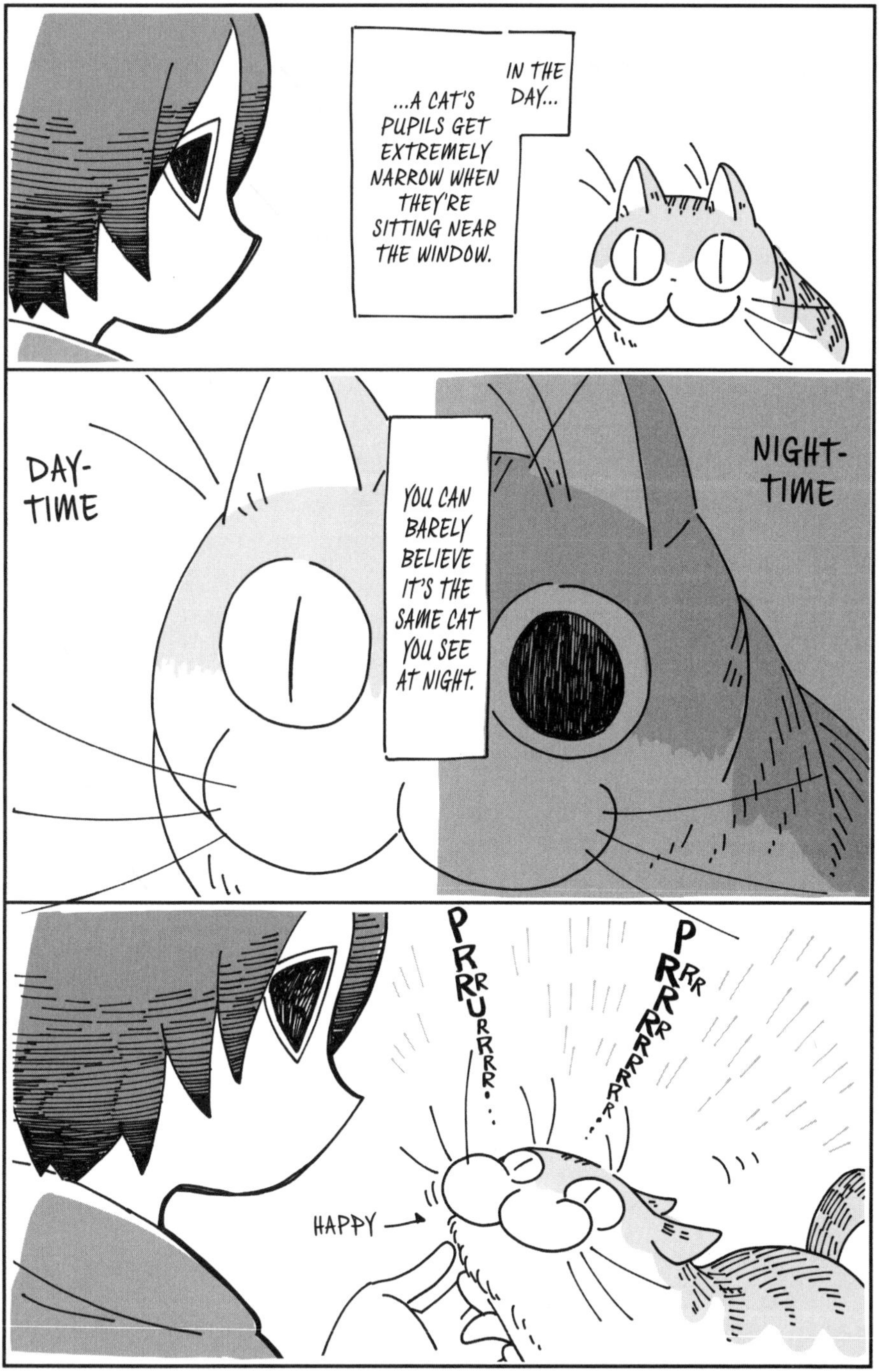
IN THE DAY...
...A CAT'S PUPILS GET EXTREMELY NARROW WHEN THEY'RE SITTING NEAR THE WINDOW.
NIGHT-TIME
YOU CAN BARELY BELIEVE IT'S THE SAME CAT YOU SEE AT NIGHT.
DAY-TIME
PRRRRRRRRRRR...
PRRURRRRR...
HAPPY

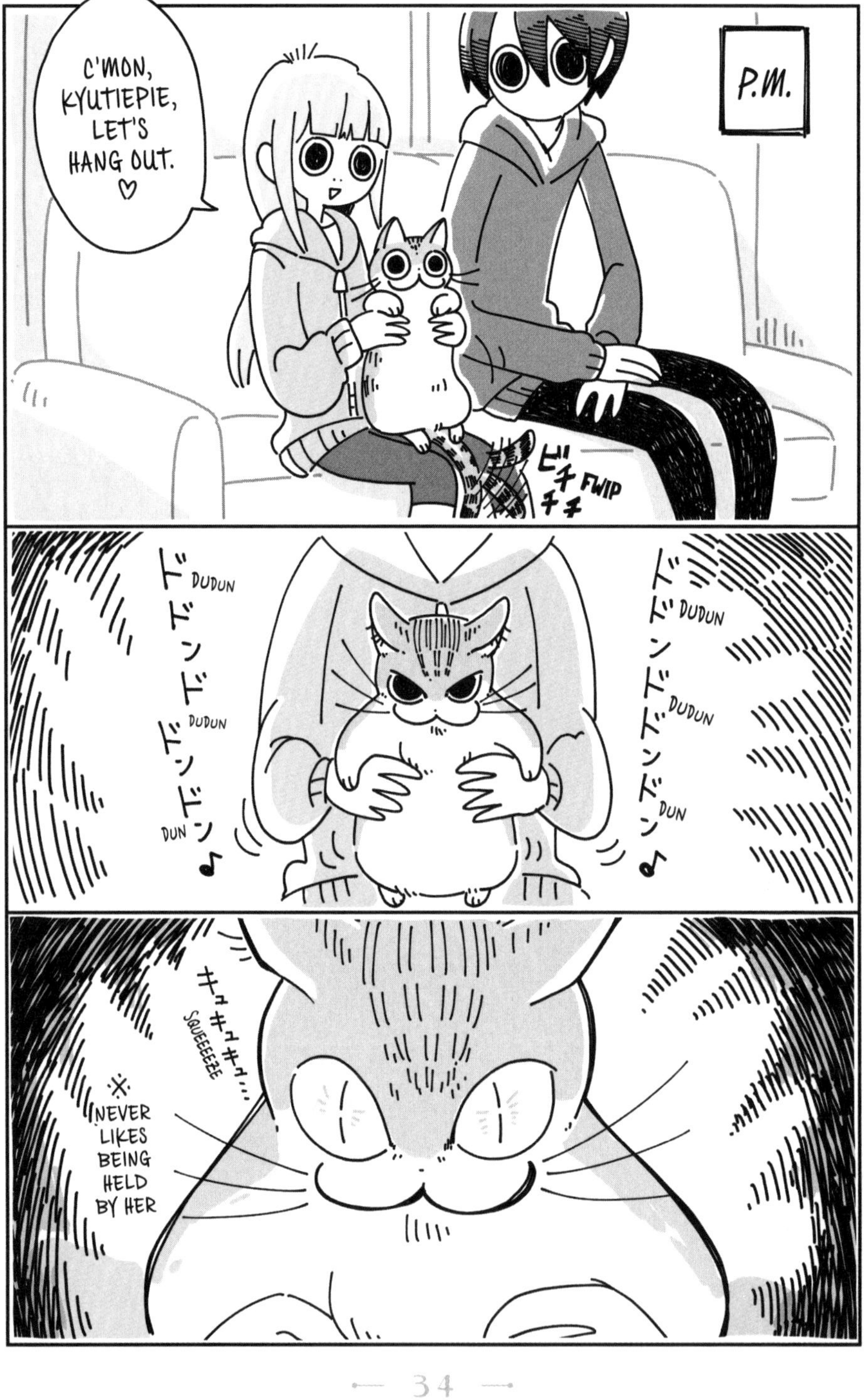
P.M.
C'MON, KYUTIEPIE, LET'S HANG OUT. ♡
ビチチチ FWIP
ドドンドドンドン♪
DUDUN DUDUN DUN
ドドンドドンドン♪
DUDUN DUDUN DUN
キュキュキュ…
SQUEEEEEZE
※NEVER LIKES BEING HELD BY HER

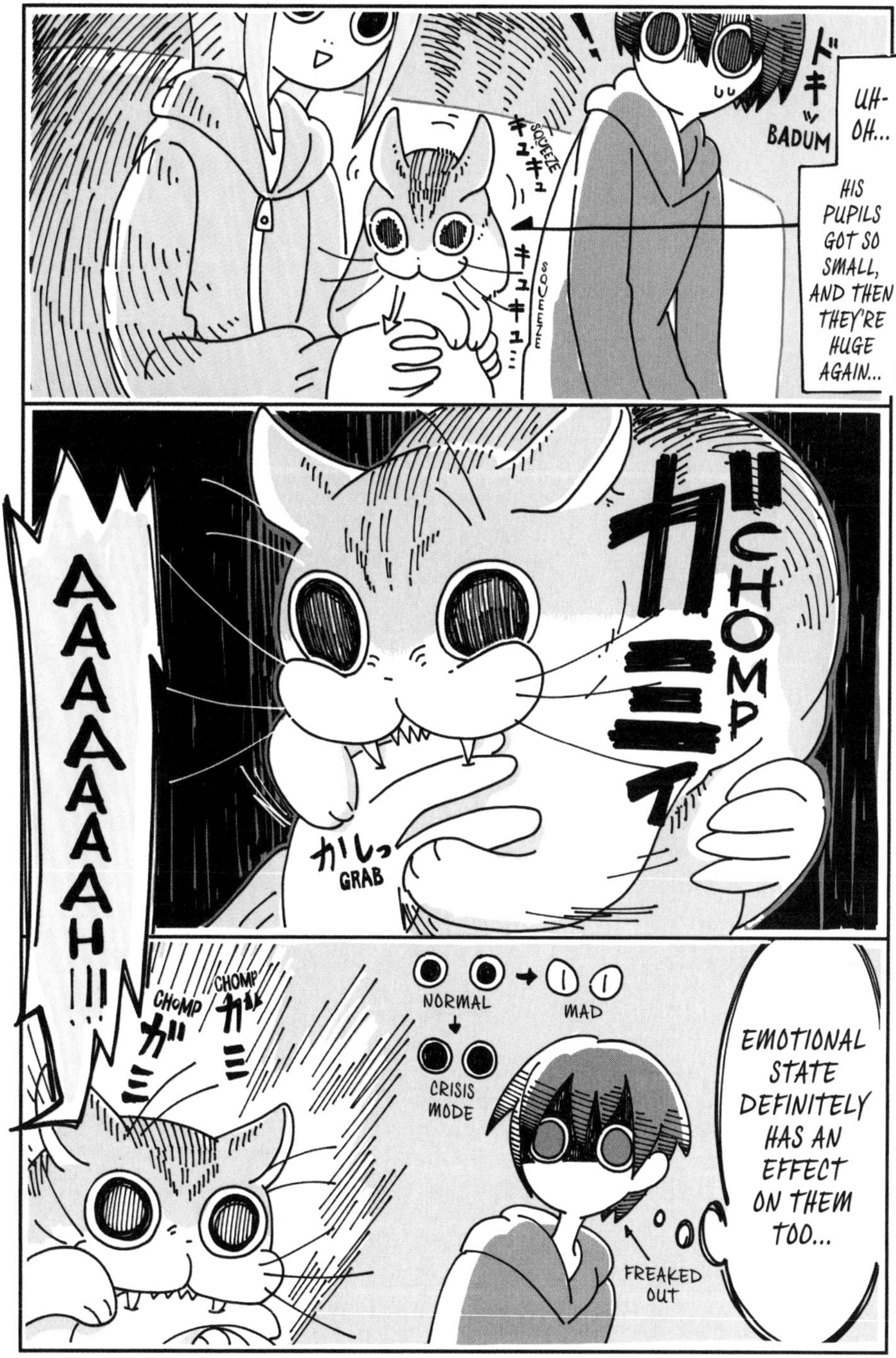
UH-OH...
ドキッ BADUM
HIS PUPILS GOT SO SMALL, AND THEN THEY'RE HUGE AGAIN...
キュキュ SQUEEZE
キュキュ... SQUEEZE
ガミッ CHOMP
カしっ GRAB
AAAAAAAH!!!
EMOTIONAL STATE DEFINITELY HAS AN EFFECT ON THEM TOO...
NORMAL
MAD
CRISIS MODE
FREAKED OUT
ガミ CHOMP
ガミ CHOMP

Cat Grooming Hurts

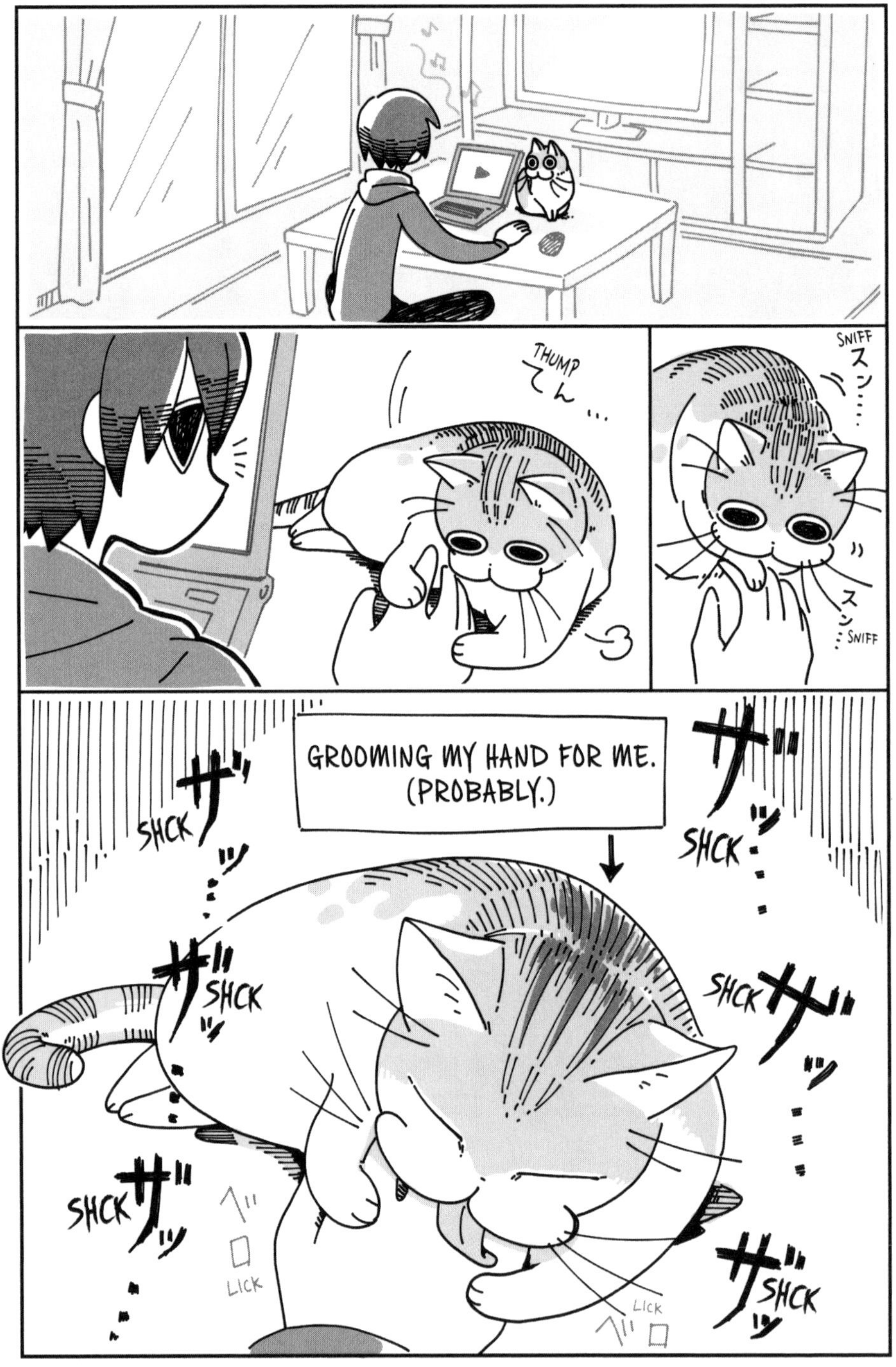

SNIFF
スン…
スン…
SNIFF
THUMP
てん…
GROOMING MY HAND FOR ME. (PROBABLY.)
SHCK
ザッ…
SHCK
ザッ…
SHCK
ザッ…
SHCK
ザッ
SHCK
ザッ…
SHCK
ザッ…
ベロ
LICK
ベロ
LICK

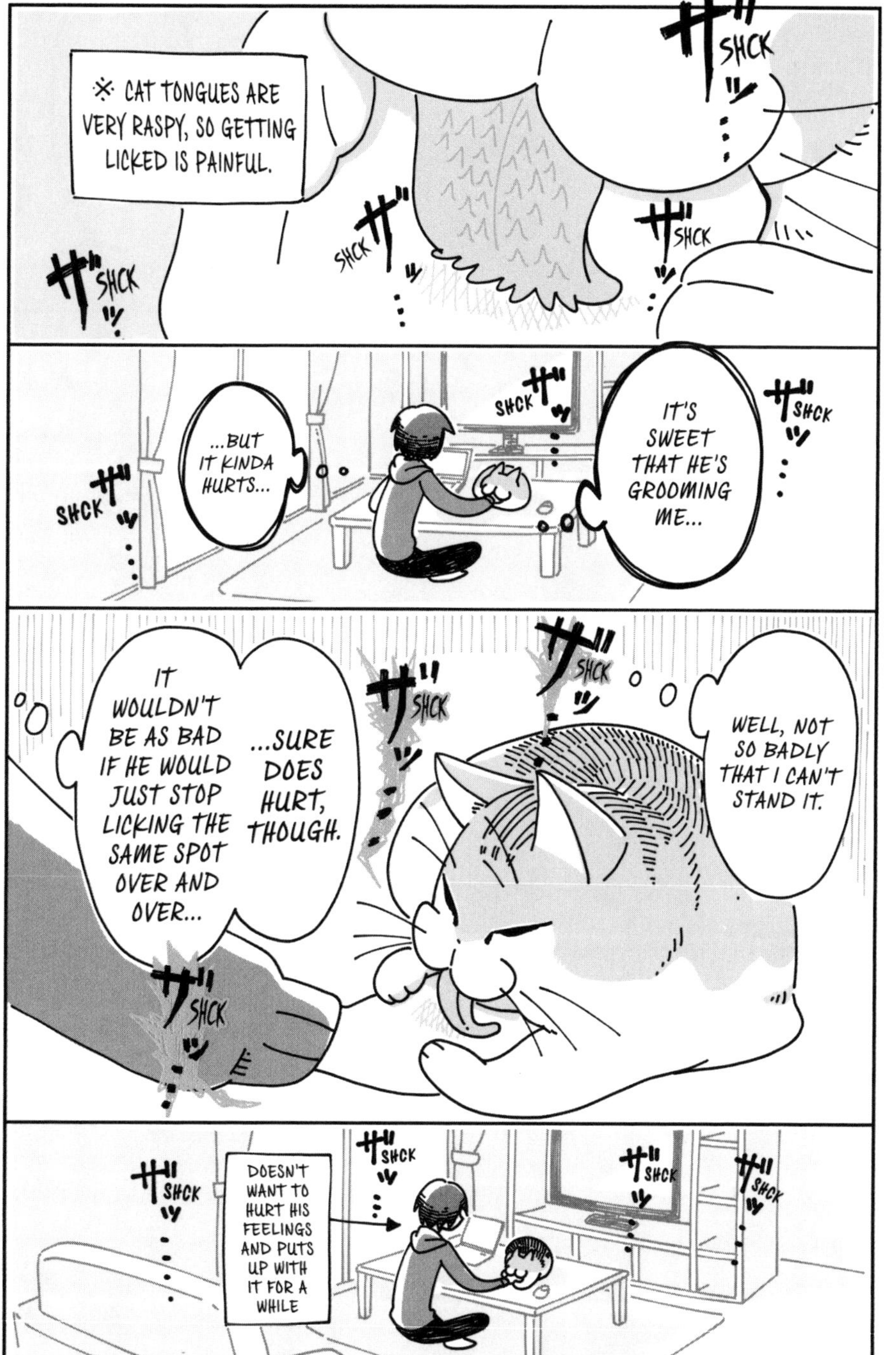
ザッ SHCK
ザッ SHCK
※ CAT TONGUES ARE VERY RASPY, SO GETTING LICKED IS PAINFUL.
ザッ SHCK
ザッ SHCK
ザッ SHCK
IT'S SWEET THAT HE'S GROOMING ME...
ザッ SHCK
...BUT IT KINDA HURTS...
ザッ SHCK
WELL, NOT SO BADLY THAT I CAN'T STAND IT.
ザッ SHCK
ザッ SHCK
...SURE DOES HURT, THOUGH.
IT WOULDN'T BE AS BAD IF HE WOULD JUST STOP LICKING THE SAME SPOT OVER AND OVER...
ザッ SHCK
ザッ SHCK
ザッ SHCK
ザッ SHCK
DOESN'T WANT TO HURT HIS FEELINGS AND PUTS UP WITH IT FOR A WHILE
ザッ SHCK

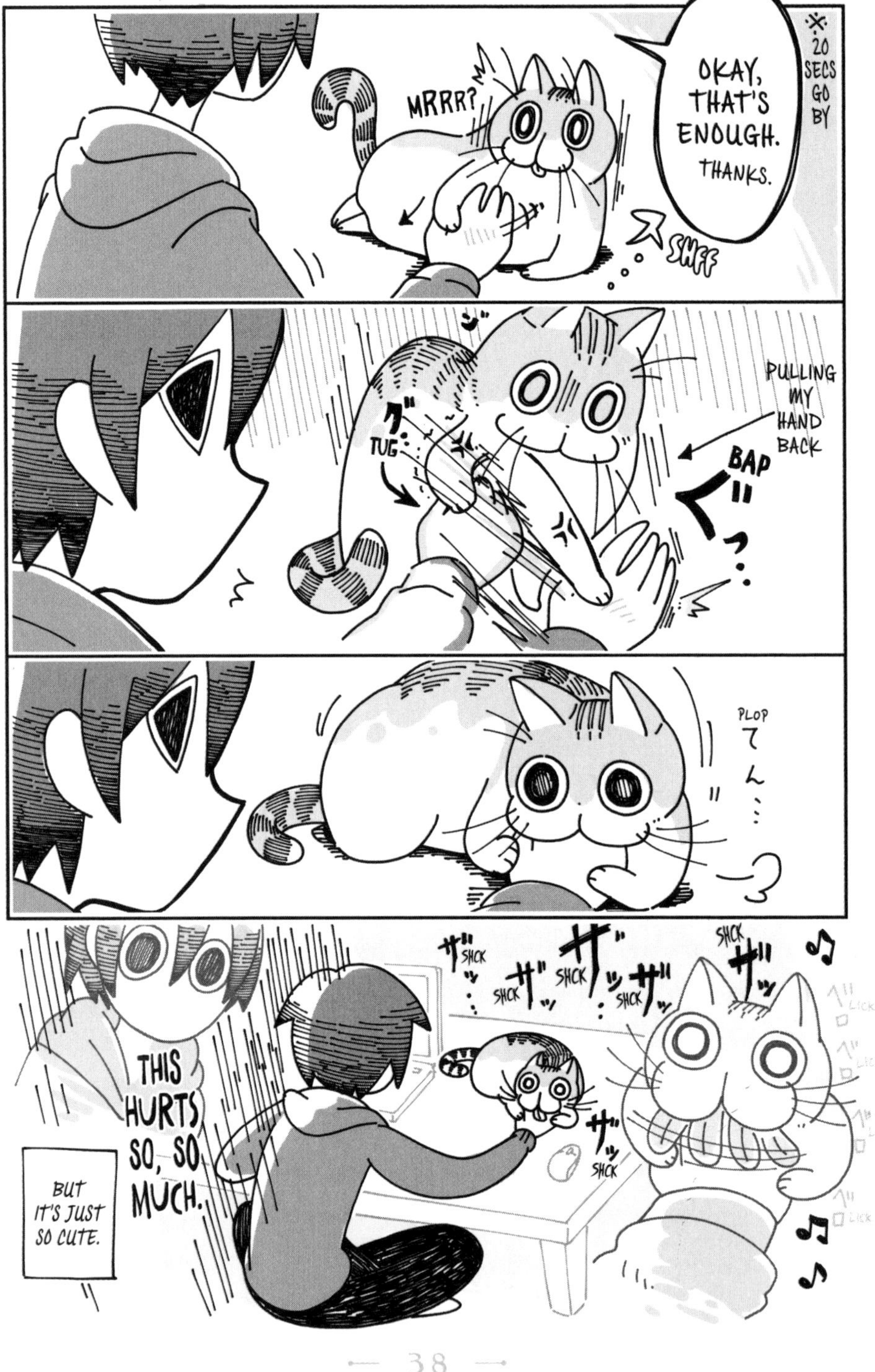
※20 SECS GO BY
OKAY, THAT'S ENOUGH.
THANKS.
SHFF
MRRR?
PULLING MY HAND BACK
BAP
TUG
PLOP
てん
LICK
LICK
LICK
LICK
SHCK
SHCK
SHCK
SHCK
SHCK
SHCK
THIS HURTS SO, SO MUCH.
BUT IT'S JUST SO CUTE.

No Matter How Much You Want to Touch the Whiskers...Don't

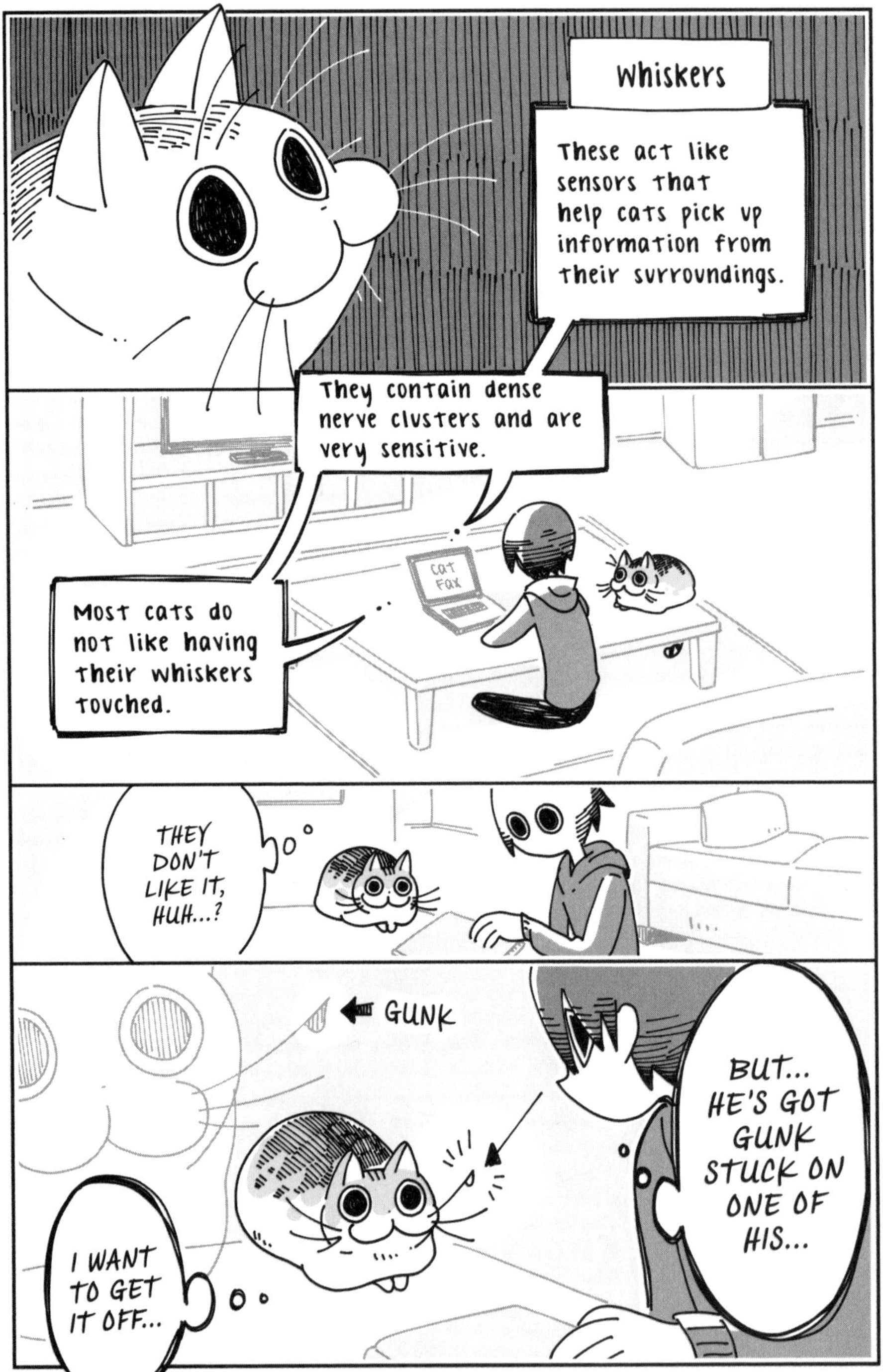

Whiskers
These act like sensors that help cats pick up information from their surroundings.
They contain dense nerve clusters and are very sensitive.
Cat Fax
Most cats do not like having their whiskers touched.
THEY DON'T LIKE IT, HUH...?
...
BUT... HE'S GOT GUNK STUCK ON ONE OF HIS...
GUNK
I WANT TO GET IT OFF...

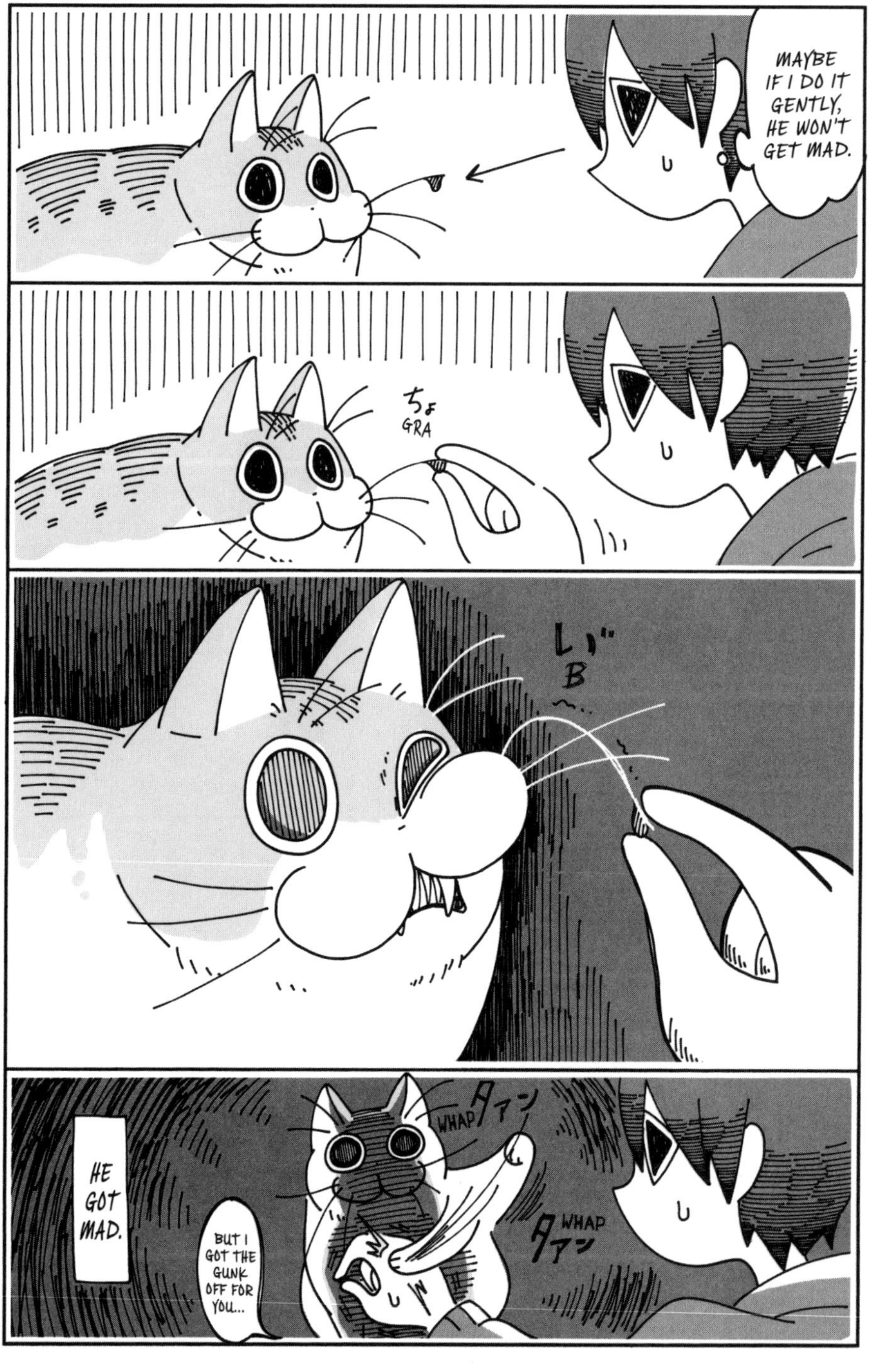
MAYBE IF I DO IT GENTLY, HE WON'T GET MAD.
ちょ
GRA
じ
B
WHAP タァン
WHAP タァン
HE GOT MAD.
BUT I GOT THE GUNK OFF FOR YOU...

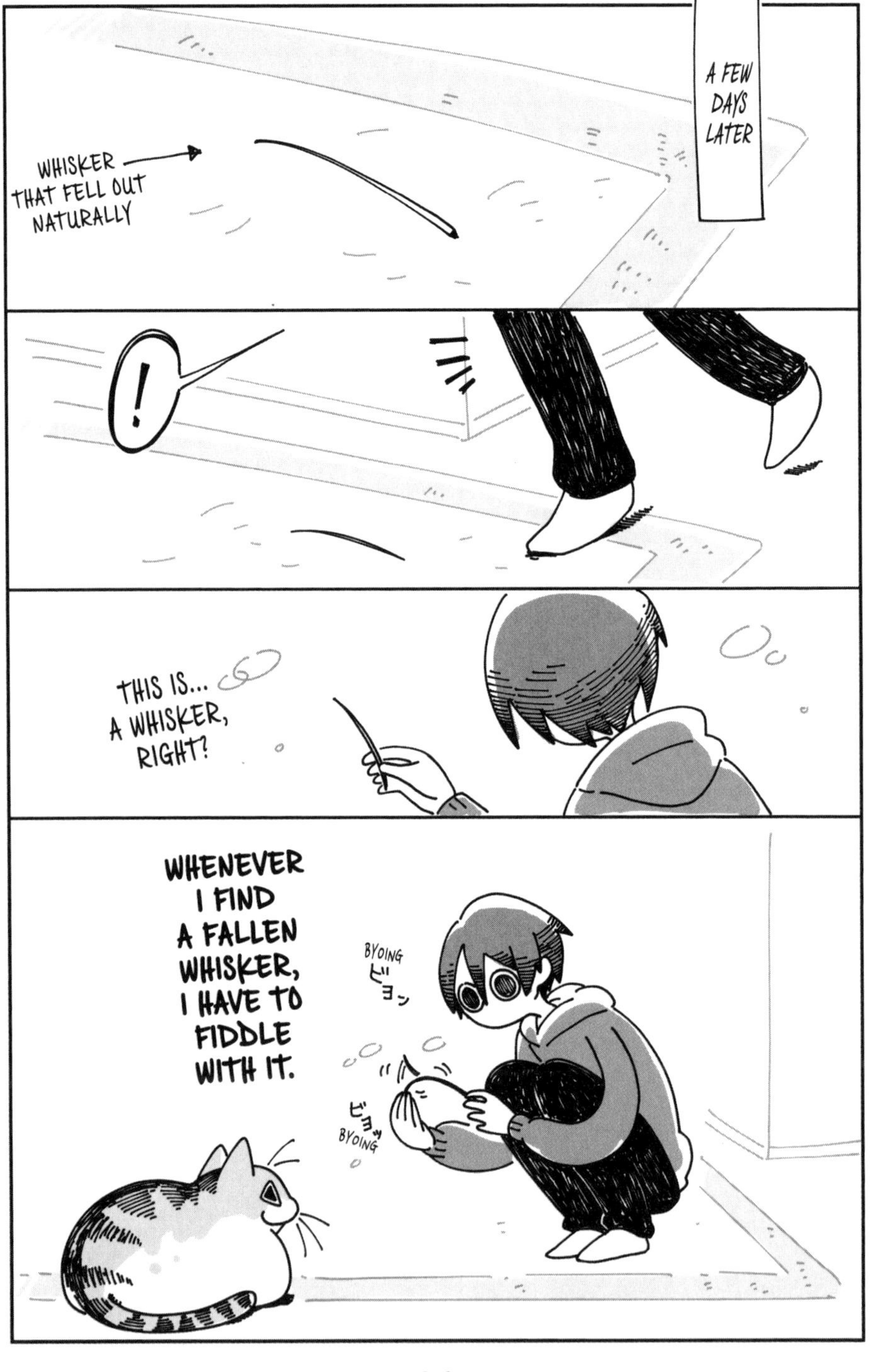
A FEW DAYS LATER
WHISKER THAT FELL OUT NATURALLY
!
THIS IS... A WHISKER, RIGHT?
WHENEVER I FIND A FALLEN WHISKER, I HAVE TO FIDDLE WITH IT.
BYOING
ビヨッ
ビヨッ
BYOING

SOMETIMES HE JUST MAKES THIS FACE ON HIS OWN.

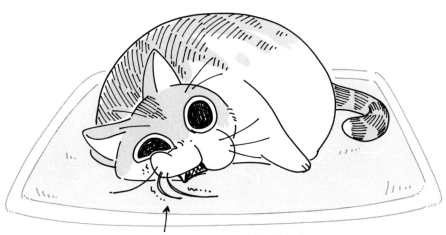

WHISKERS BENT AGAINST THE GROUND

Catmouflage

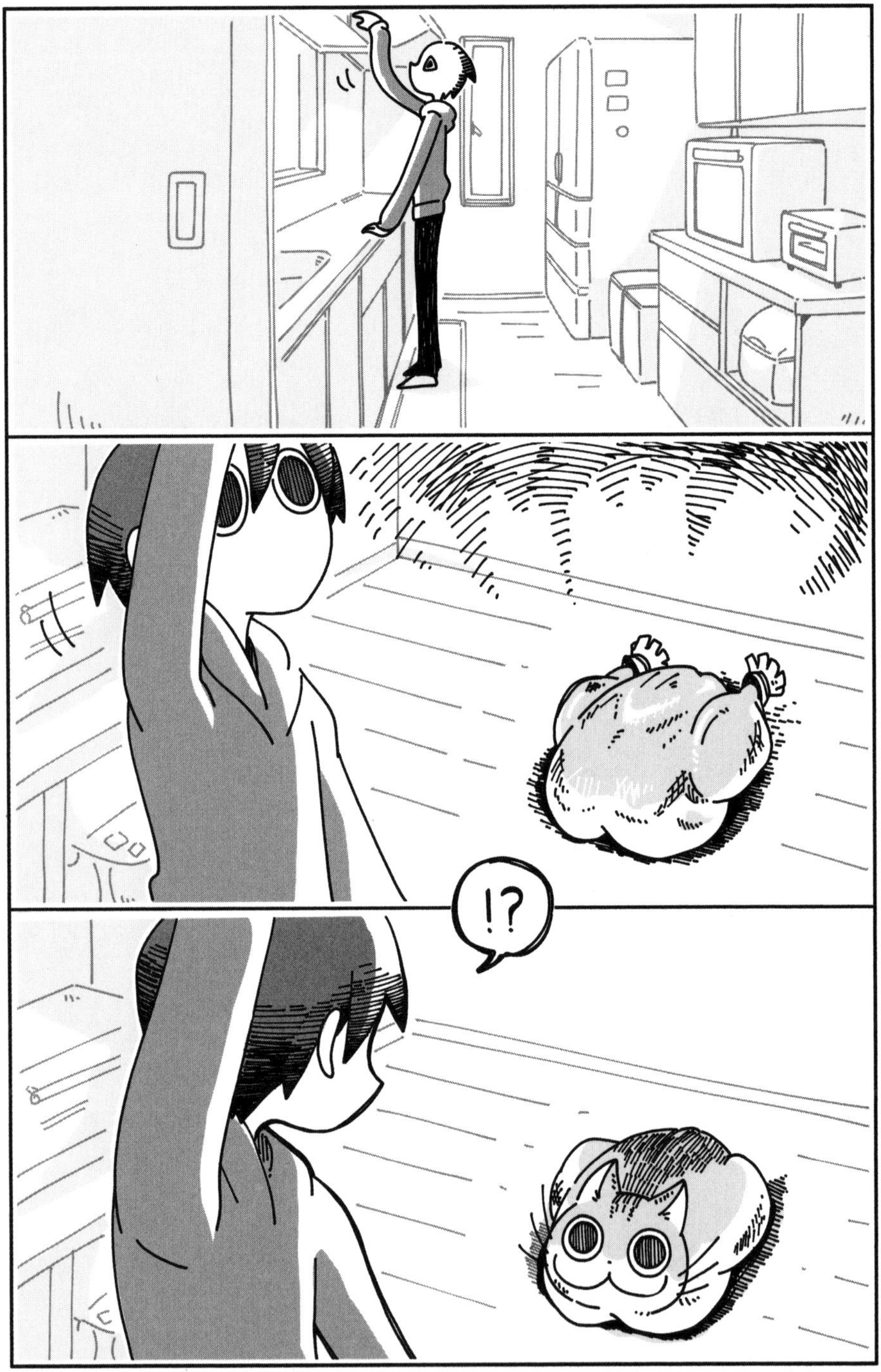
!?

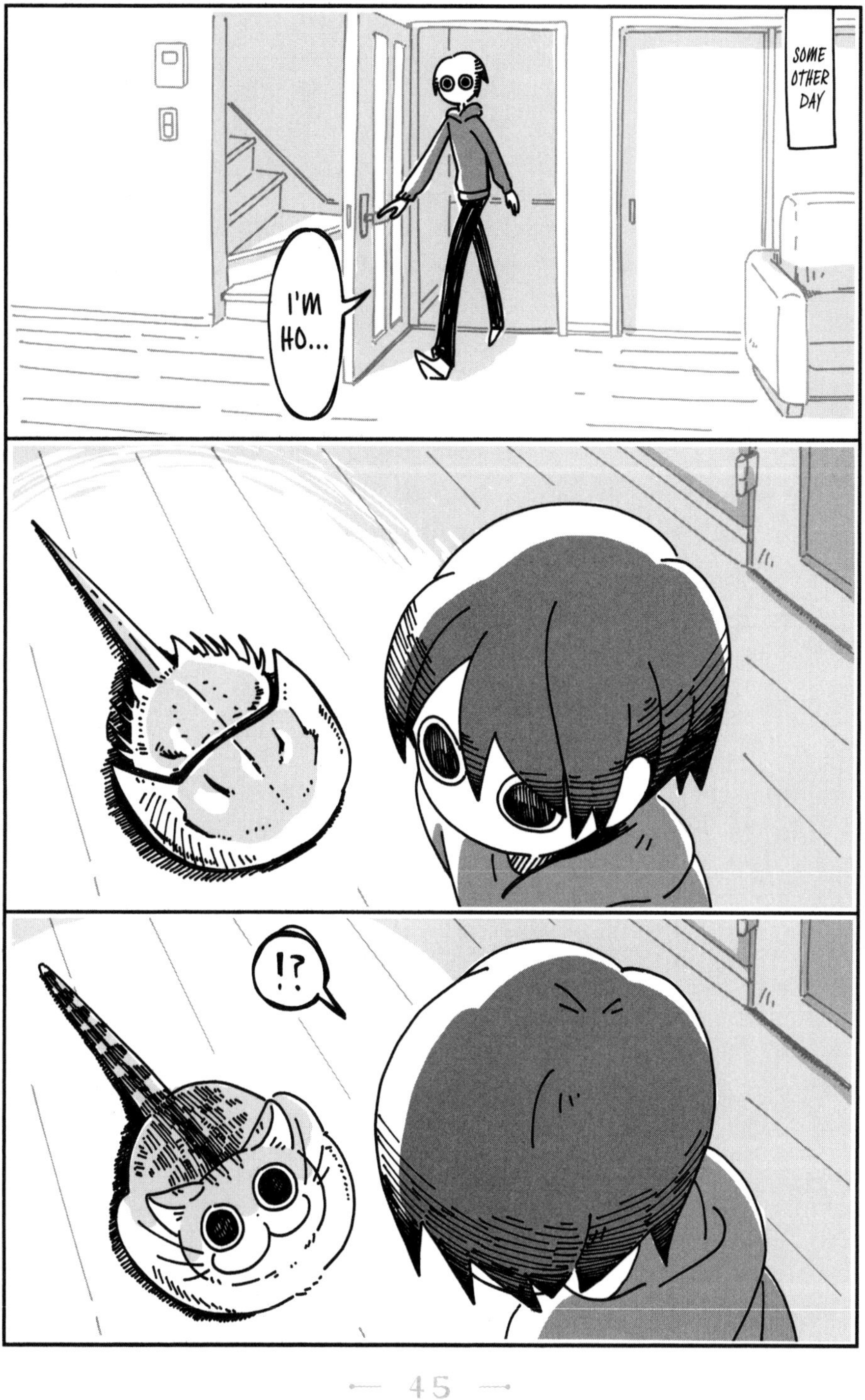
SOME OTHER DAY
I'M HO...
!?

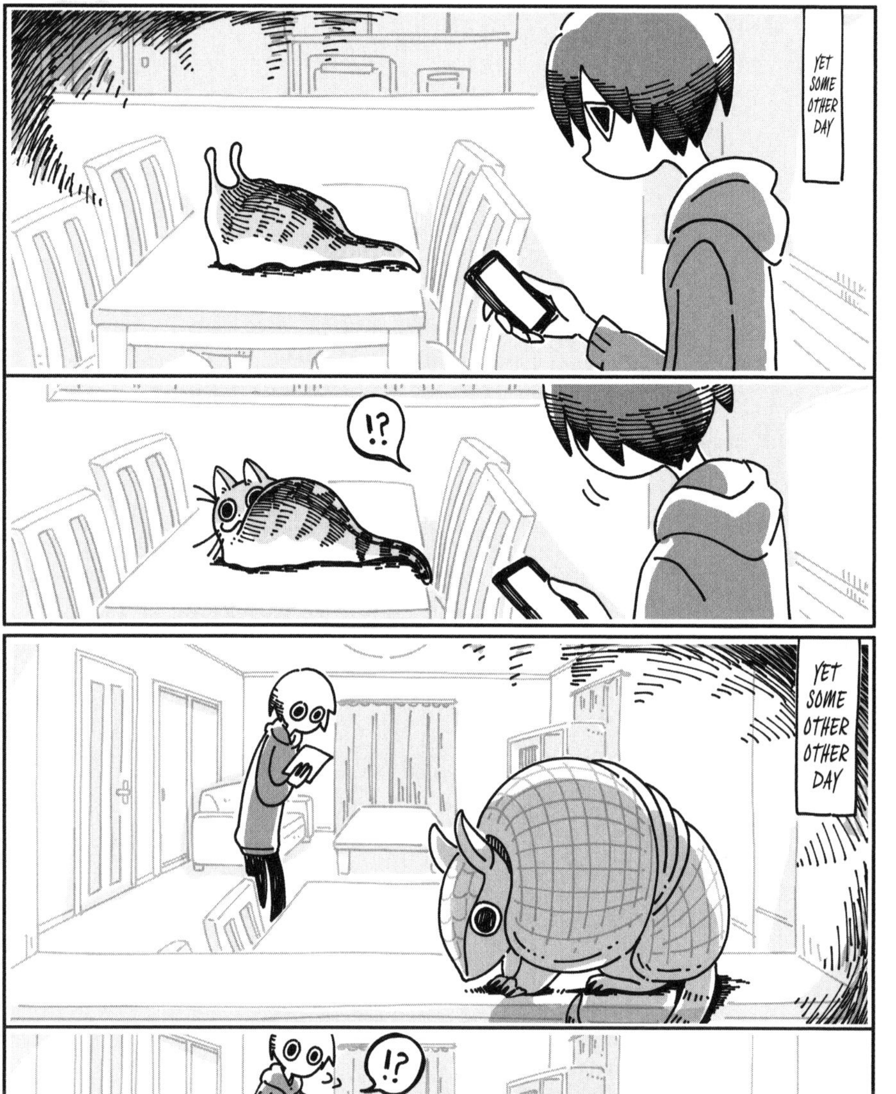
YET SOME OTHER DAY
!?
YET SOME OTHER OTHER DAY
!?

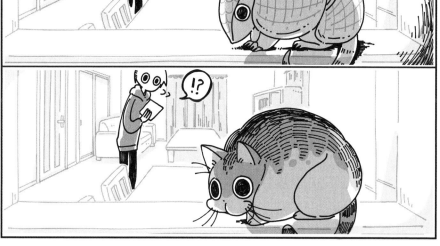

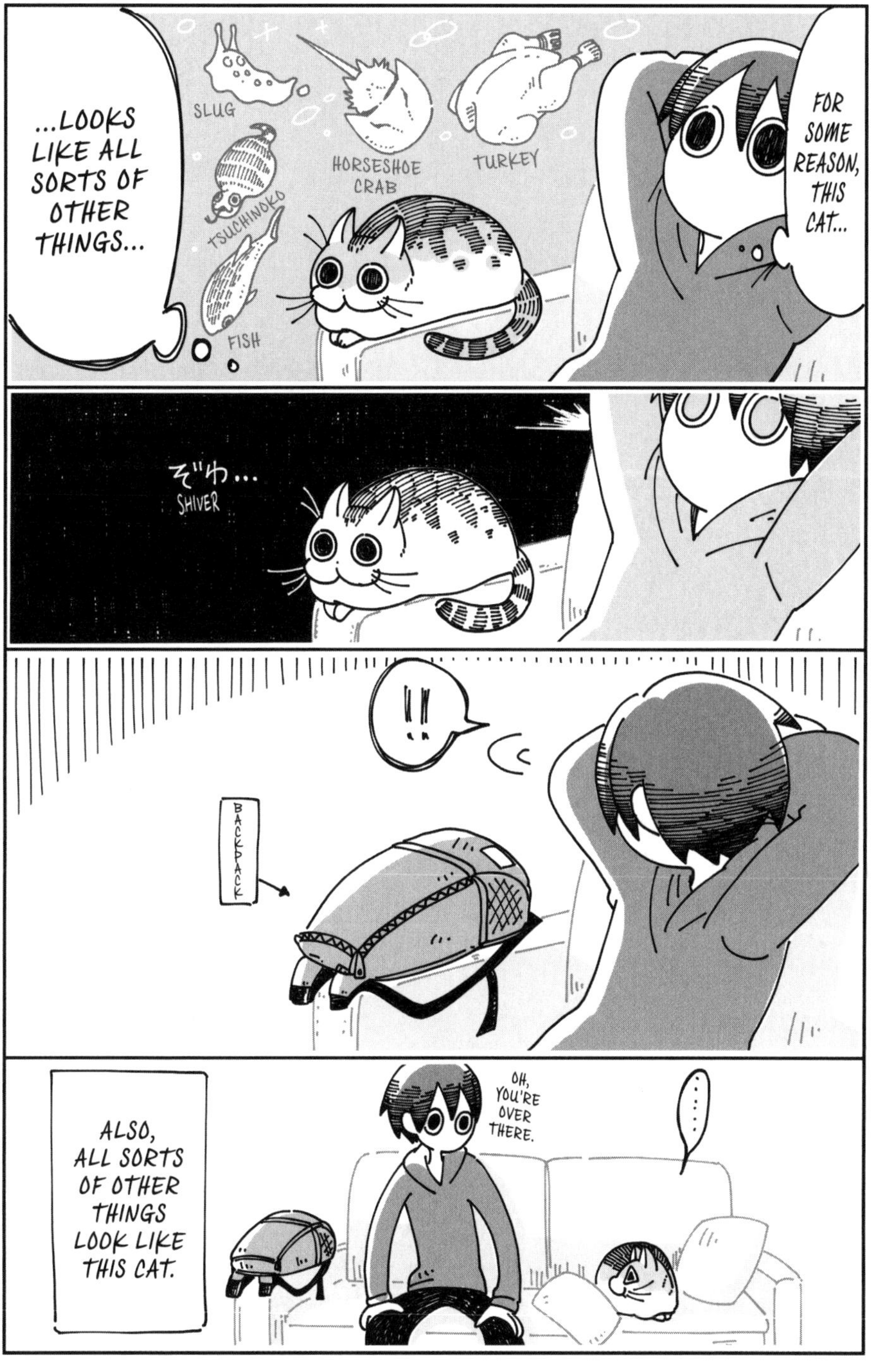
FOR SOME REASON, THIS CAT...
SLUG
HORSESHOE CRAB
TURKEY
TSUCHINOKO
FISH
...LOOKS LIKE ALL SORTS OF OTHER THINGS...
ぞわ...
SHIVER
!!
BACKPACK
......
OH, YOU'RE OVER THERE.
ALSO, ALL SORTS OF OTHER THINGS LOOK LIKE THIS CAT.

My Cat Has Lag

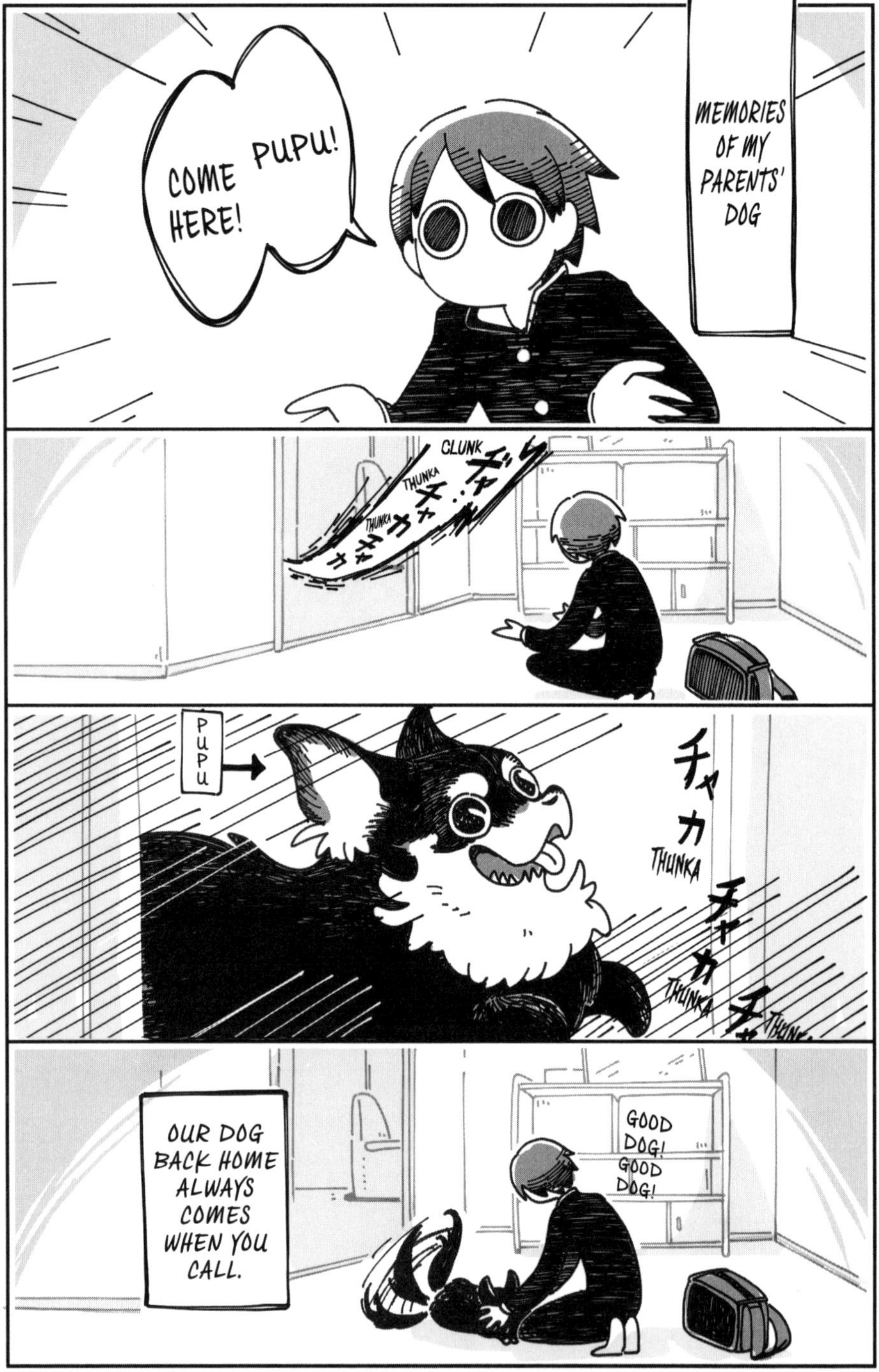

MEMORIES OF MY PARENTS' DOG
PUPU! COME HERE!
CLUNK
THUNKA
THUNKA
PUPU
チャカ
THUNKA
チャカ
THUNKA
GOOD DOG! GOOD DOG!
OUR DOG BACK HOME ALWAYS COMES WHEN YOU CALL.

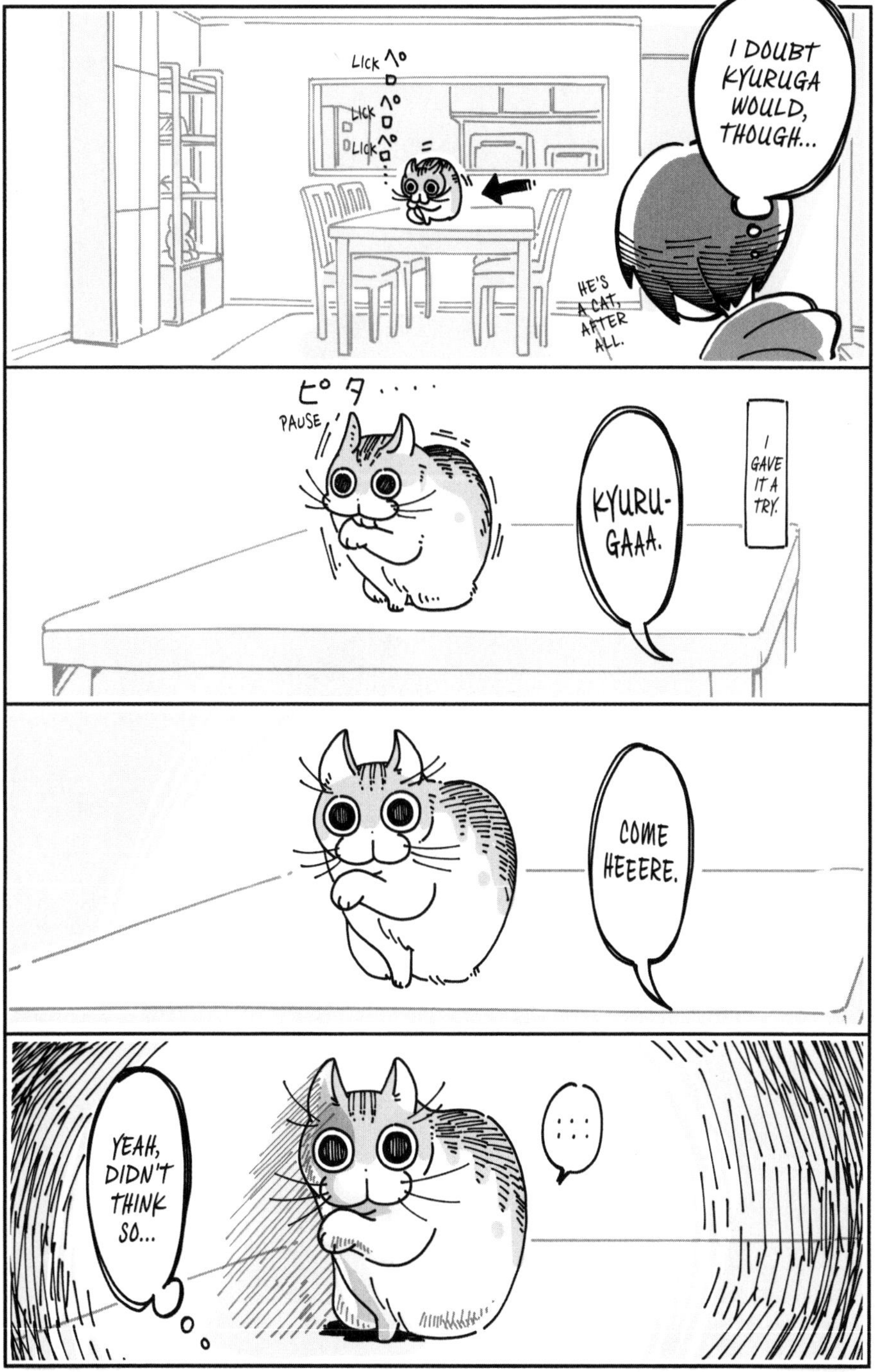
I DOUBT KYURUGA WOULD, THOUGH...
HE'S A CAT, AFTER ALL.
LICK ペロ
LICK ペロ
LICK ペロ
I GAVE IT A TRY.
KYURU-GAAA.
ピタ....
PAUSE
COME HEEERE.
......
YEAH, DIDN'T THINK SO...

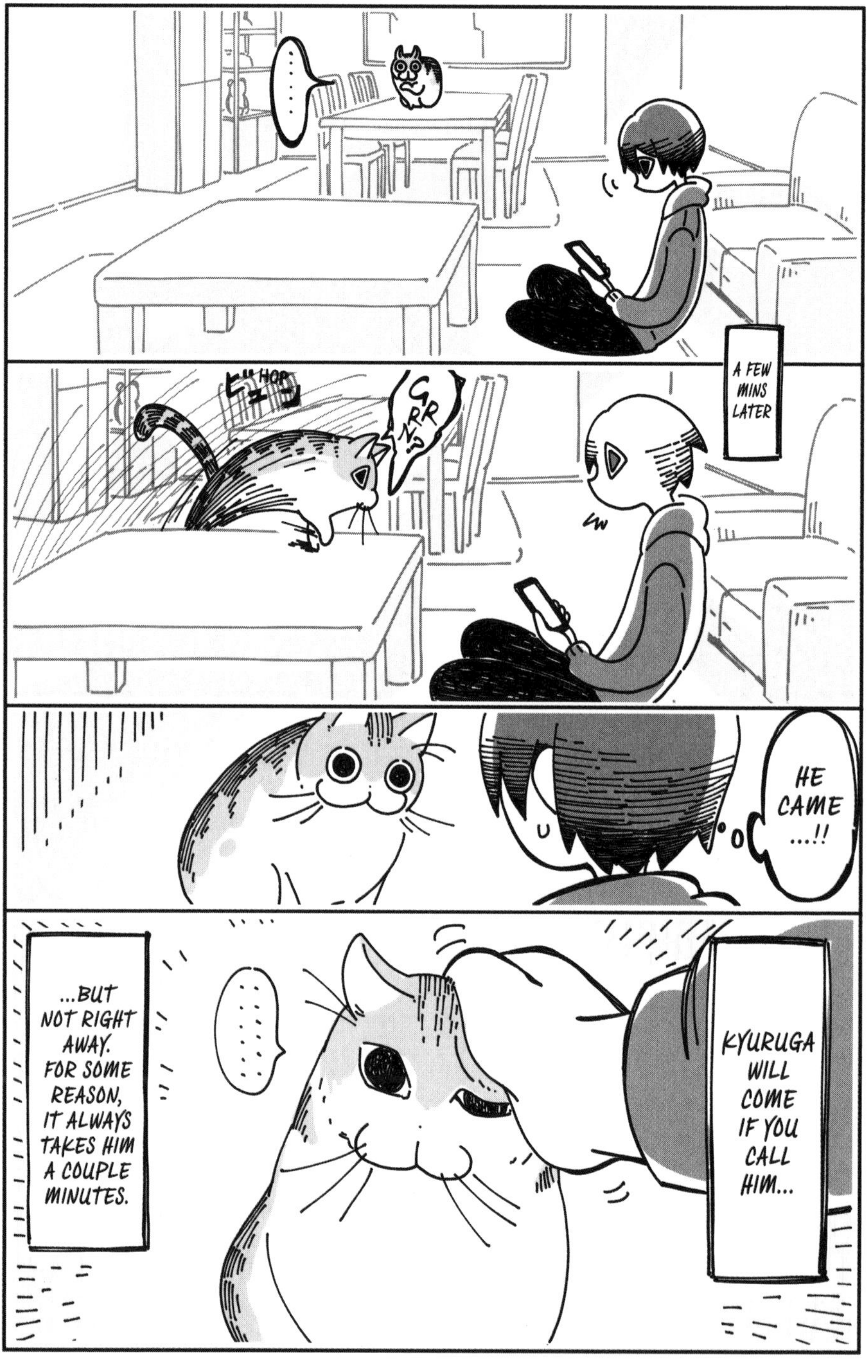
......
A FEW MINS LATER
GRRN?
ビョン
HOP
HE CAME ...!!
KYURUGA WILL COME IF YOU CALL HIM...
......
...BUT NOT RIGHT AWAY. FOR SOME REASON, IT ALWAYS TAKES HIM A COUPLE MINUTES.

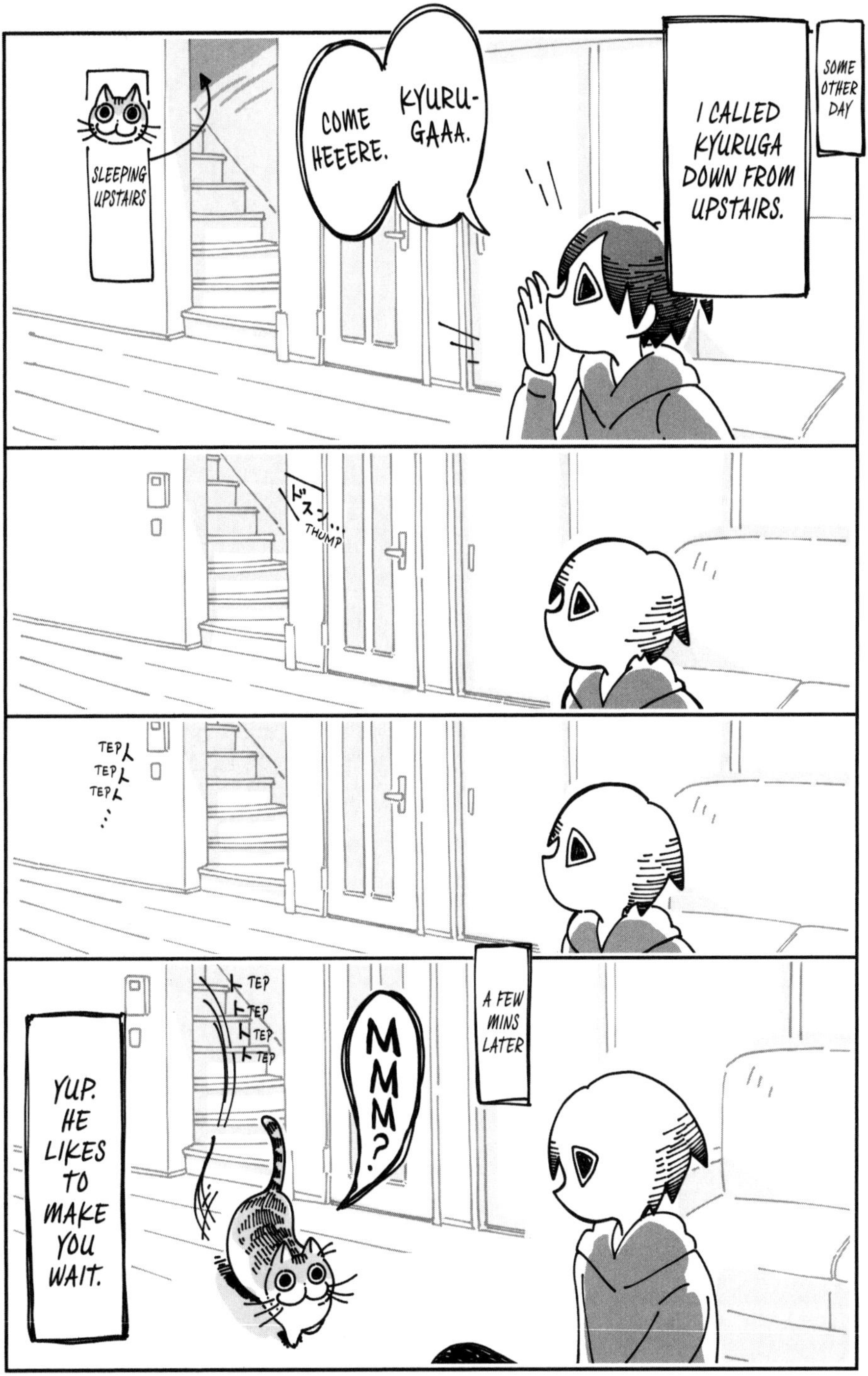
SOME OTHER DAY
I CALLED KYURUGA DOWN FROM UPSTAIRS.
KYURU-GAAA. COME HEEERE.
SLEEPING UPSTAIRS
ドスン… THUMP
TEP TEP TEP…
A FEW MINS LATER
MMM?
TEP TEP TEP TEP
YUP. HE LIKES TO MAKE YOU WAIT.

The Allure of Inside-Out Cat Ears

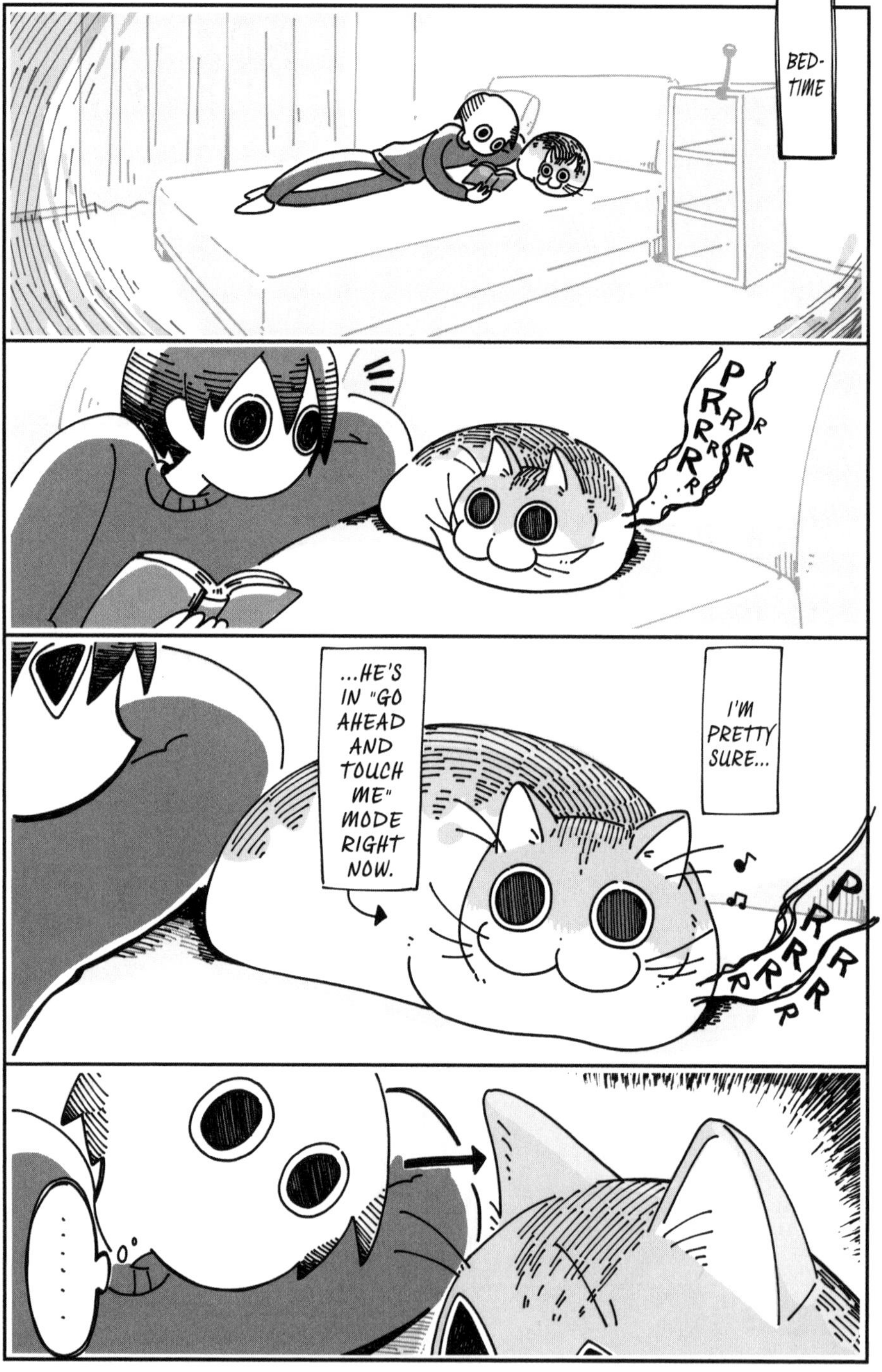
BED-TIME
PRRRRRRRRR
I'M PRETTY SURE...
...HE'S IN "GO AHEAD AND TOUCH ME" MODE RIGHT NOW.
PRRRRRRRRR
......

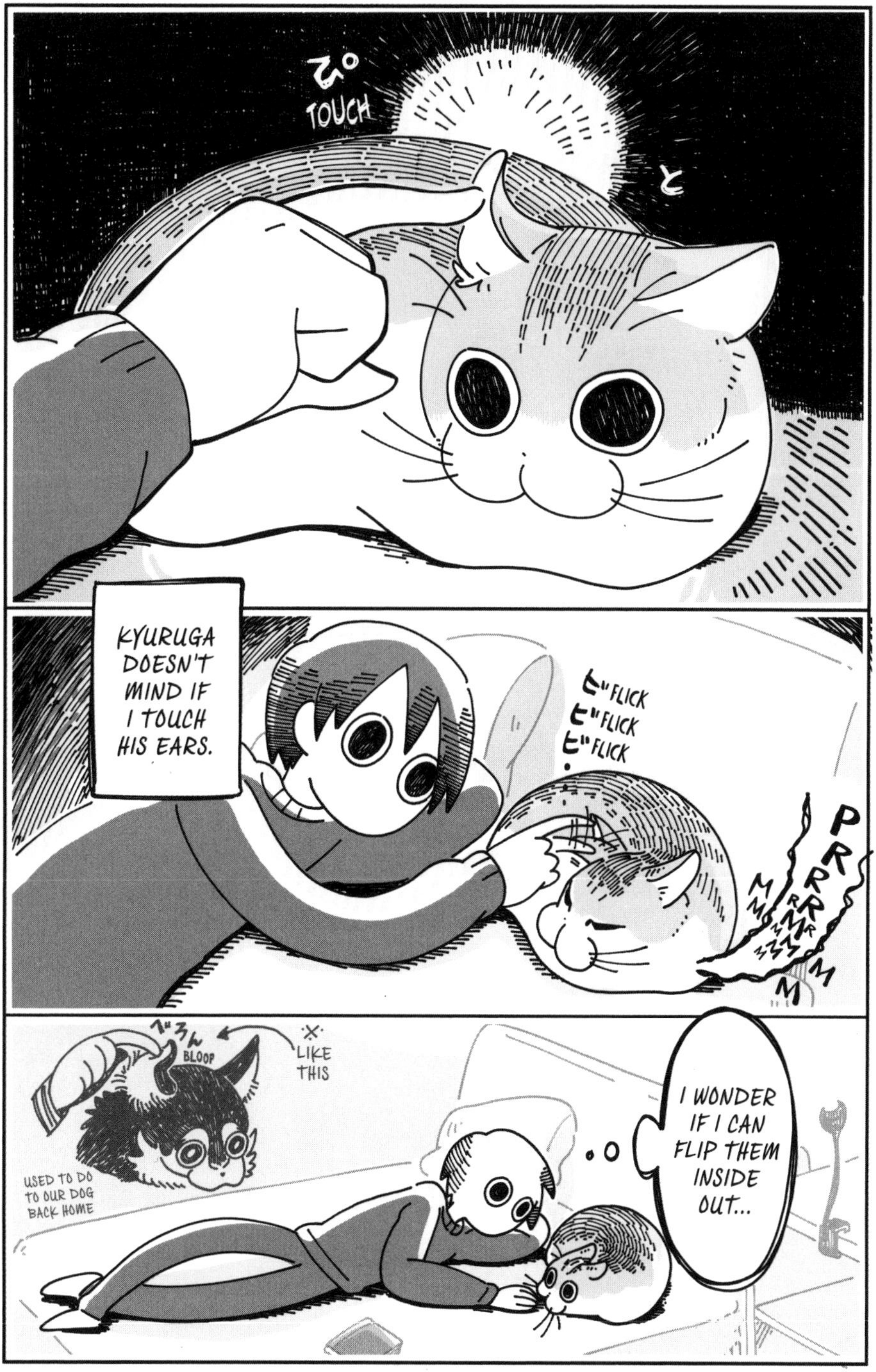

と
ぴ TOUCH
KYURUGA DOESN'T MIND IF I TOUCH HIS EARS.
ビ FLICK
ビ FLICK
ビ FLICK
PRRRRRRRM
MMMMMMM
I WONDER IF I CAN FLIP THEM INSIDE OUT...
※ LIKE THIS
べろん BLOOP
USED TO DO TO OUR DOG BACK HOME

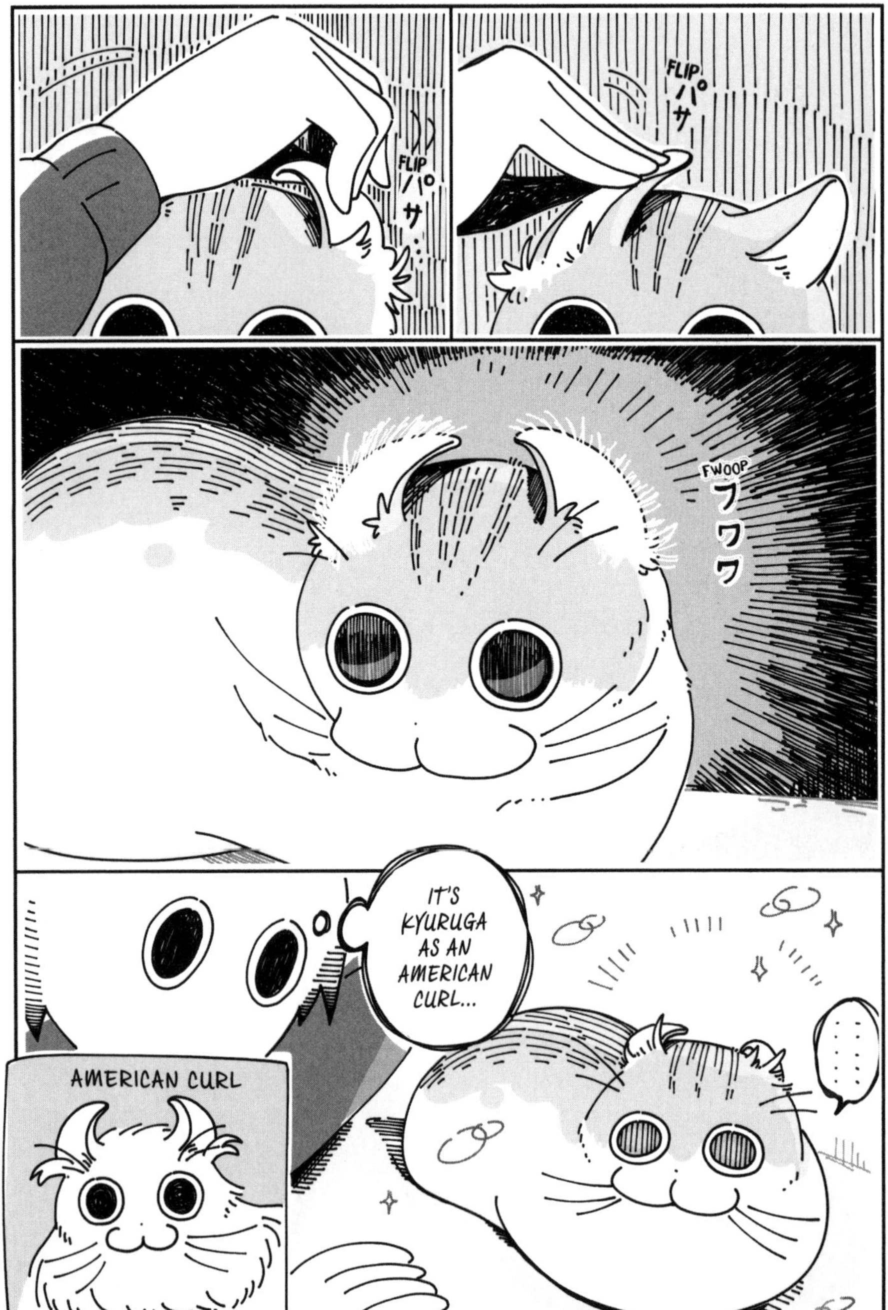
FLIP
パサ
FLIP
パサ…
FWOOP
フワワ
IT'S KYURUGA AS AN AMERICAN CURL...
AMERICAN CURL
A BREED WITH CURLED EARS

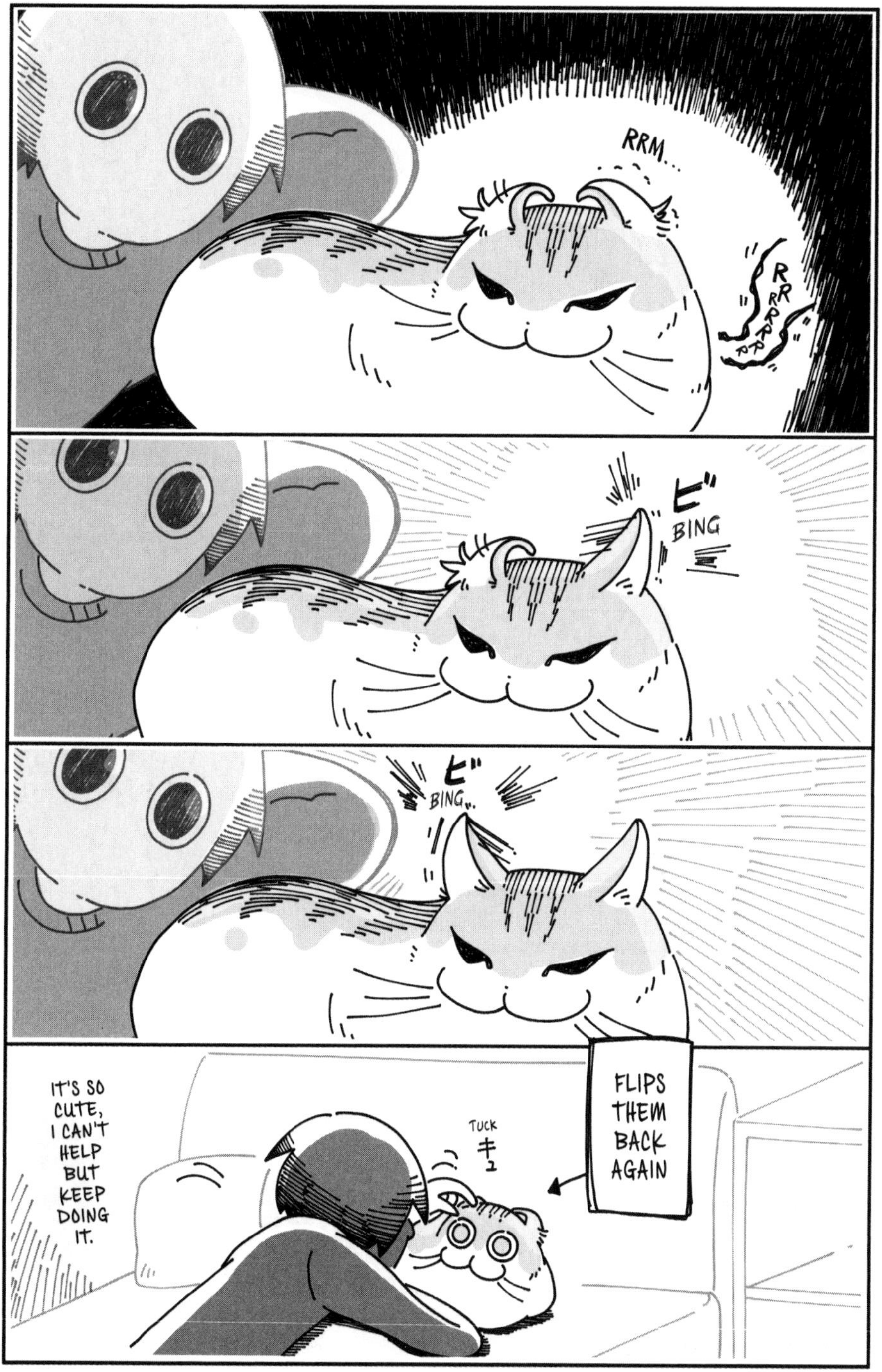
RRM...
RRRRRR
ビ
BING
ビ
BING..
FLIPS THEM BACK AGAIN
TUCK
キュ
IT'S SO CUTE, I CAN'T HELP BUT KEEP DOING IT.

Cats Can Squeeze Through If Their Head Fits

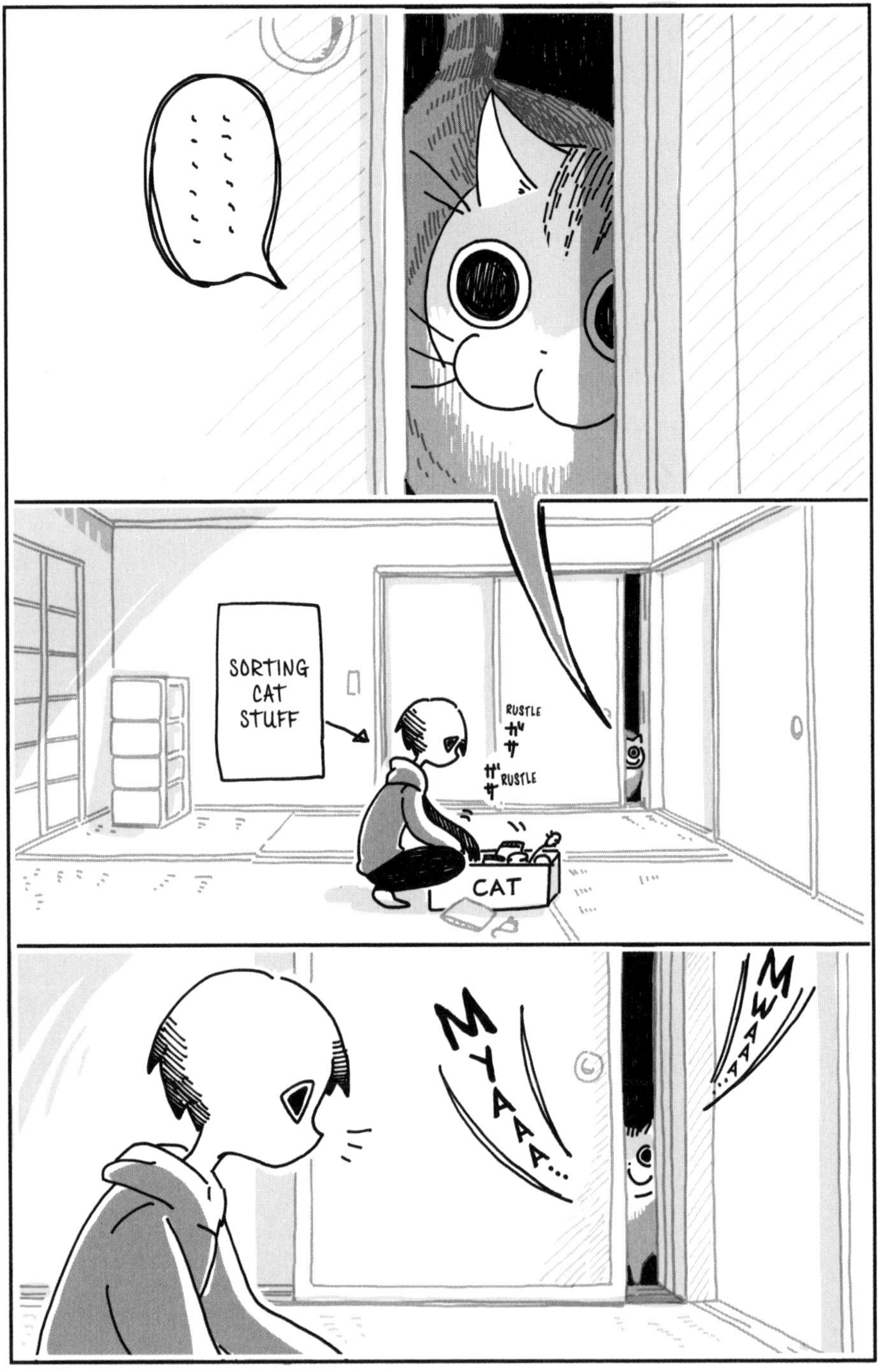
......
SORTING CAT STUFF
RUSTLE
ガサ
ガサ
RUSTLE
CAT
MWAAA...
MYAAAA...

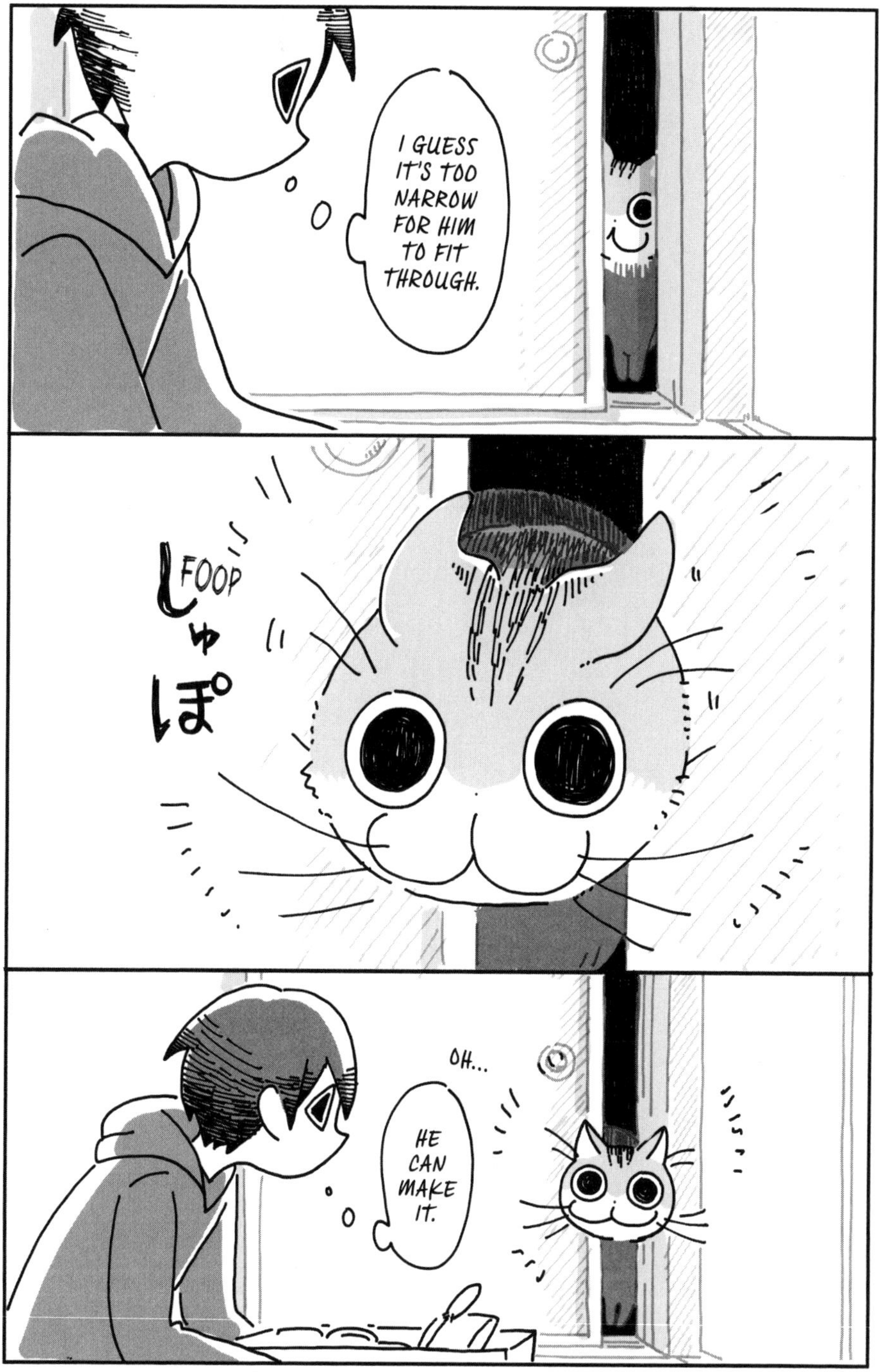
I GUESS IT'S TOO NARROW FOR HIM TO FIT THROUGH.
しゅぽ FOOP
OH...
HE CAN MAKE IT.

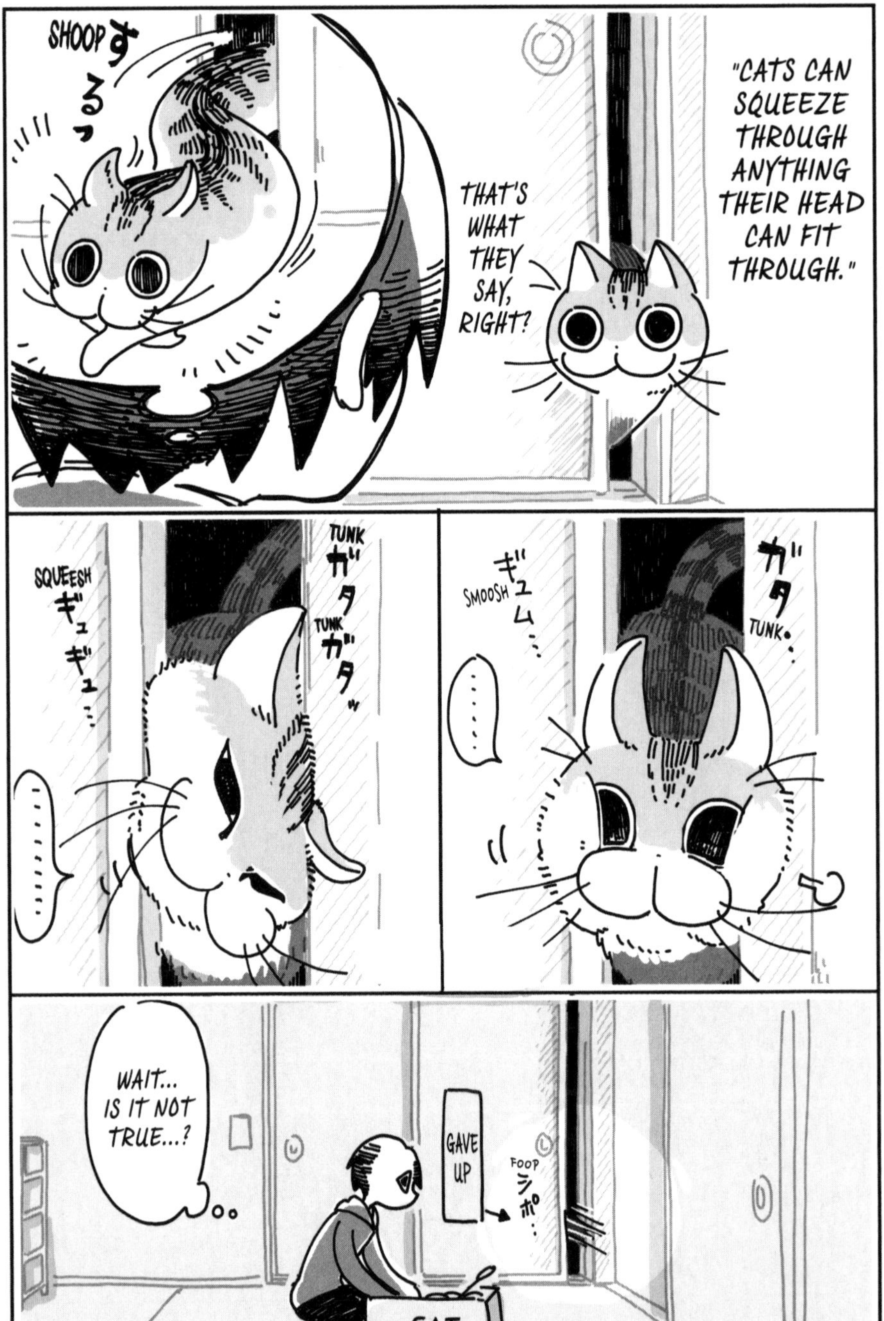
"CATS CAN SQUEEZE THROUGH ANYTHING THEIR HEAD CAN FIT THROUGH."
THAT'S WHAT THEY SAY, RIGHT?
SHOOP するっ
ガタ TUNK.
SMOOSH ギュム…
……
TUNK ガタ
TUNK ガタッ
SQUEESH ギュギュ…
……
FOOP シポ…
GAVE UP
CAT
WAIT... IS IT NOT TRUE...?

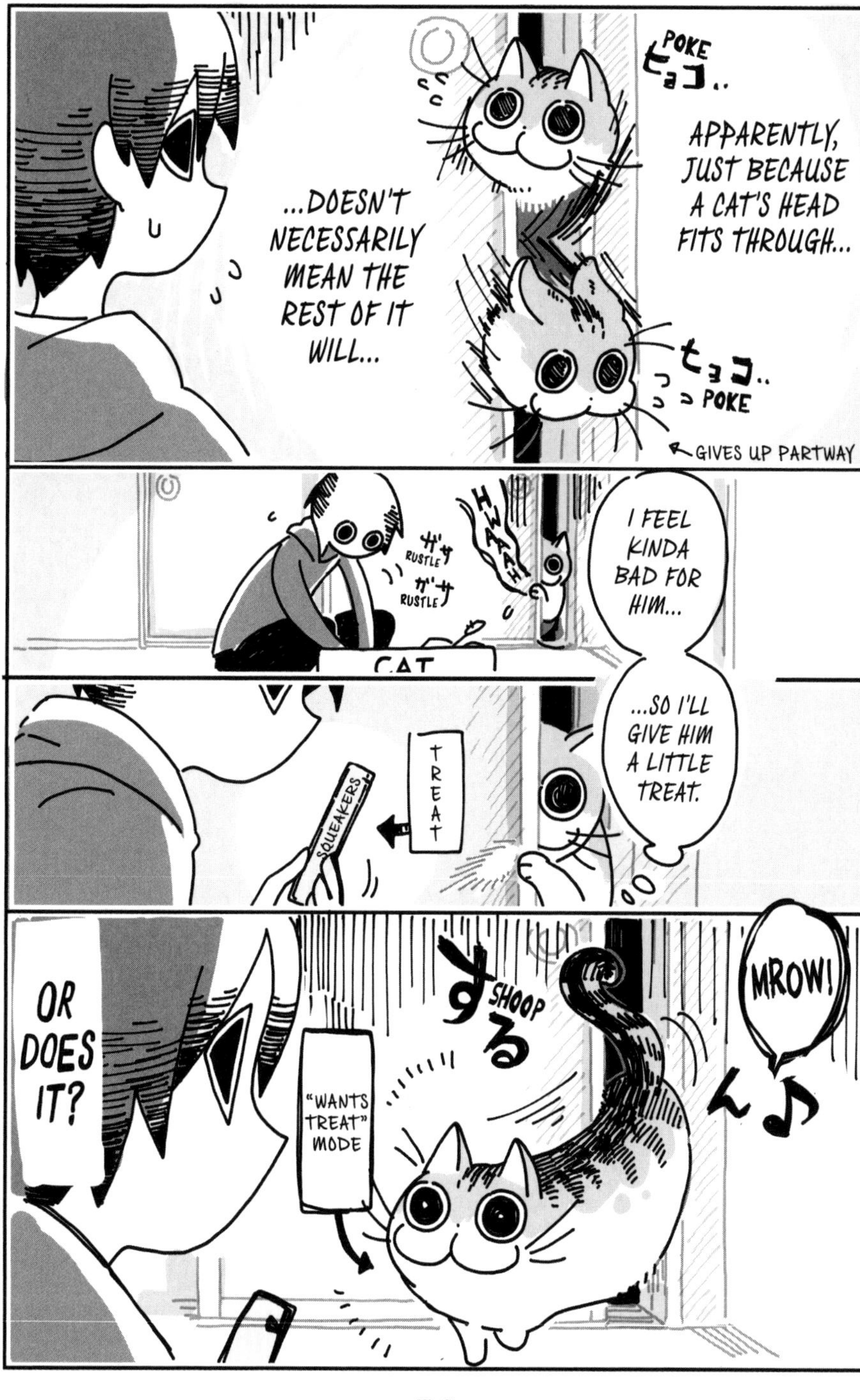
ヒョコ..
POKE
APPARENTLY, JUST BECAUSE A CAT'S HEAD FITS THROUGH...
...DOESN'T NECESSARILY MEAN THE REST OF IT WILL...
ヒョコ..
POKE
GIVES UP PARTWAY
I FEEL KINDA BAD FOR HIM...
HWAAAH
ガサ
RUSTLE
ガサ
RUSTLE
CAT
...SO I'LL GIVE HIM A LITTLE TREAT.
TREAT
SQUEAKERS
MROW!
ん♪
する
SHOOP
"WANTS TREAT" MODE
OR DOES IT?

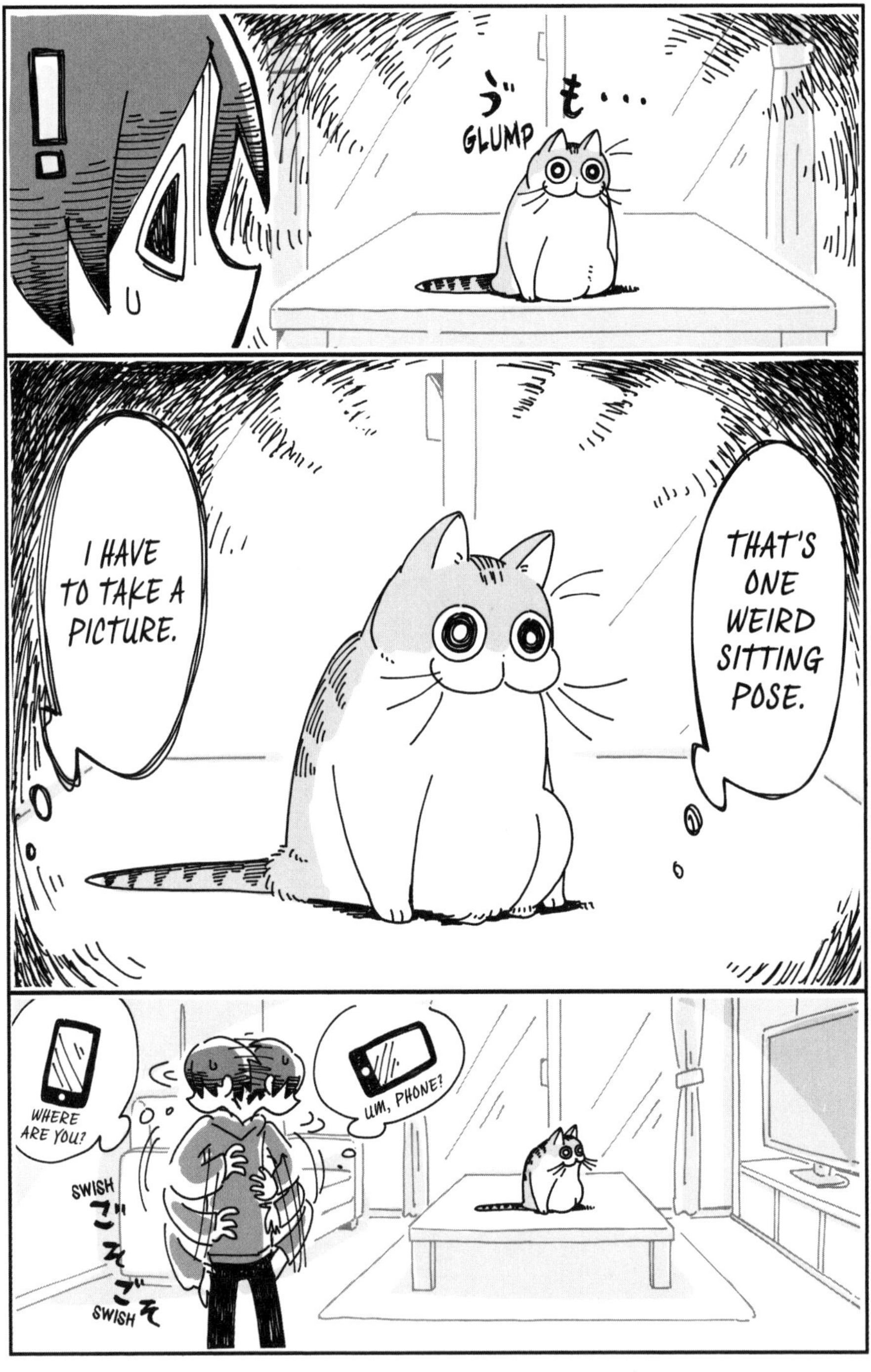
ゔも…
GLUMP
!
THAT'S ONE WEIRD SITTING POSE.
I HAVE TO TAKE A PICTURE.
UM, PHONE?
WHERE ARE YOU?
SWISH
ごそごそ
SWISH

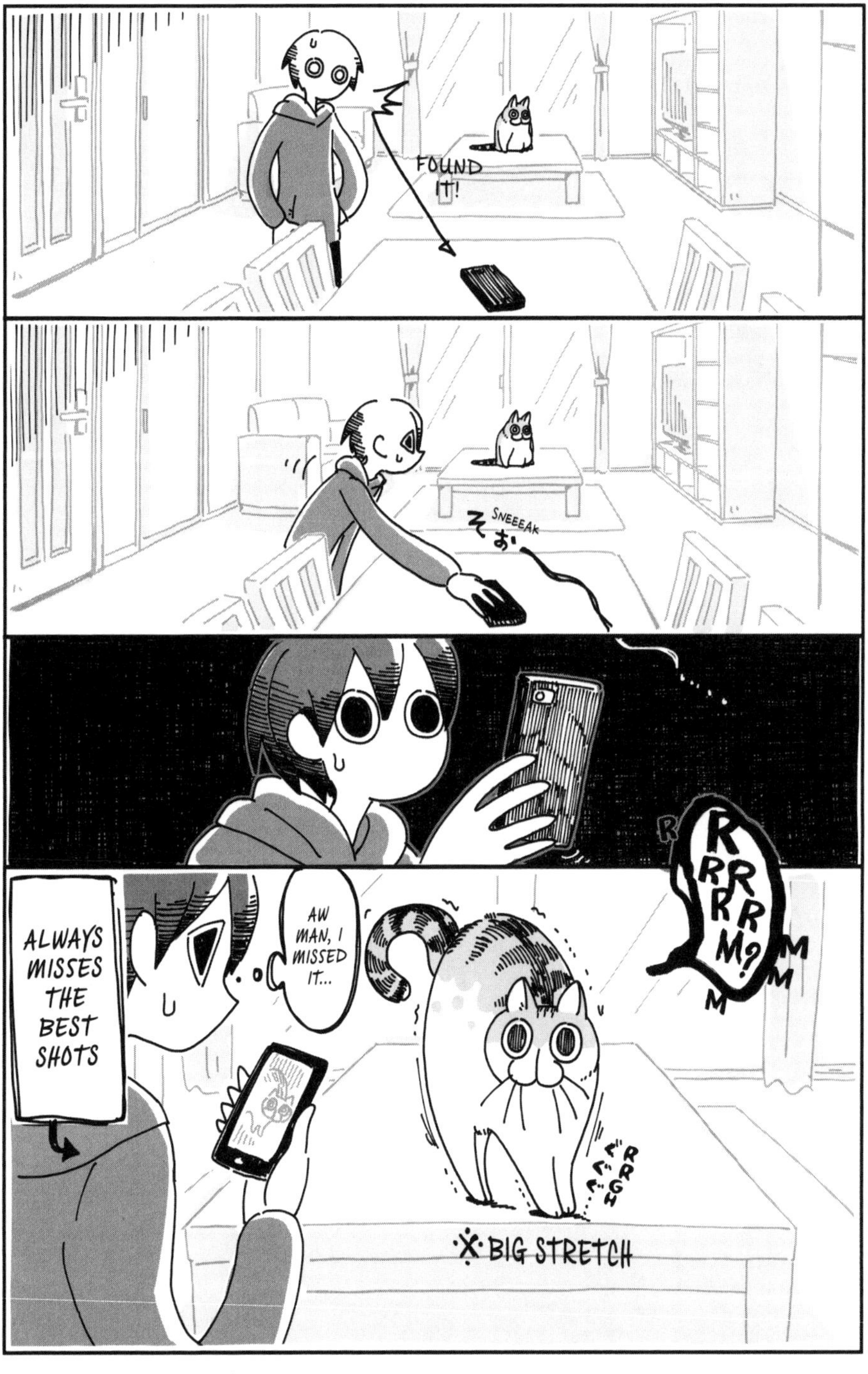
FOUND IT!
SNEEEAK
RRRRRM?
AW MAN, I MISSED IT...
ALWAYS MISSES THE BEST SHOTS
※BIG STRETCH

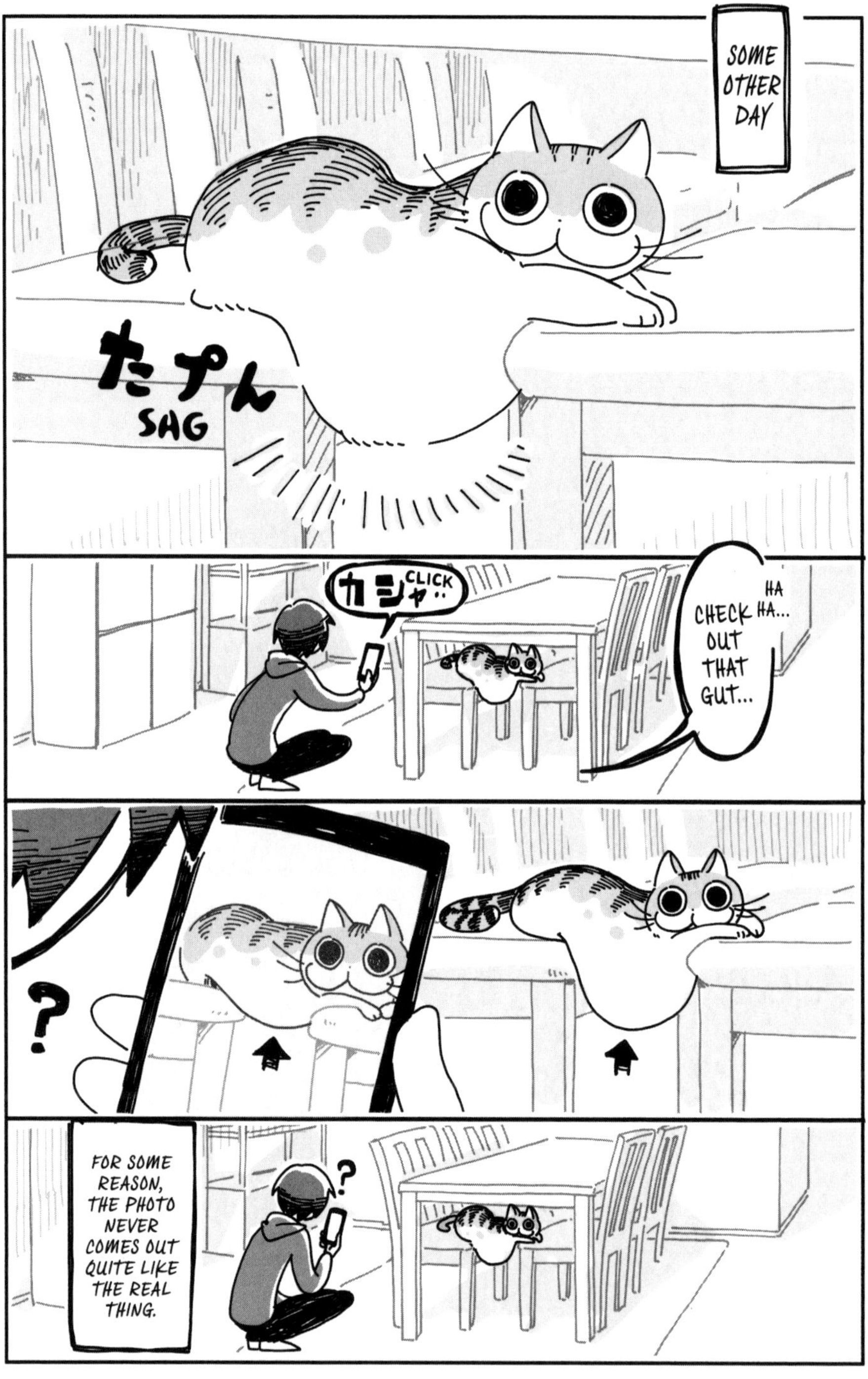
SOME OTHER DAY
たぷん
SAG
CHECK OUT THAT GUT...
HA HA...
カシャ‥
CLICK
?
?
FOR SOME REASON, THE PHOTO NEVER COMES OUT QUITE LIKE THE REAL THING.

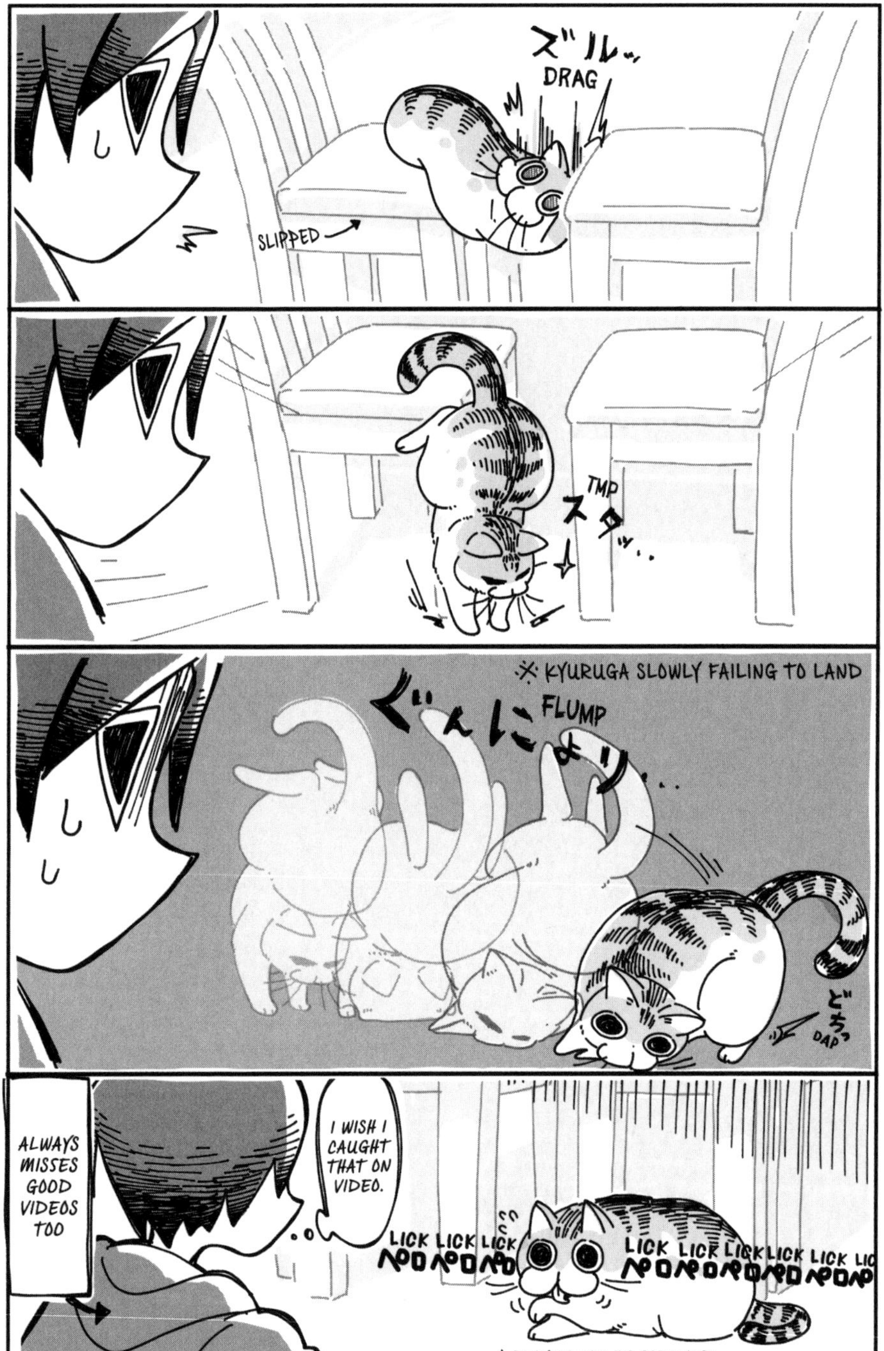
ズルッ
DRAG
SLIPPED
TMP
スタッ
※KYURUGA SLOWLY FAILING TO LAND
ぐんにょり
FLUMP
どちっ
DAP
LICK LICK LICK LICK LICK LICK
ペロペロペロペロペロペロ
LICK LICK LICK
ペロペロペロ
I WISH I CAUGHT THAT ON VIDEO.
ALWAYS MISSES GOOD VIDEOS TOO
※PLAYING OFF HIS SCREWUP

Coming Home to Aggressive Love

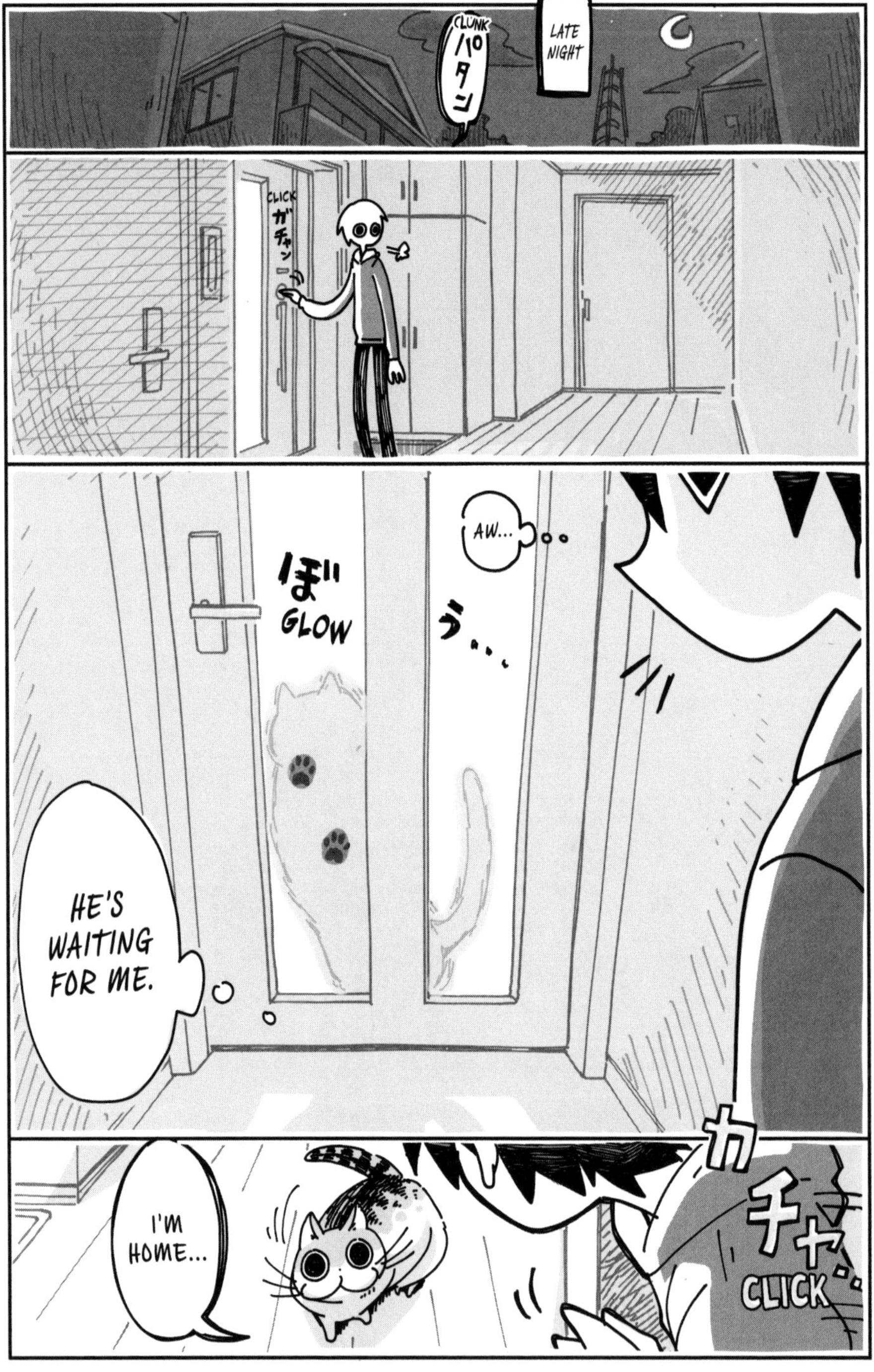
LATE NIGHT
CLUNK
パタン
CLICK
ガチャン
AW...
ぼう...
GLOW
HE'S WAITING FOR ME.
カチャ
CLICK
I'M HOME...

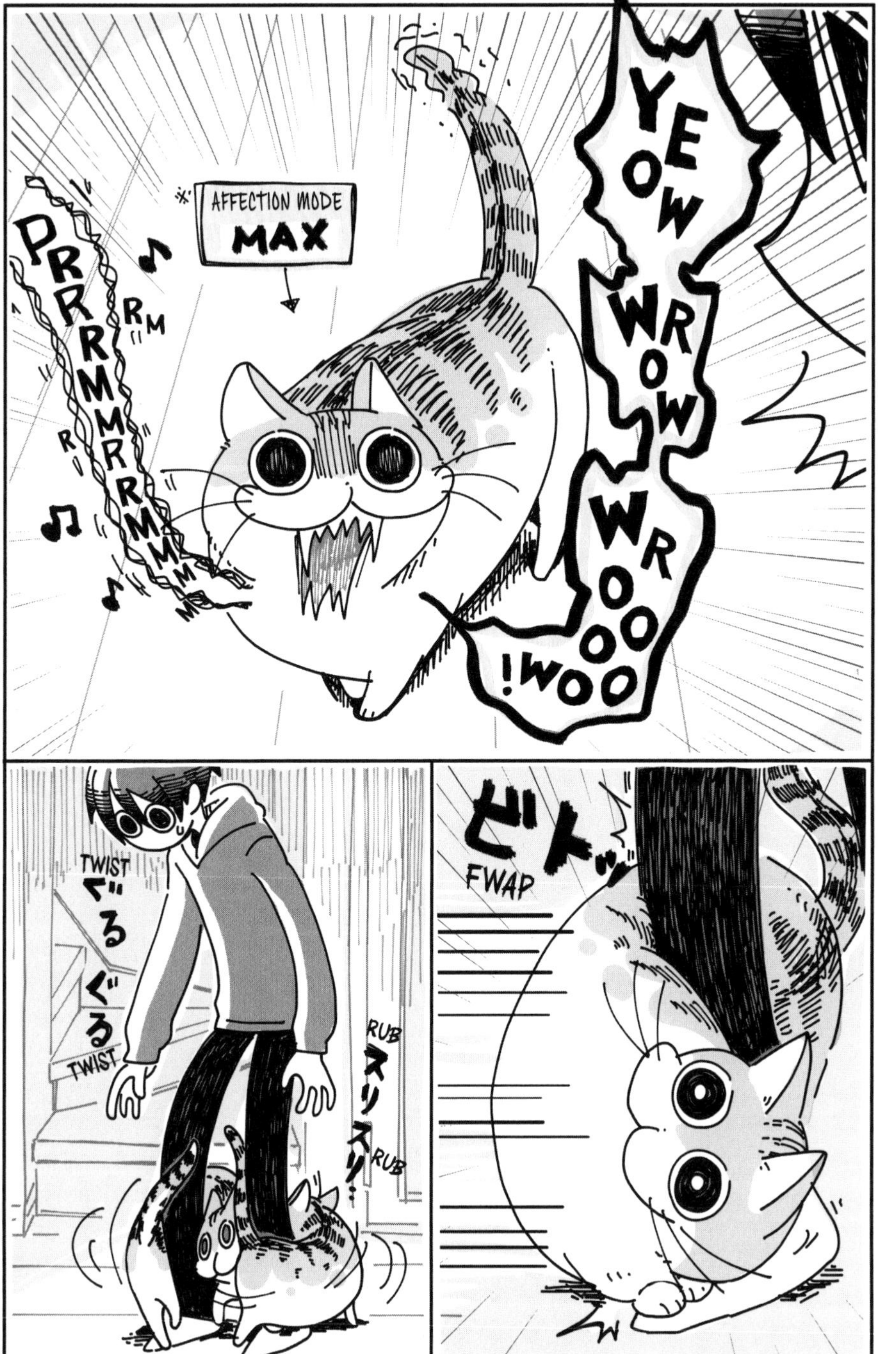
YEOW WROW WROOOOOM!
AFFECTION MODE MAX
PRRRMMRRRMMMM
RM
R
ドドッ
FWAP
TWIST ぐるぐる TWIST
RUB スリスリ… RUB

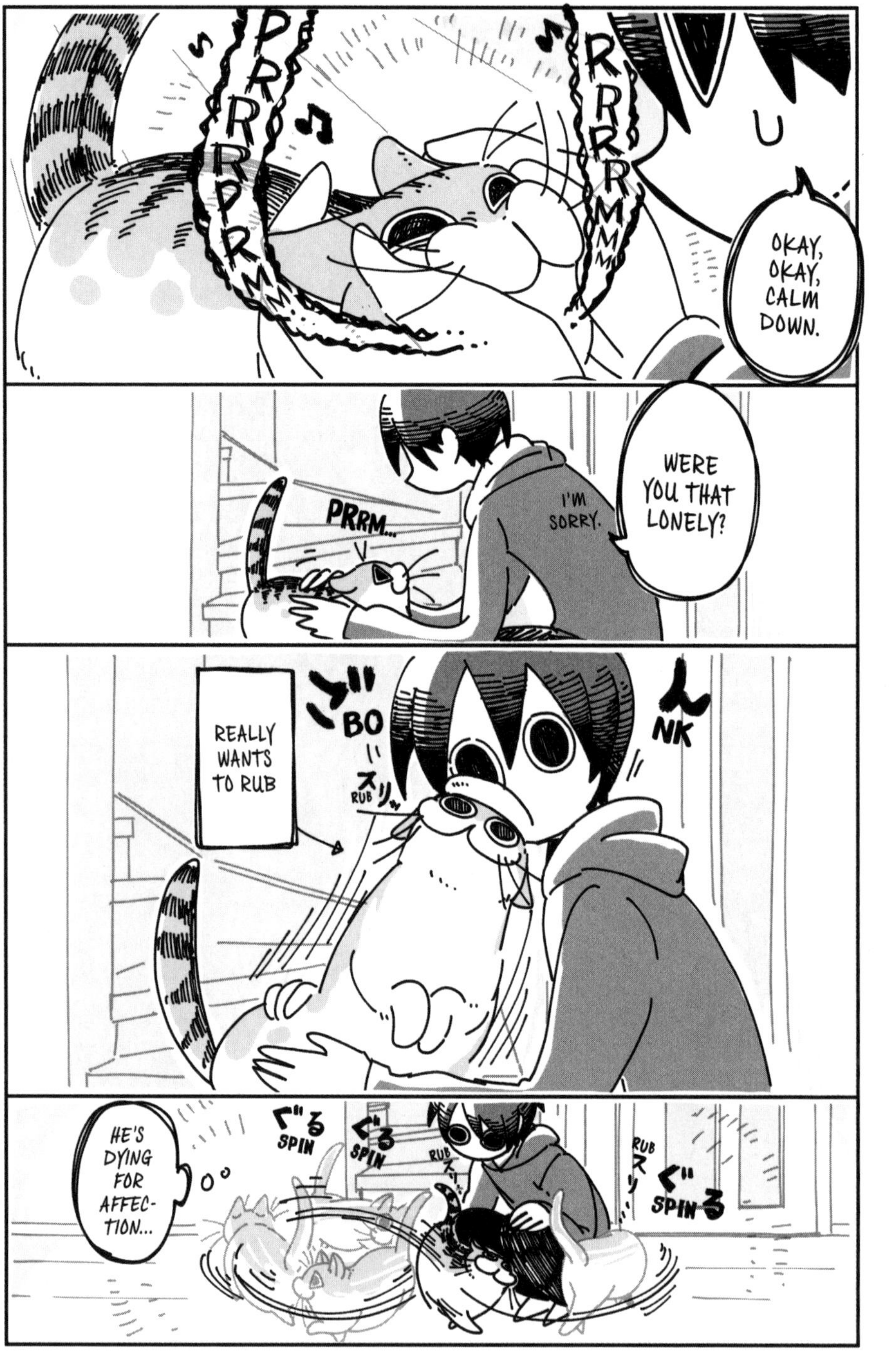
U...
OKAY, OKAY, CALM DOWN.
RRRRMMM
PRRRPRRM
WERE YOU THAT LONELY?
I'M SORRY.
PRRM...
ん NK
ご BO
いスリ RUB
REALLY WANTS TO RUB
ぐる SPIN
スリ RUB
スリ RUB
ぐる SPIN
ぐる SPIN
HE'S DYING FOR AFFEC-TION...

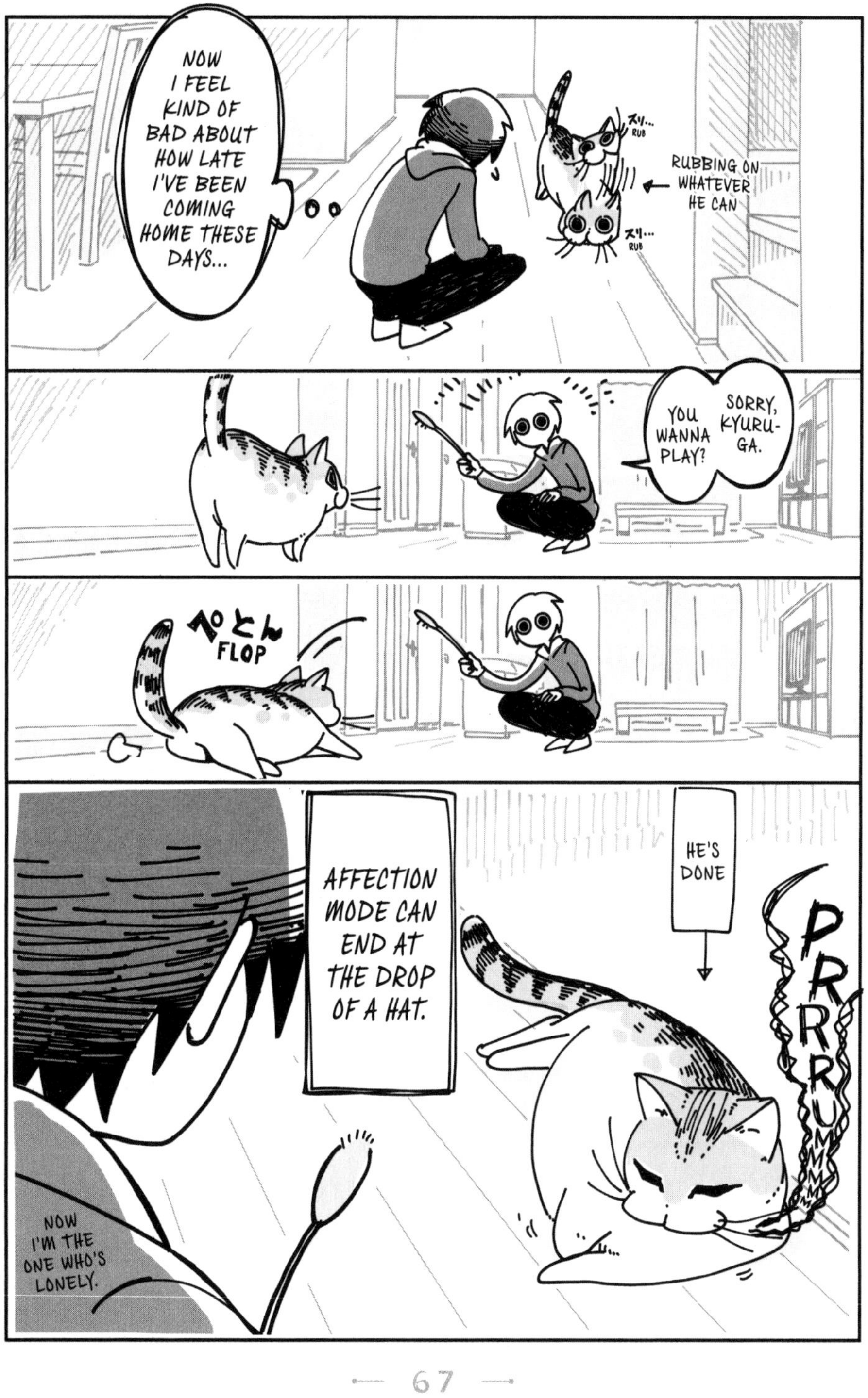
RUBBING ON WHATEVER HE CAN
スリ… RUB
スリ… RUB
NOW I FEEL KIND OF BAD ABOUT HOW LATE I'VE BEEN COMING HOME THESE DAYS...
SORRY, KYURU-GA.
YOU WANNA PLAY?
ぺとん FLOP
PRRRUMMMMM
HE'S DONE
AFFECTION MODE CAN END AT THE DROP OF A HAT.
NOW I'M THE ONE WHO'S LONELY.

A Cat Who Observes Grilled Fish

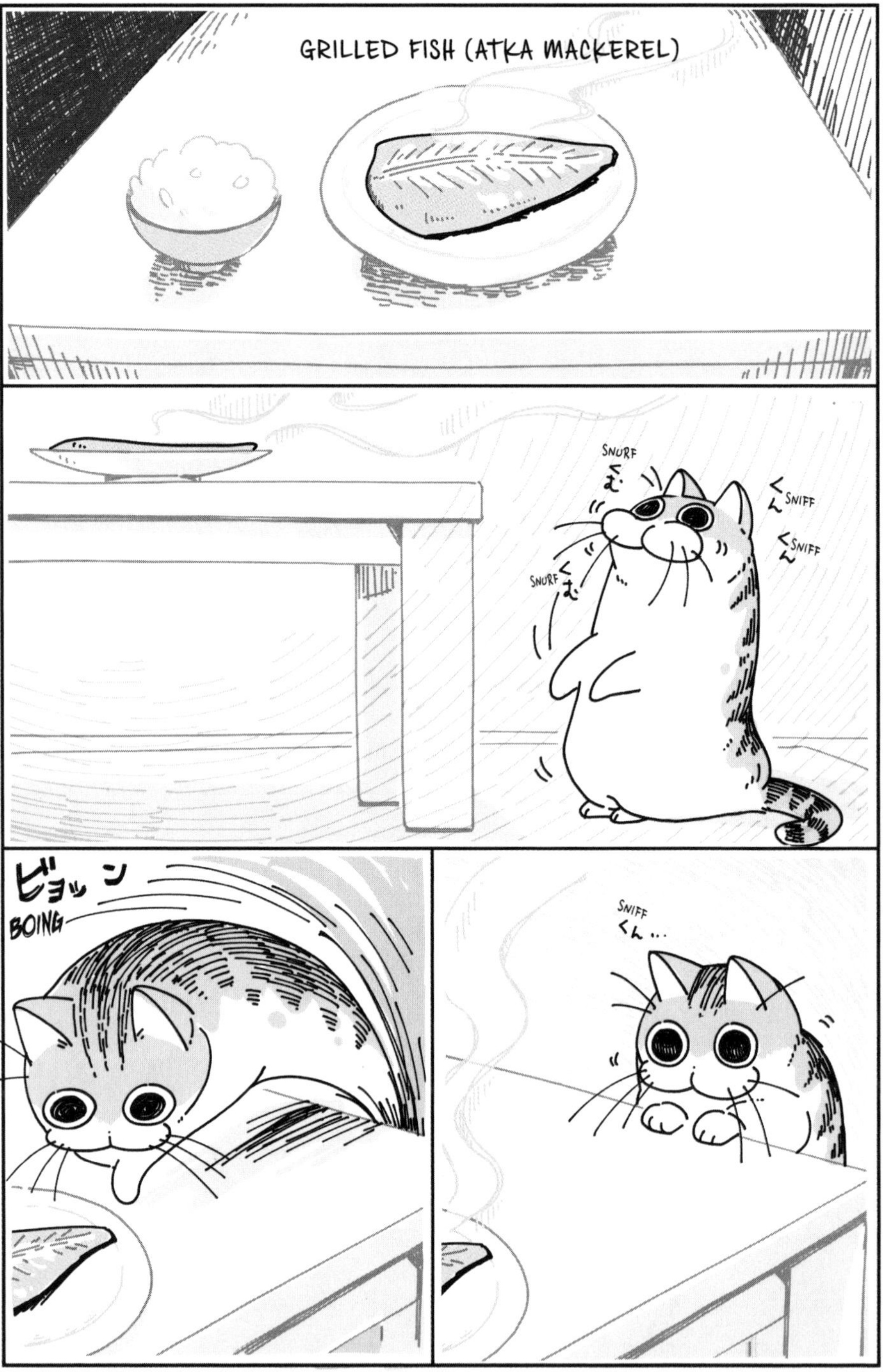
GRILLED FISH (ATKA MACKEREL)
くん SNIFF
くん SNIFF
SNURF くむ
SNURF くむ
SNIFF くん…
ビョッン
BOING

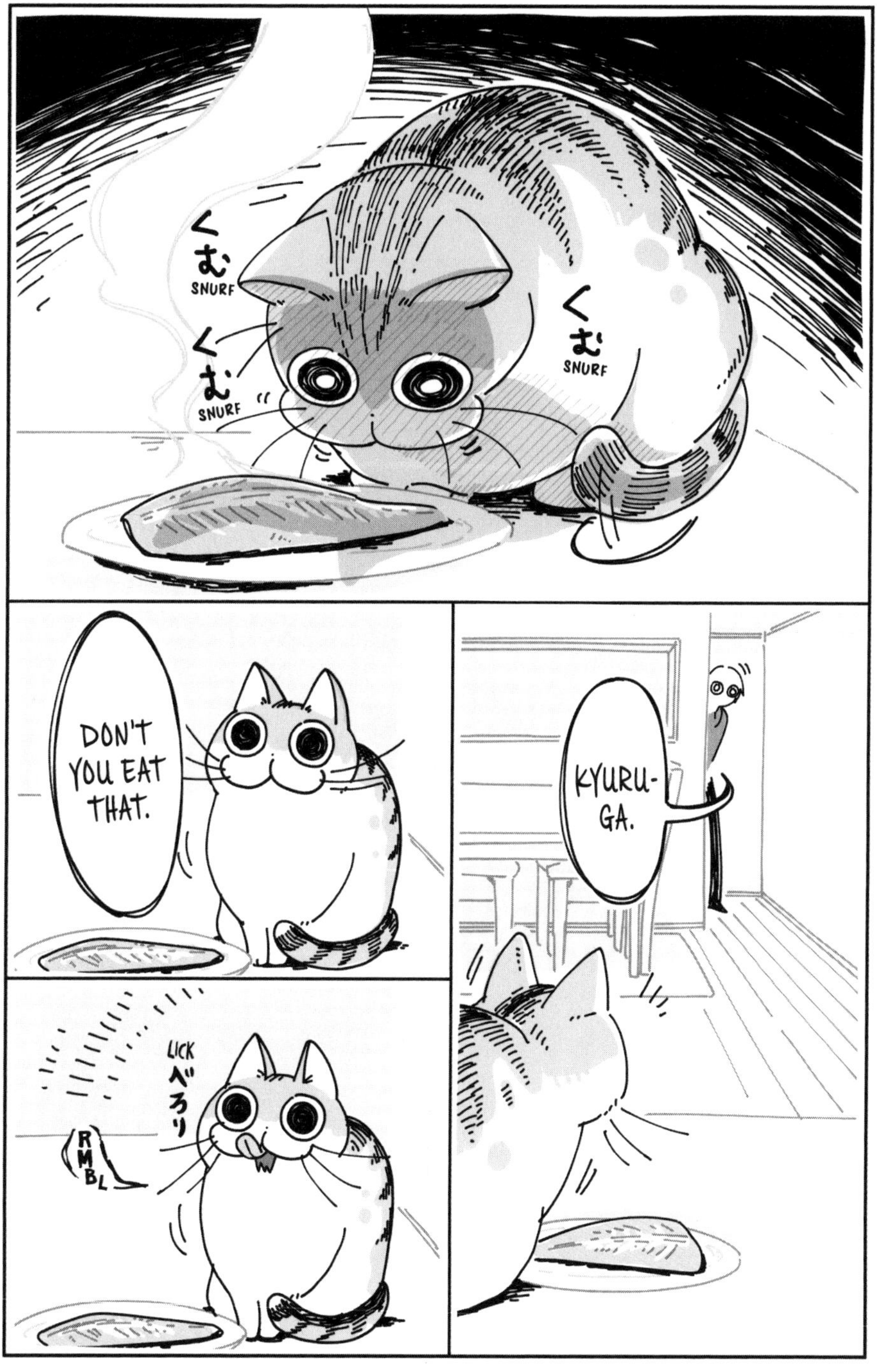
くむ
SNURF
くむ
SNURF
くむ
SNURF
KYURU-GA.
DON'T YOU EAT THAT.
LICK
べろり
RMBL

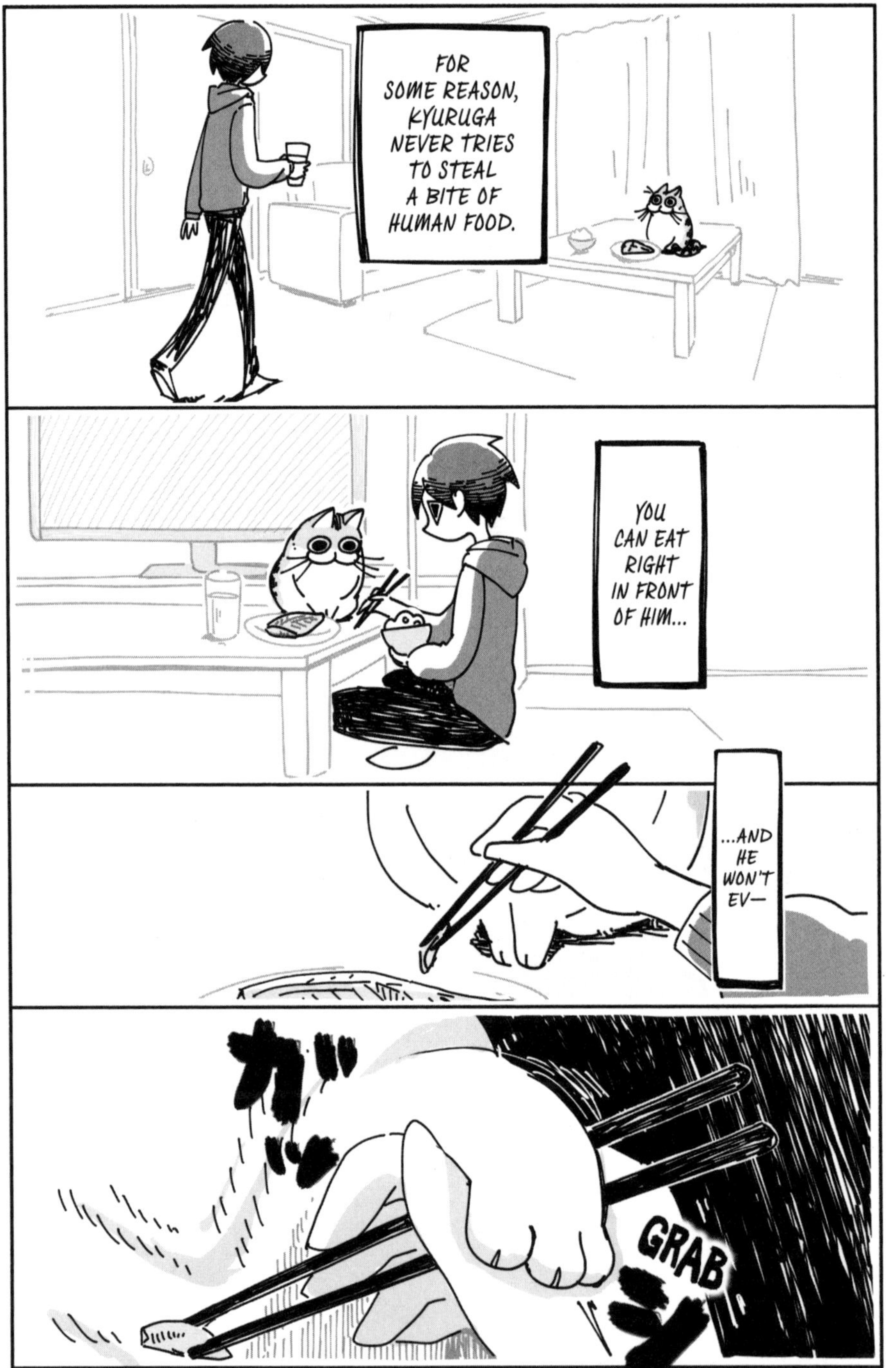
FOR SOME REASON, KYURUGA NEVER TRIES TO STEAL A BITE OF HUMAN FOOD.
YOU CAN EAT RIGHT IN FRONT OF HIM...
...AND HE WON'T EV—
ガッ
GRAB

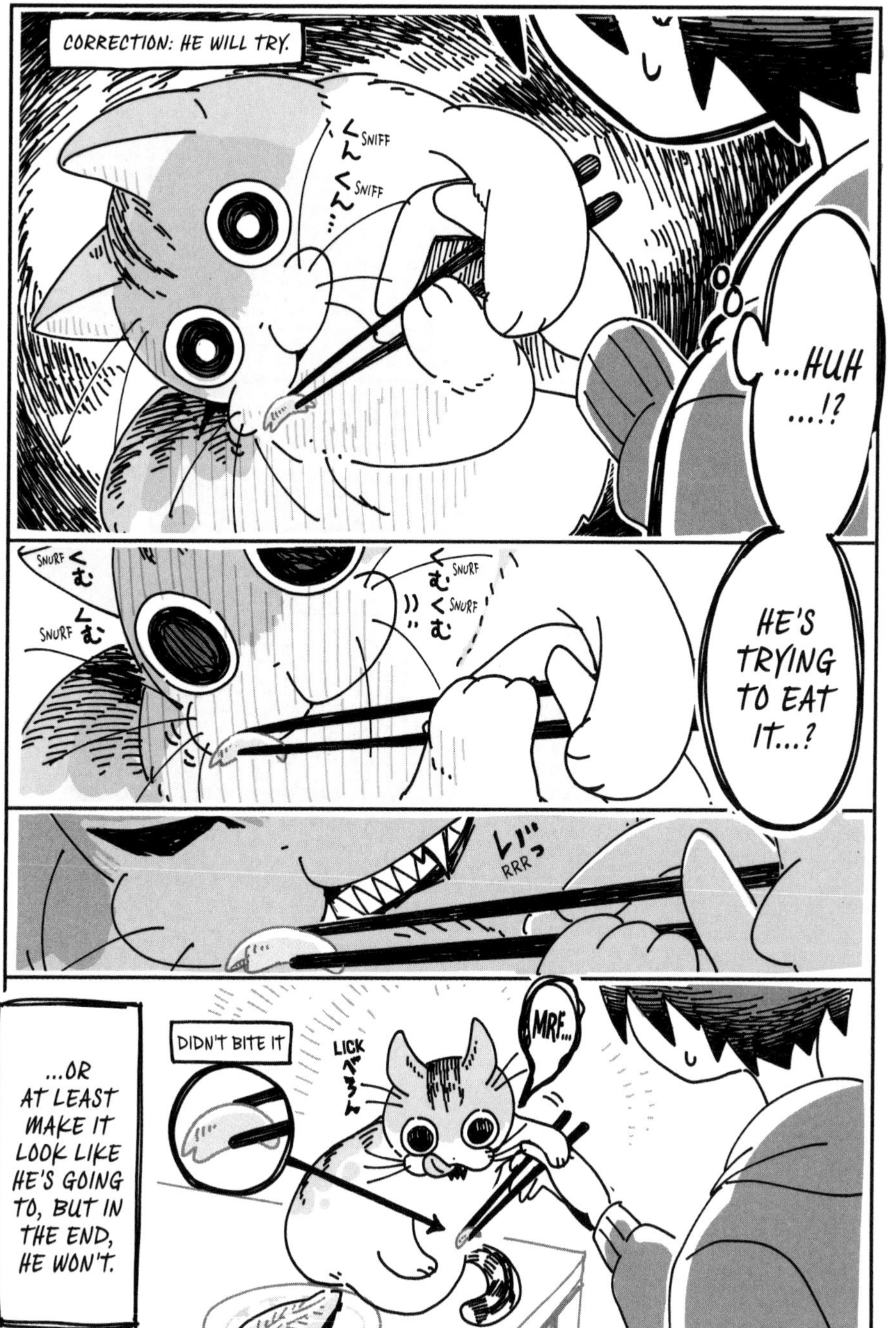
CORRECTION: HE WILL TRY.
くんくん… SNIFF SNIFF
...HUH ...!?
HE'S TRYING TO EAT IT...?
くむくむ SNURF SNURF
くむ SNURF
くむ SNURF
レじっ RRR
MRF...
LICK べろん
DIDN'T BITE IT
...OR AT LEAST MAKE IT LOOK LIKE HE'S GOING TO, BUT IN THE END, HE WON'T.

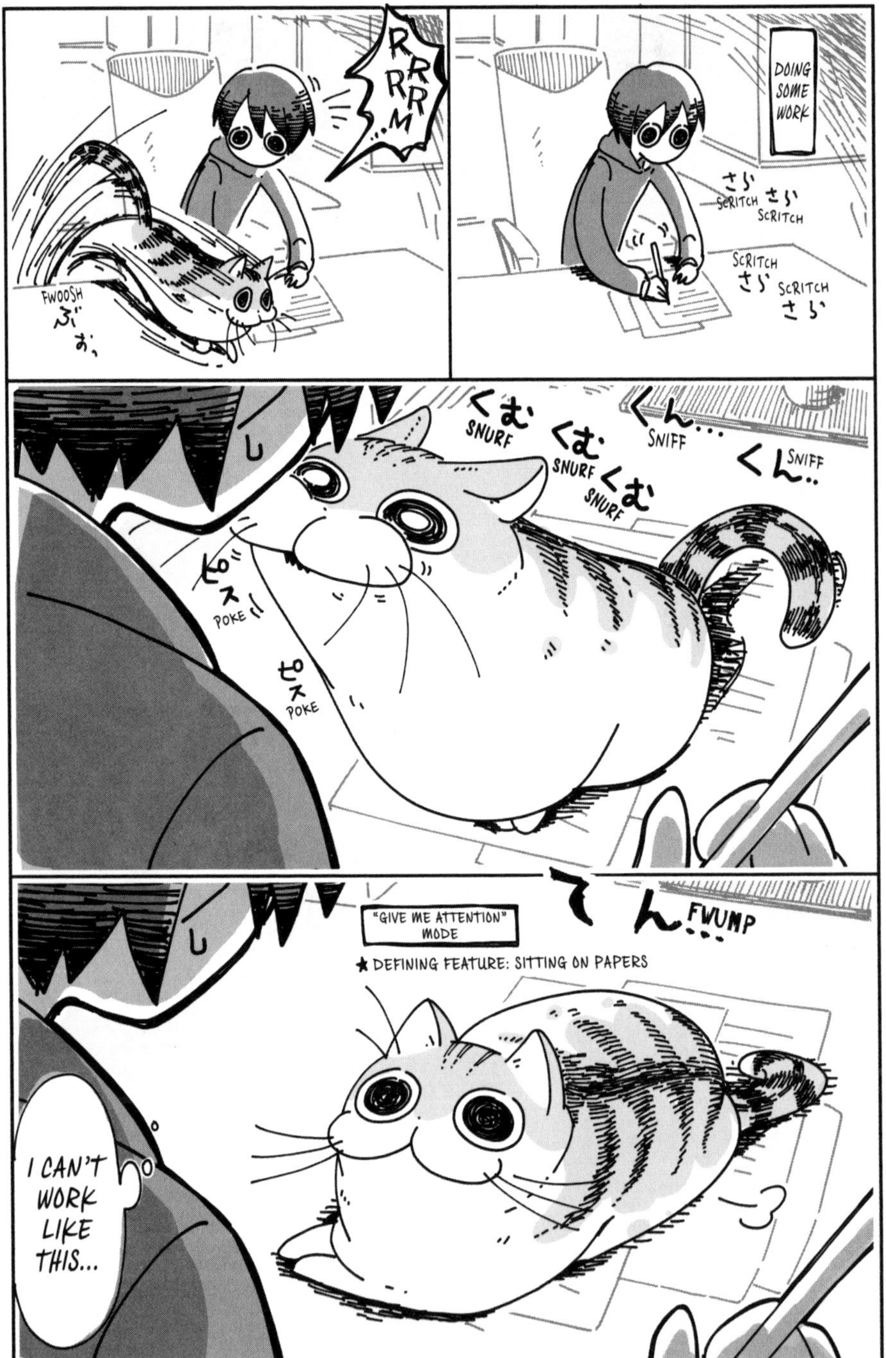
DOING SOME WORK
さら SCRITCH
さら SCRITCH
SCRITCH さら
SCRITCH さら
RRRRM...
FWOOSH ぶぉ
くん… SNIFF
くん… SNIFF
くむ SNURF
くむ SNURF
くむ SNURF
ピス POKE
ピス POKE
てん… FWUMP
"GIVE ME ATTENTION" MODE
★ DEFINING FEATURE: SITTING ON PAPERS
I CAN'T WORK LIKE THIS...

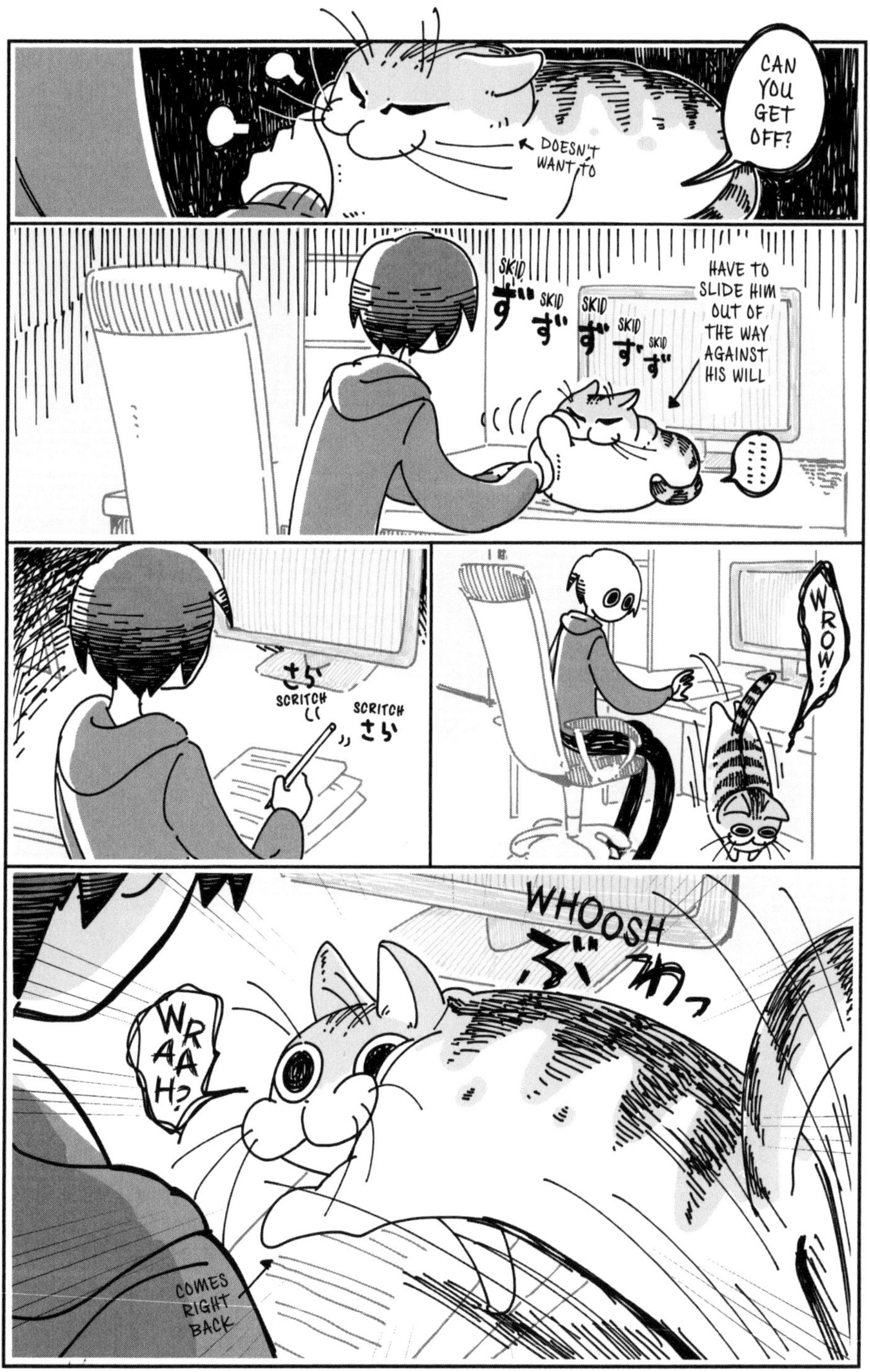
CAN YOU GET OFF?
DOESN'T WANT TO
HAVE TO SLIDE HIM OUT OF THE WAY AGAINST HIS WILL
SKID ず SKID ず SKID ず SKID ず SKID ず
WROW...
SCRITCH さら
SCRITCH さら
WHOOSH ぶわっ
WRAAH?
COMES RIGHT BACK

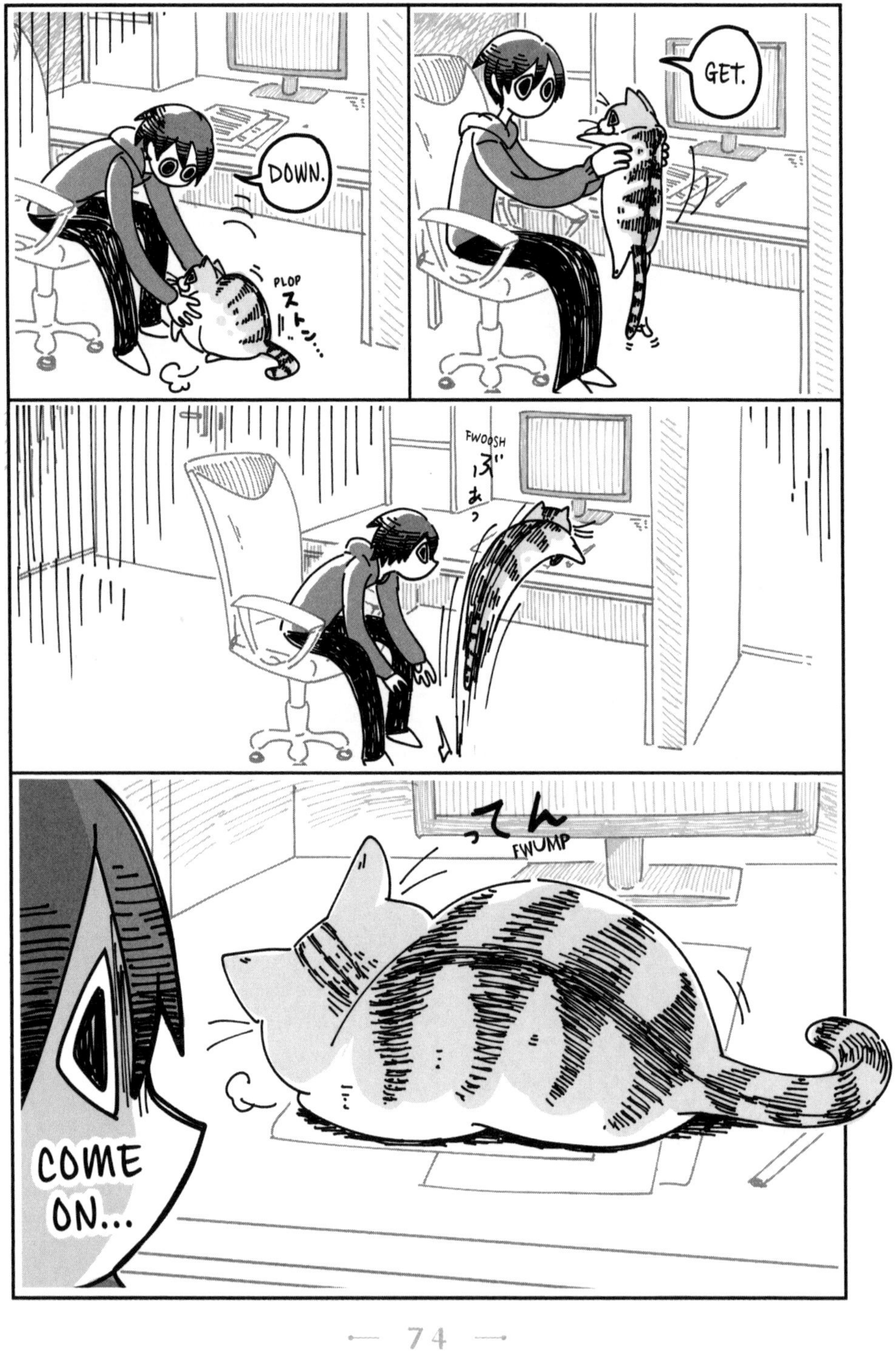
GET.
DOWN.
PLOP
ストン…
FWOOSH
ぶぁっ
ってん
FWUMP
COME ON...

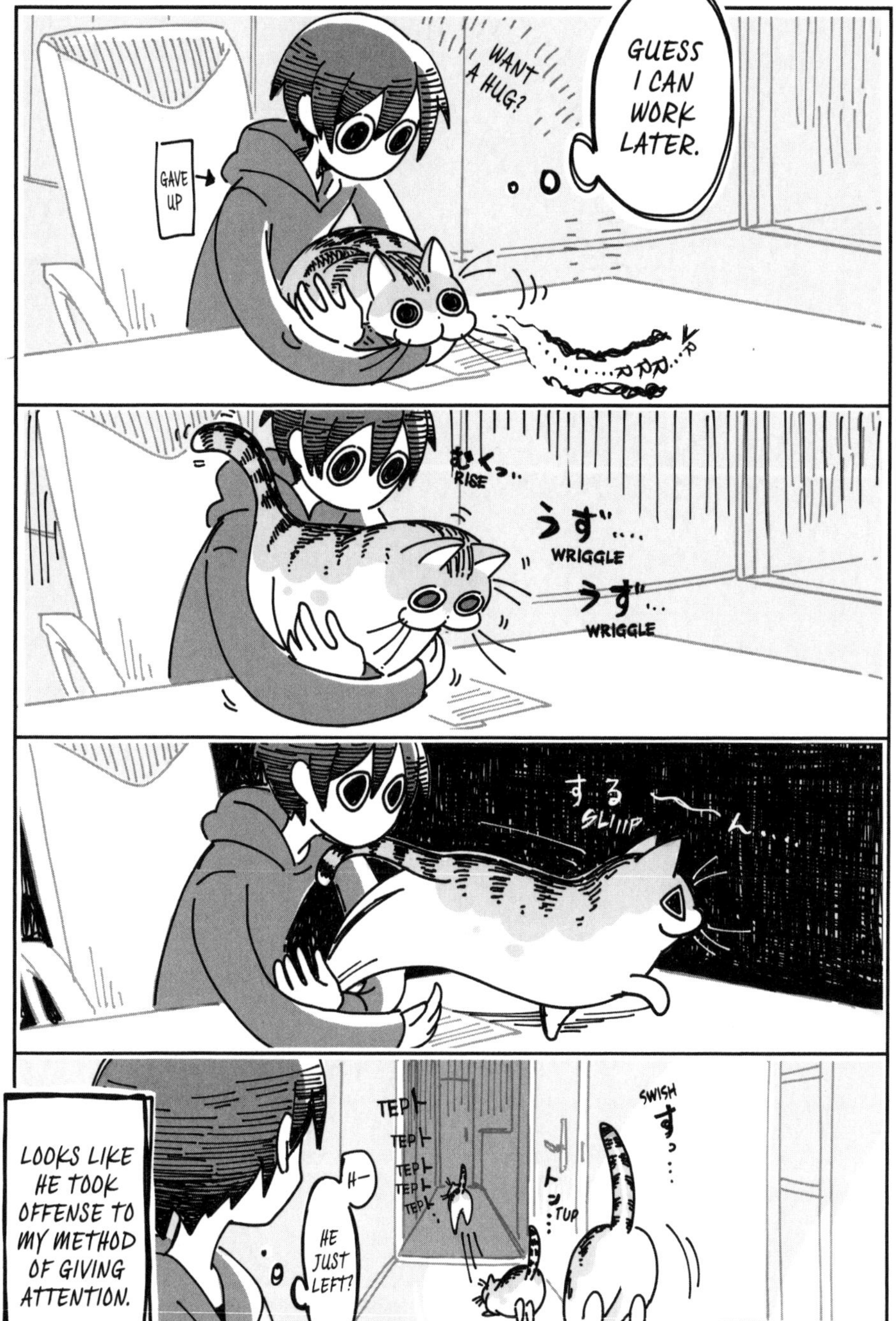

GUESS I CAN WORK LATER.
WANT A HUG?
GAVE UP
むくっ..
RISE
うず....
WRIGGLE
うず...
WRIGGLE
する〜〜ん...
SLIIIP
SWISH
すっ...
トン...
TUP
TEP
TEP
TEP
TEP
TEP
HE JUST LEFT?
H—
LOOKS LIKE HE TOOK OFFENSE TO MY METHOD OF GIVING ATTENTION.

A Cat Who Loves Knocking Stuff off Things

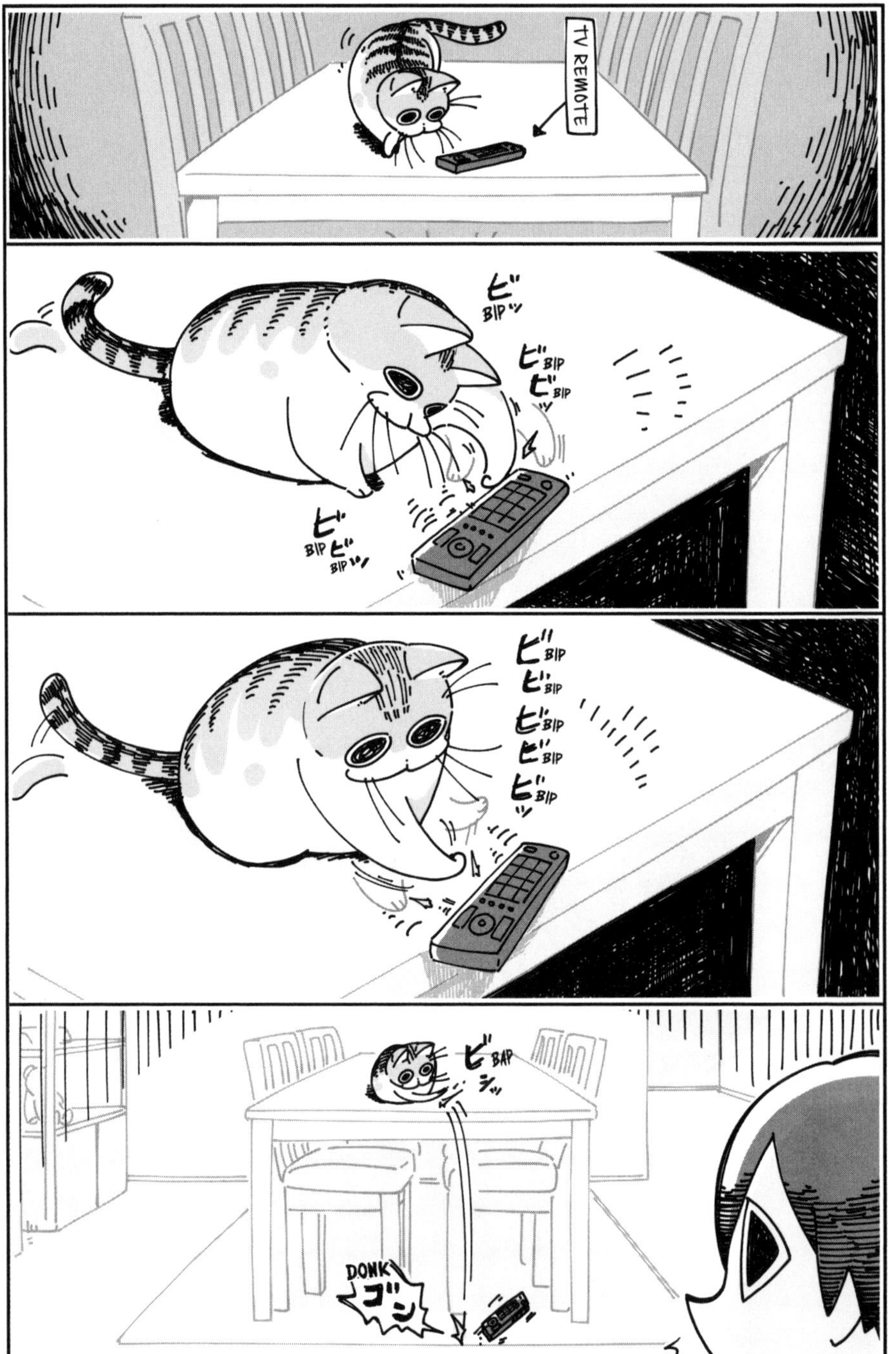
TV REMOTE
ビ BIP ッ
ビ BIP ビ BIP ッ
ビ BIP ビ BIP ッ
ビ BIP
ビ BIP
ビ BIP
ビ BIP
ビ BIP ッ
ビ BAP シッ
DONK ゴン

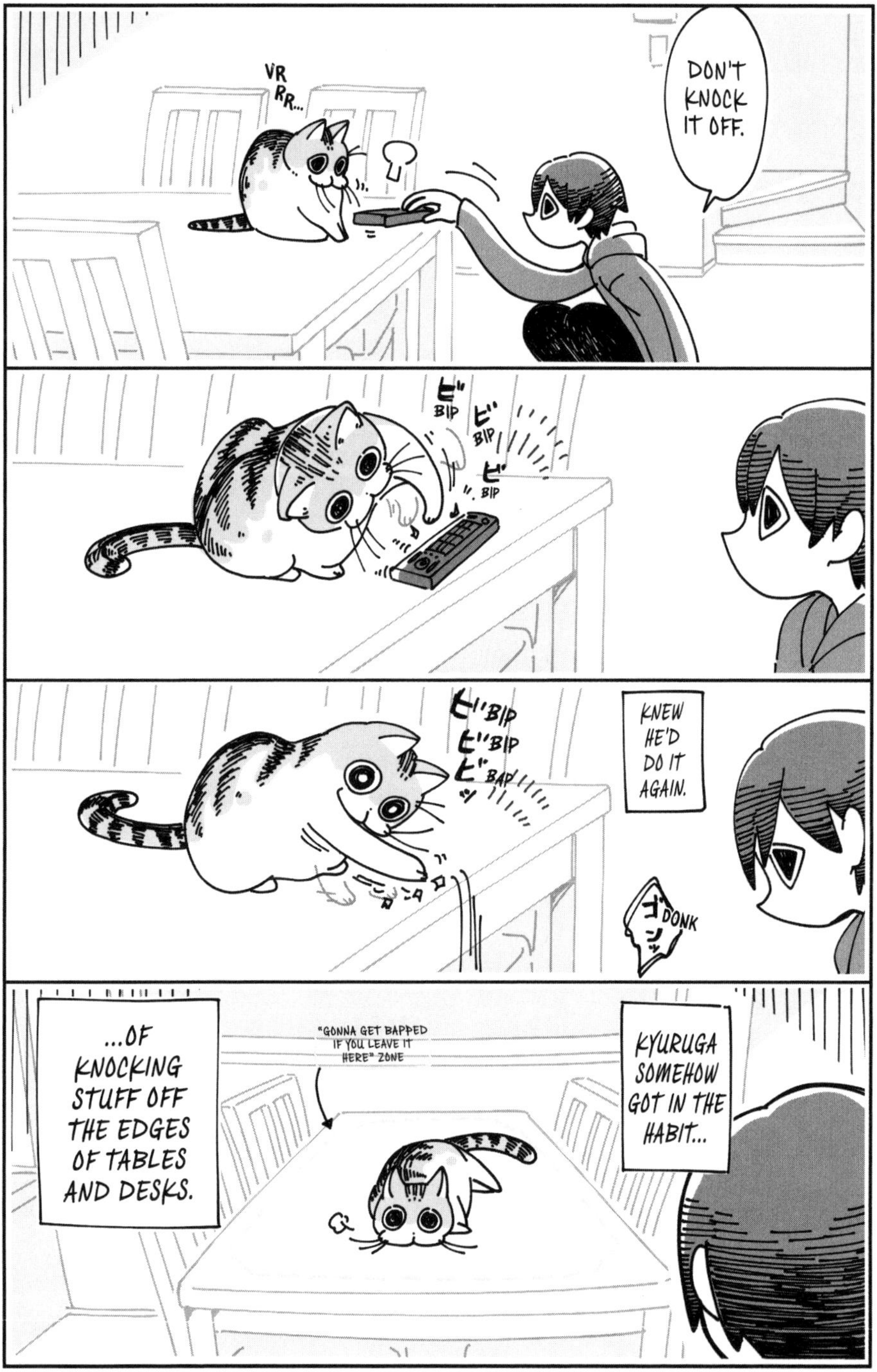
DON'T KNOCK IT OFF.
VR RR...
ビ BIP
ビ BIP
ビ BIP
KNEW HE'D DO IT AGAIN.
ゴンッ DONK
ビ BIP
ビ BIP
ビ BAP
KYURUGA SOMEHOW GOT IN THE HABIT...
"GONNA GET BAPPED IF YOU LEAVE IT HERE" ZONE
...OF KNOCKING STUFF OFF THE EDGES OF TABLES AND DESKS.

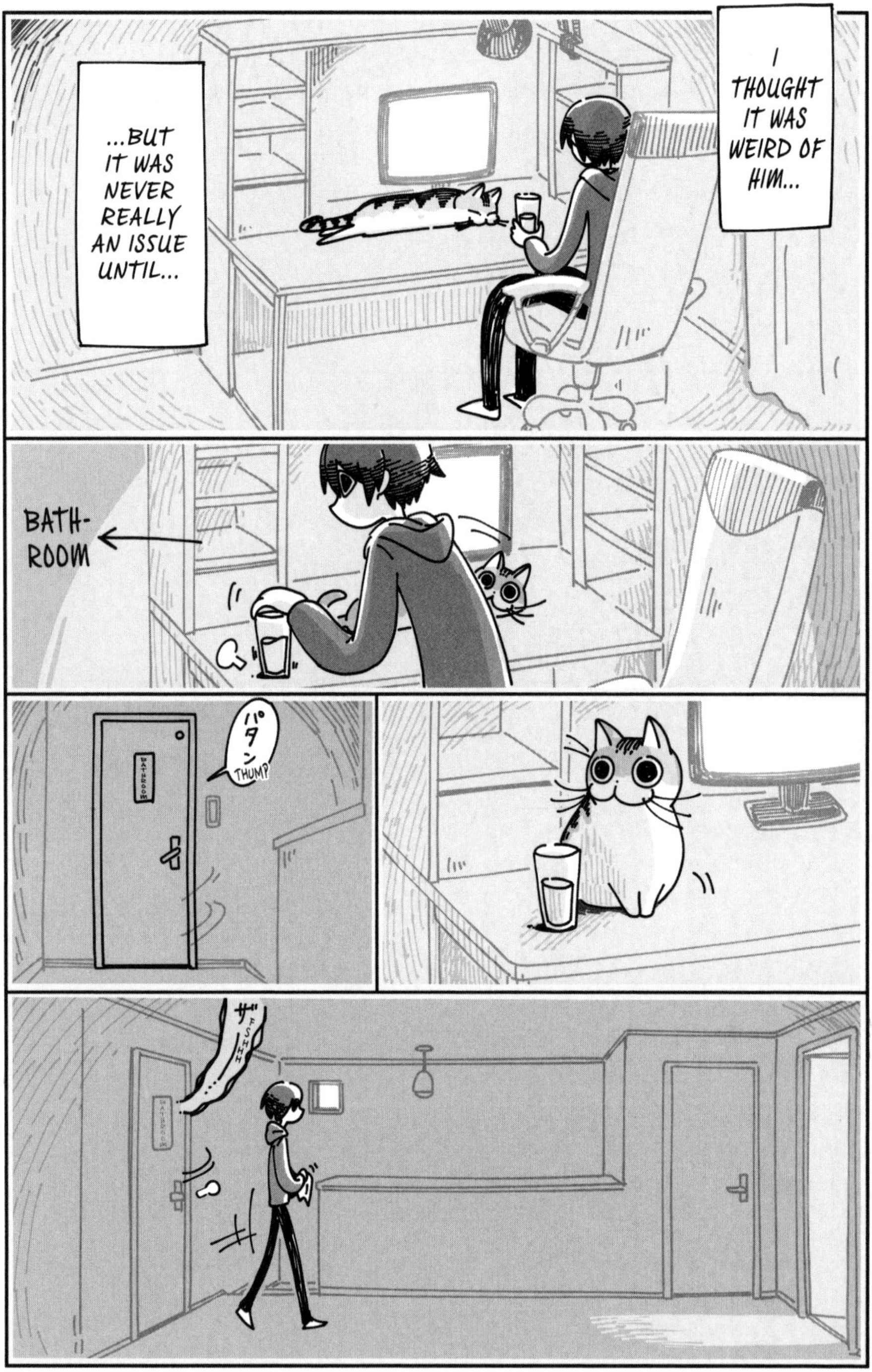
I THOUGHT IT WAS WEIRD OF HIM...
...BUT IT WAS NEVER REALLY AN ISSUE UNTIL...
BATH-ROOM
パタン
THUMP
ザ
FSHHH

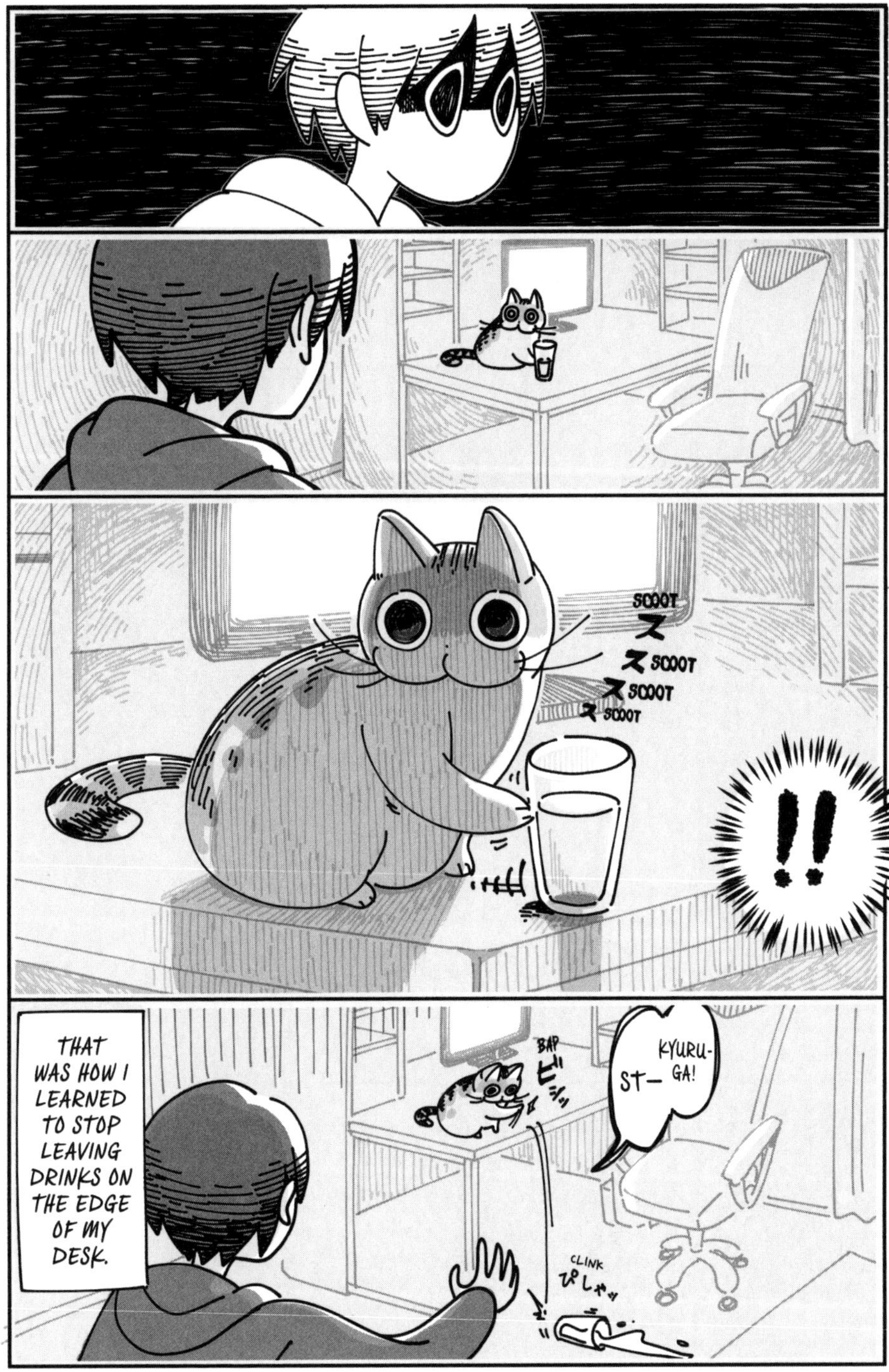
SCOOT ス
ス SCOOT
ス SCOOT
ス SCOOT
!!
ST— KYURU-GA!
BAP ビシッ
CLINK ぴしゃッ
THAT WAS HOW I LEARNED TO STOP LEAVING DRINKS ON THE EDGE OF MY DESK.

A Cat Invited Me to Play

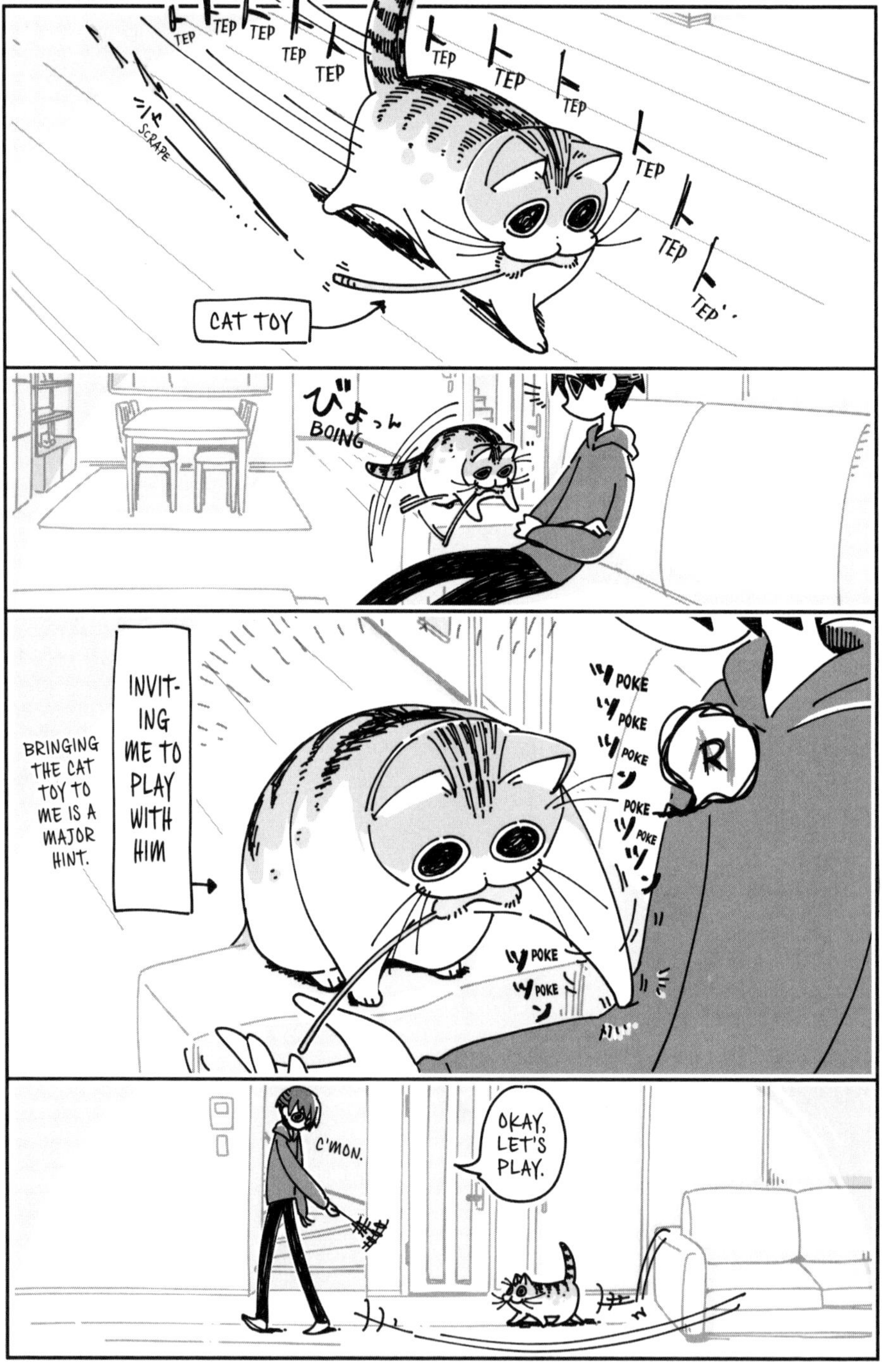
TEP TEP TEP TEP TEP TEP TEP TEP TEP TEP TEP
SCRAPE
CAT TOY
びよっん
BOING
INVITING ME TO PLAY WITH HIM
BRINGING THE CAT TOY TO ME IS A MAJOR HINT.
POKE POKE POKE POKE POKE
POKE POKE
R
OKAY, LET'S PLAY.
C'MON.

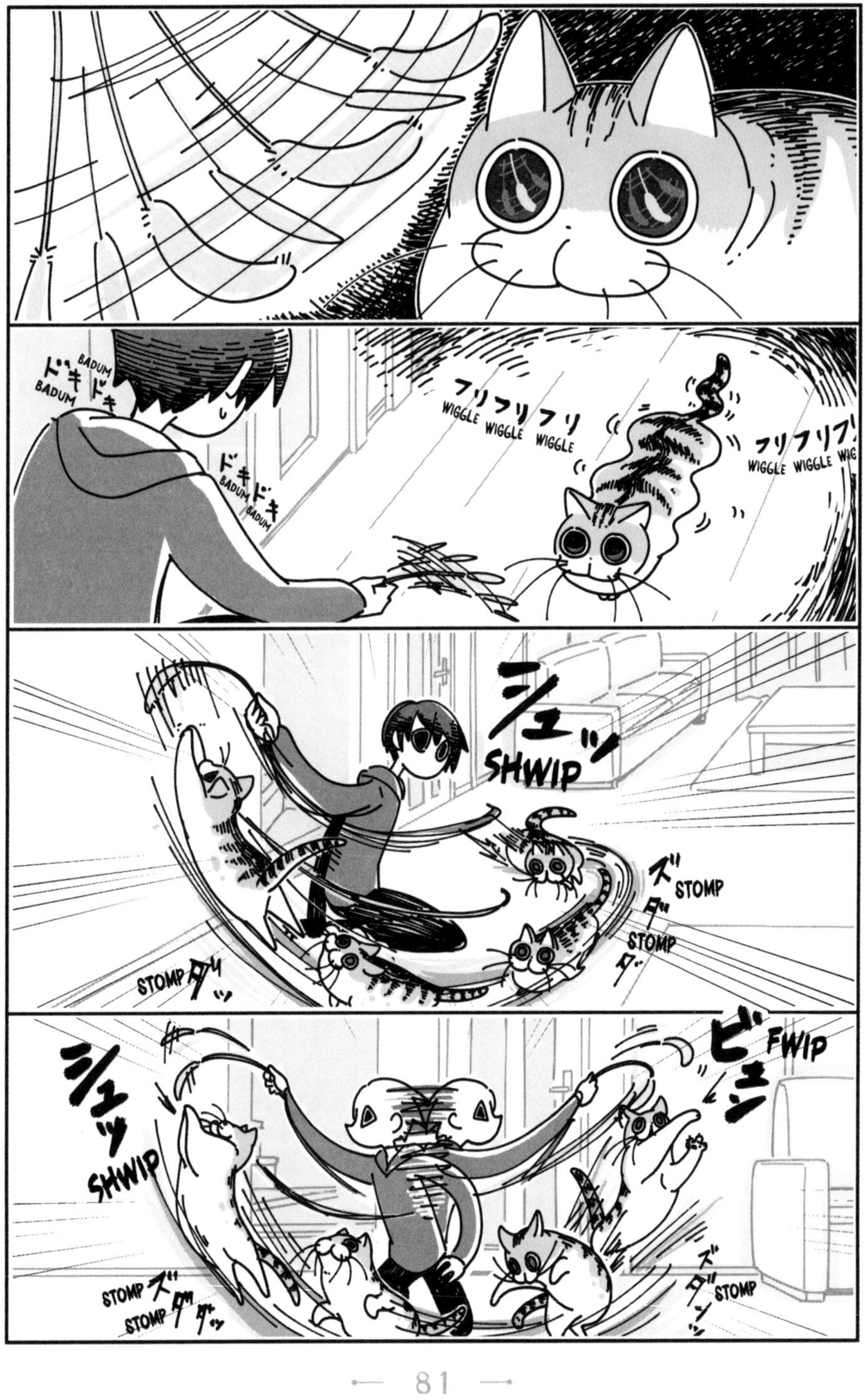
フリフリフ
WIGGLE WIGGLE WIG
フリフリフリ
WIGGLE WIGGLE WIGGLE
ドキドキ
BADUM BADUM
ドキドキ
BADUM BADUM
シュッ
SHWIP
ズダ
STOMP STOMP
ダ
ダッ
STOMP
ビュン
FWIP
ズダッ
STOMP
シュッ
SHWIP
ズダダッ
STOMP STOMP

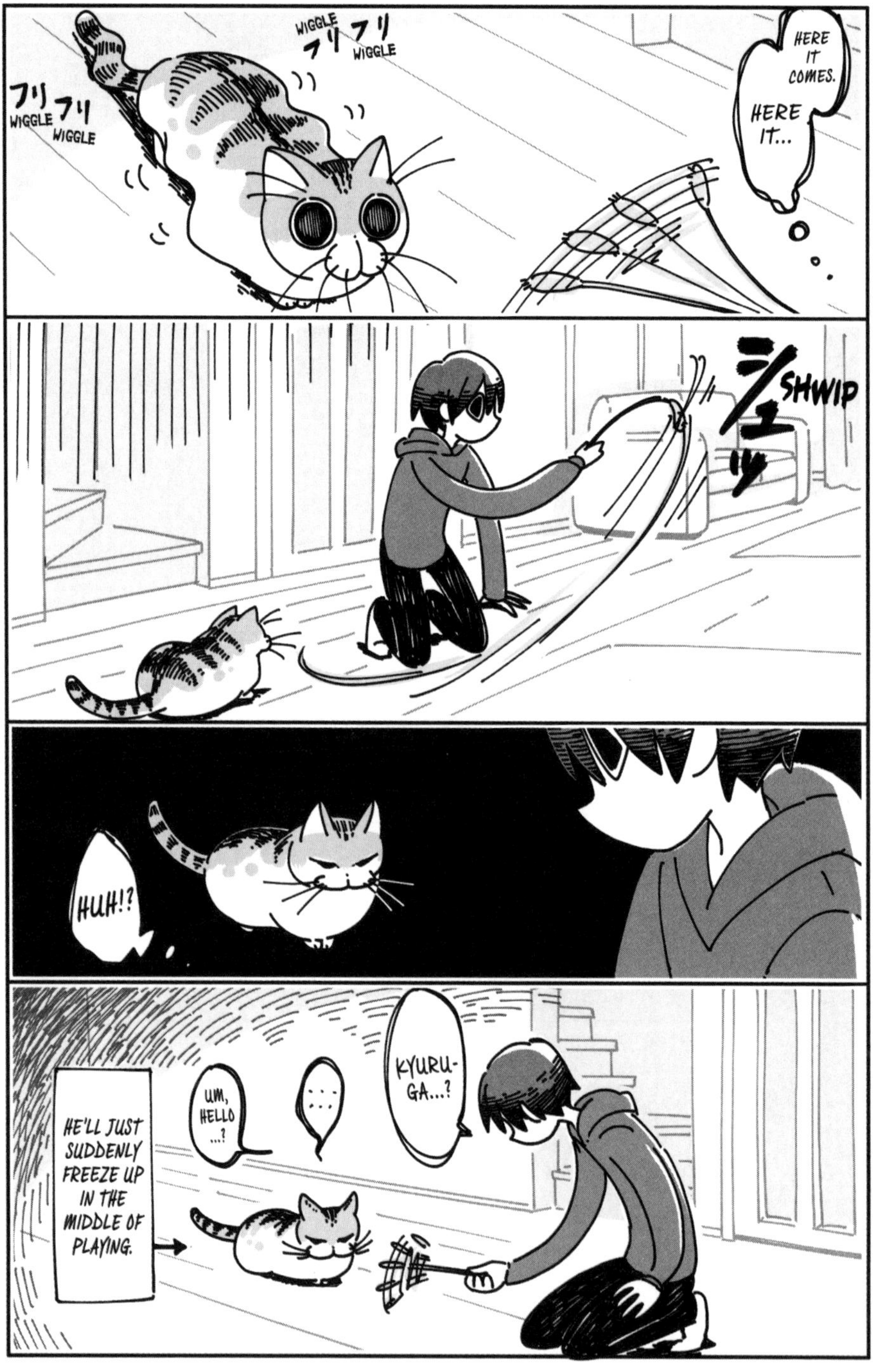
HERE IT COMES. HERE IT...
フリフリ WIGGLE WIGGLE
フリフリ WIGGLE WIGGLE
シュッ SHWIP
HUH!?
KYURU-GA...?
......
UM, HELLO...?
HE'LL JUST SUDDENLY FREEZE UP IN THE MIDDLE OF PLAYING.

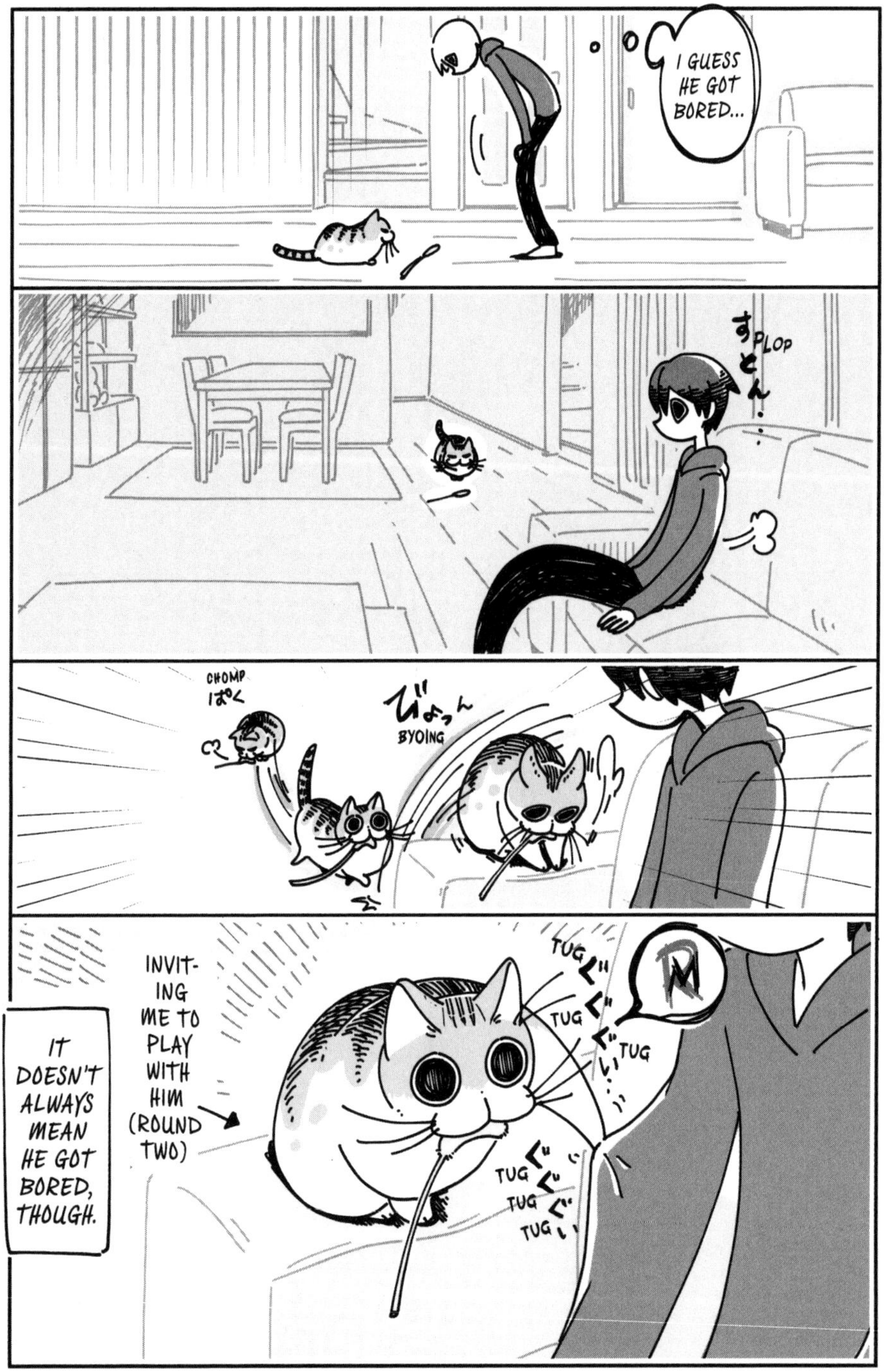
I GUESS HE GOT BORED...
すとん… PLOP
びよっん BYOING
CHOMP ぱく
TUG ぐいぐい
TUG ぐいぐい
TUG ぐいぐい…
TUG ぐいぐい
TUG ぐいぐい
TUG ぐいぐい
INVITING ME TO PLAY WITH HIM (ROUND TWO)
IT DOESN'T ALWAYS MEAN HE GOT BORED, THOUGH.

A Cat Comes to Check

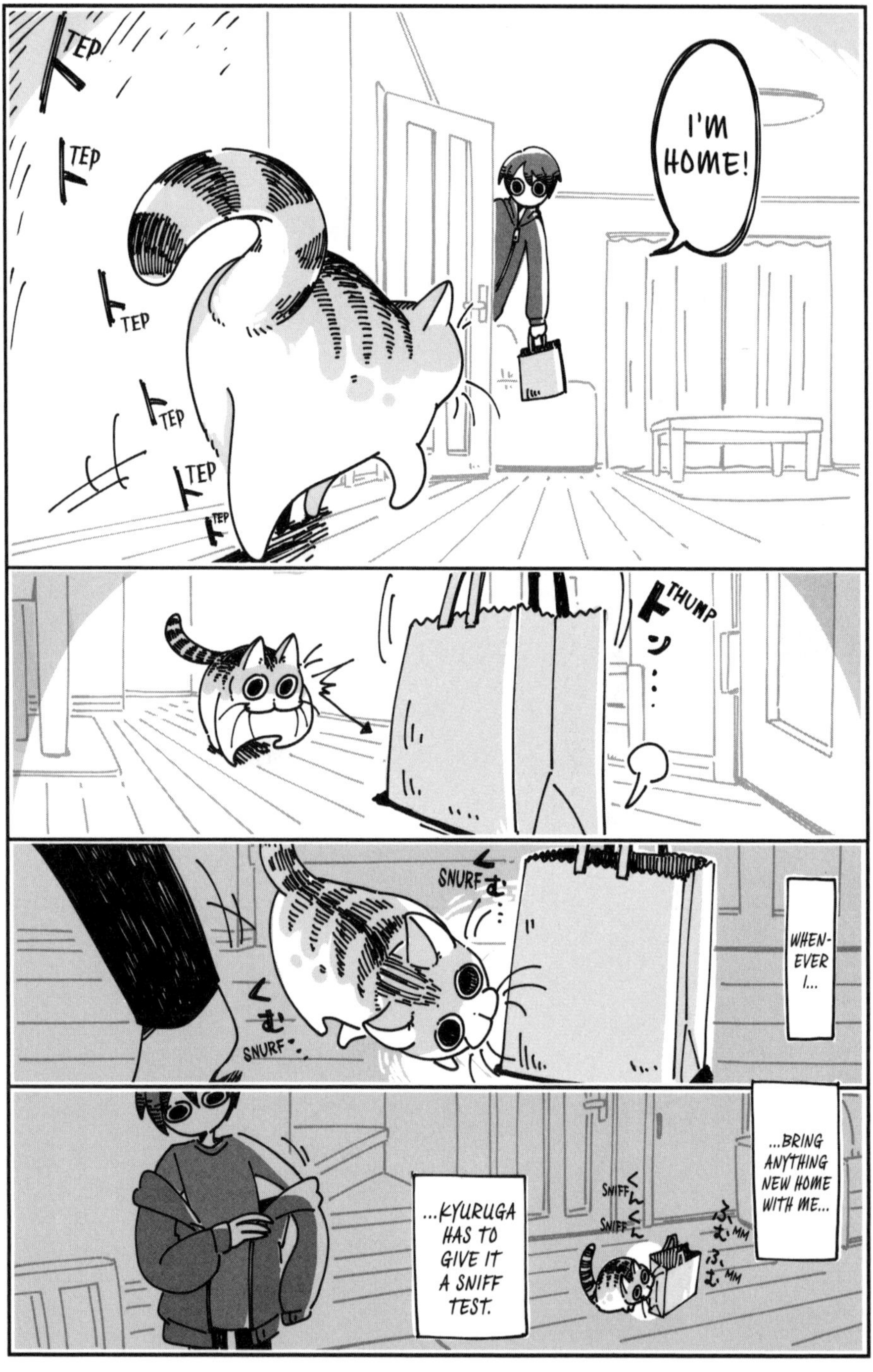
I'M HOME!
TEP
TEP
TEP
TEP
TEP
TEP
THUMP
SNURF
SNURF
WHEN-EVER I...
...BRING ANYTHING NEW HOME WITH ME...
SNIFF
SNIFF
MM
MM
...KYURUGA HAS TO GIVE IT A SNIFF TEST.

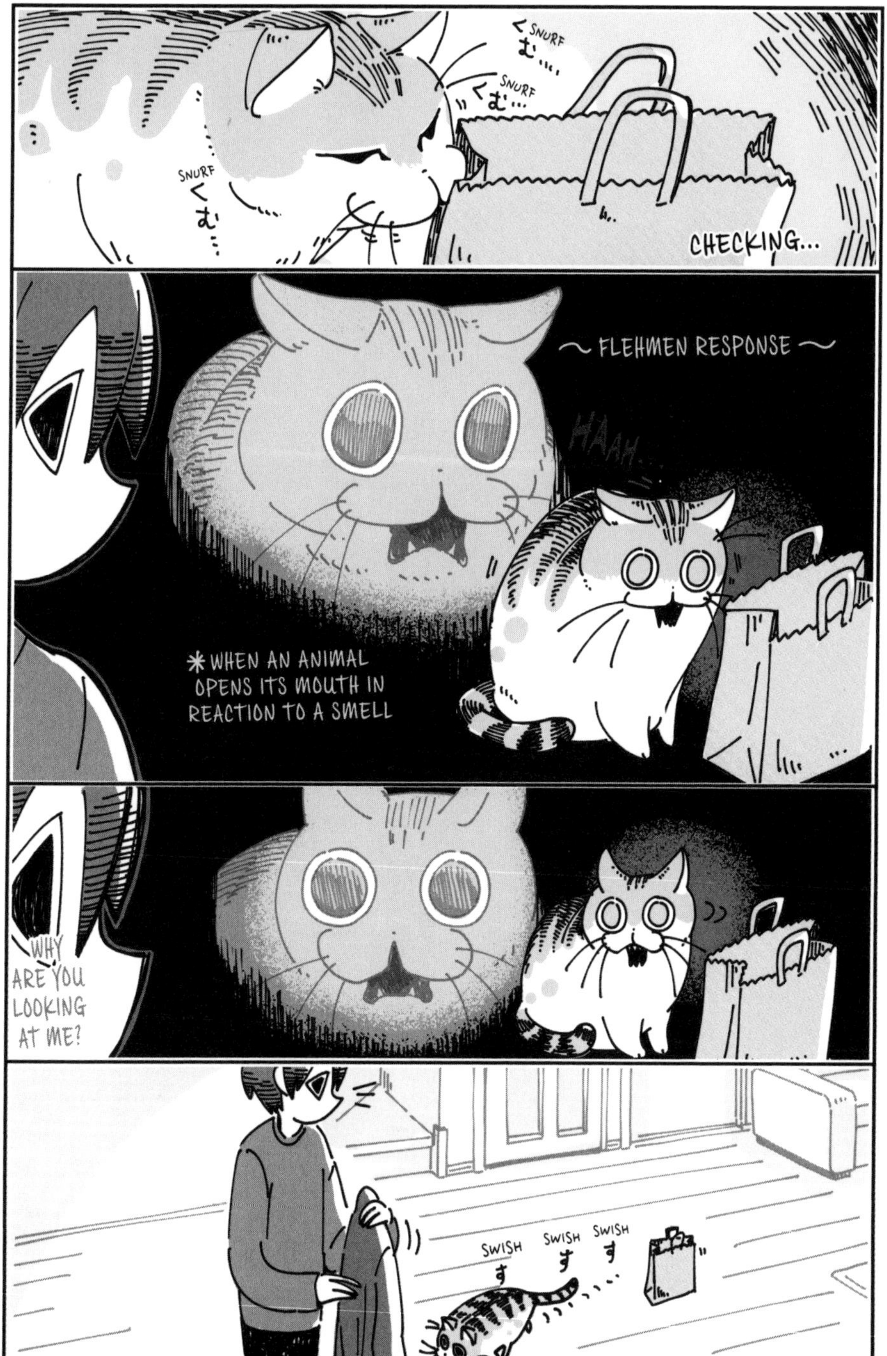
SNURF
くむ…
SNURF
くむ…
SNURF
くむ…
CHECKING…
~ FLEHMEN RESPONSE ~
HAAH…
*WHEN AN ANIMAL OPENS ITS MOUTH IN REACTION TO A SMELL
WHY ARE YOU LOOKING AT ME?
SWISH
す
SWISH
す
SWISH
す

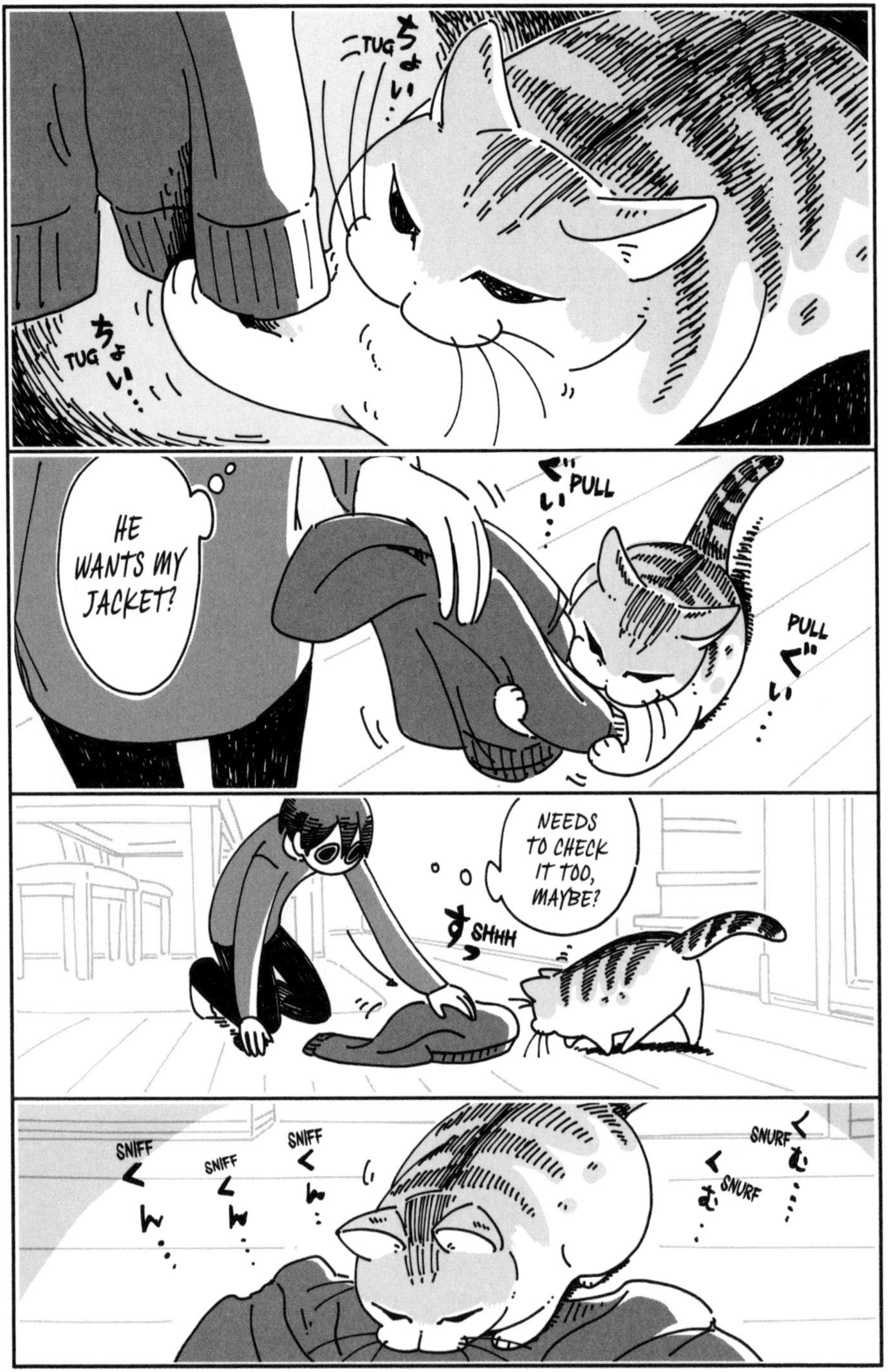
ちょい…
TUG
ちょい…
TUG
ぐい…
PULL
PULL
ぐい…
HE WANTS MY JACKET?
NEEDS TO CHECK IT TOO, MAYBE?
す
SHHH
くむ…
SNURF
くむ…
SNURF
くん…
SNIFF
くん…
SNIFF
くん…
SNIFF

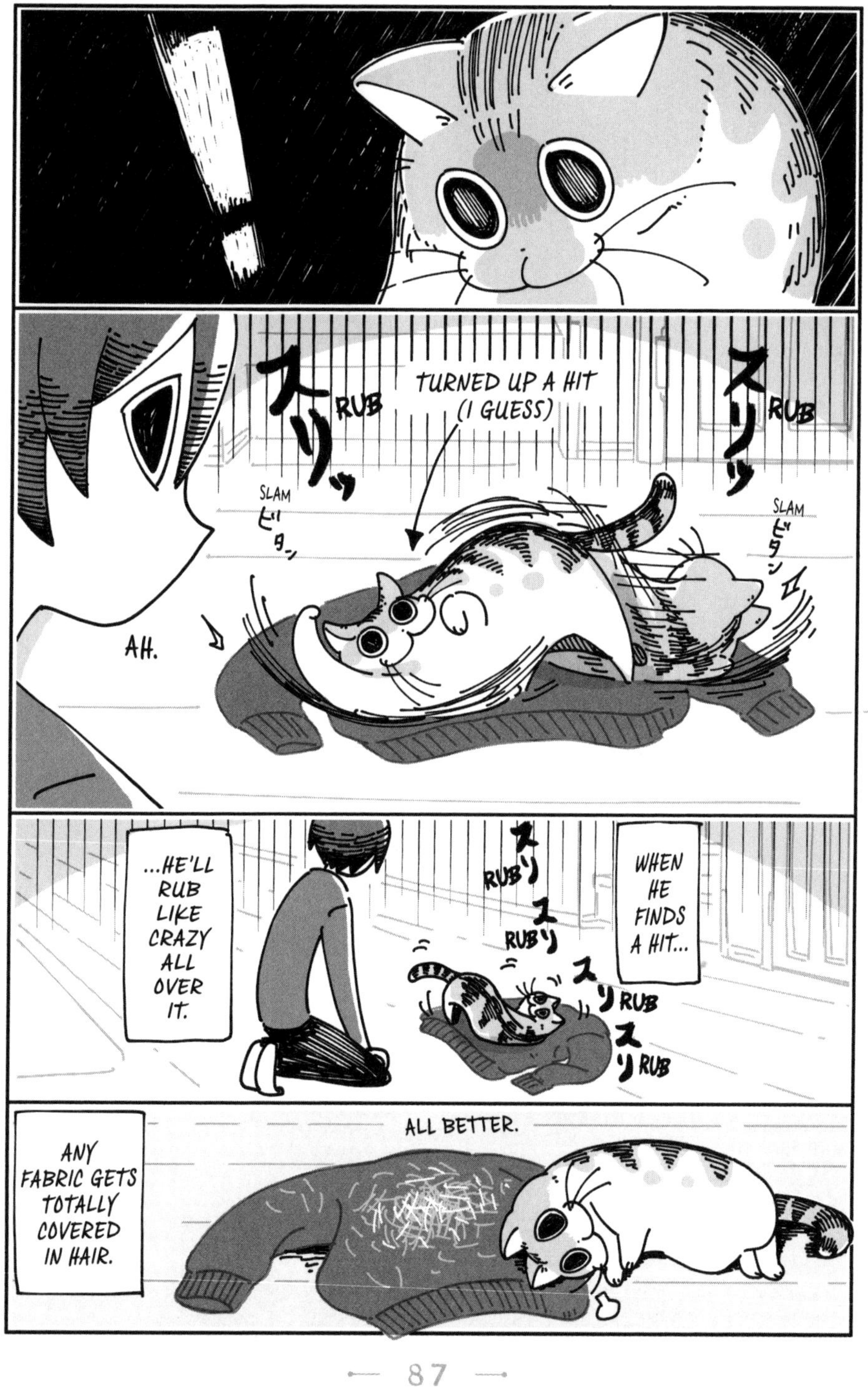
!
スリッ
RUB
SLAM
ビタン
TURNED UP A HIT (I GUESS)
スリッ
RUB
SLAM
ビタン
AH.
WHEN HE FINDS A HIT...
スリ
RUB
スリ
RUB
スリ
RUB
スリ
RUB
...HE'LL RUB LIKE CRAZY ALL OVER IT.
ALL BETTER.
ANY FABRIC GETS TOTALLY COVERED IN HAIR.

Putting Stuff on a Cat

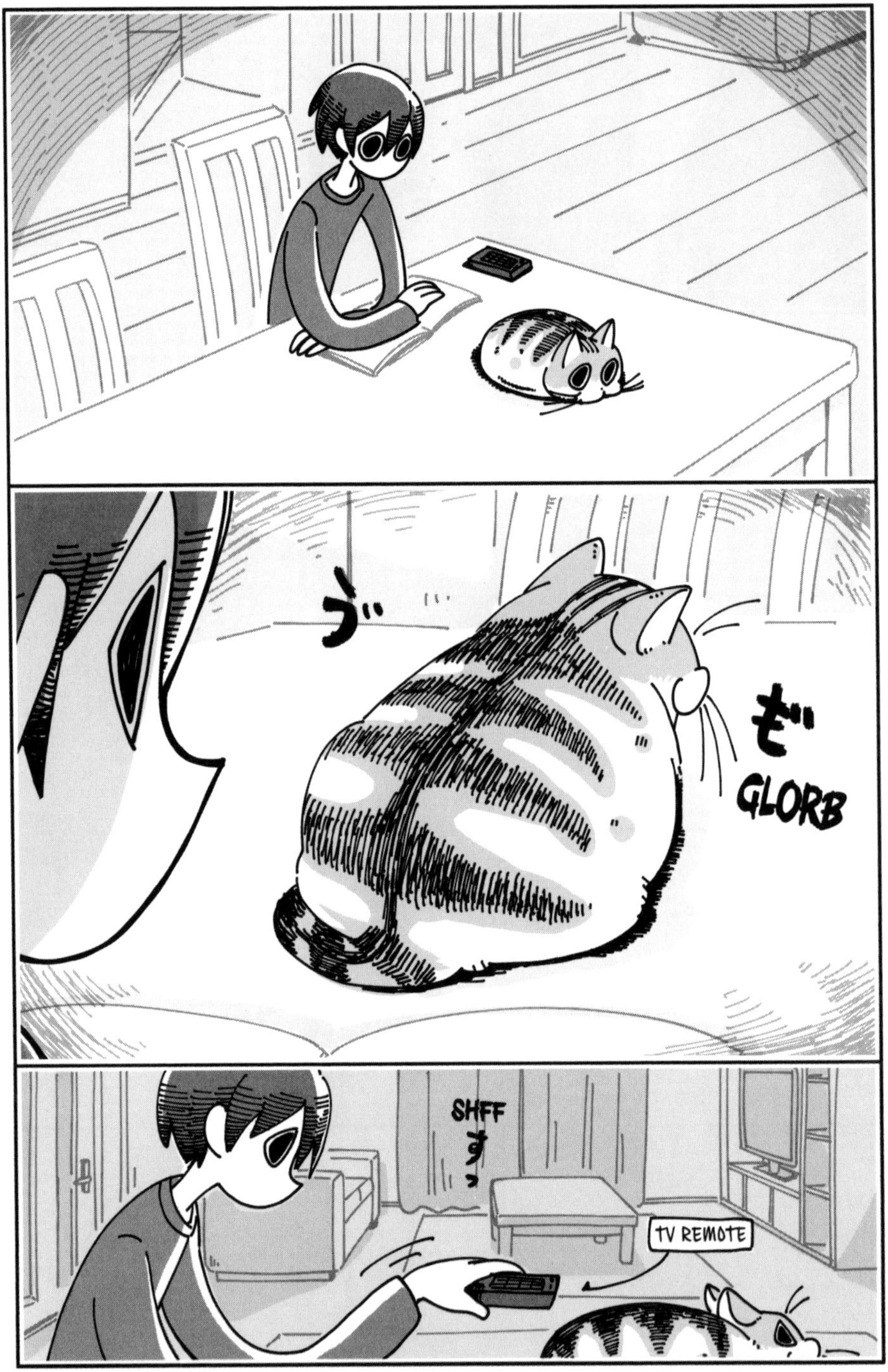
ぎ
GLORB
う゛
TV REMOTE
SHFF
すっ

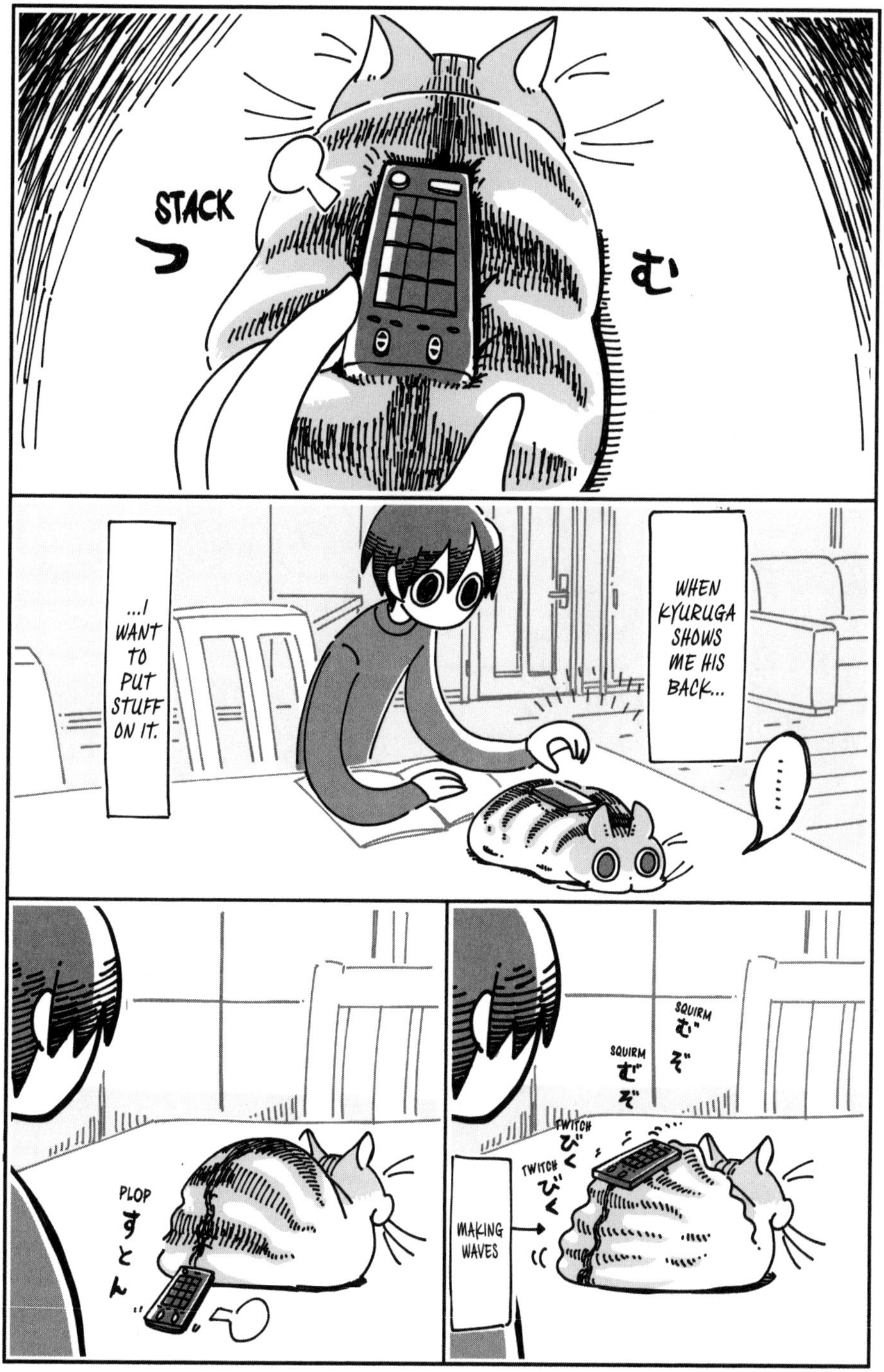
STACK
つむ
WHEN KYURUGA SHOWS ME HIS BACK...
...I WANT TO PUT STUFF ON IT.
......
SQUIRM
むぞ
SQUIRM
ずぞ
TWITCH
びく
TWITCH
びく
MAKING WAVES
PLOP
すとん

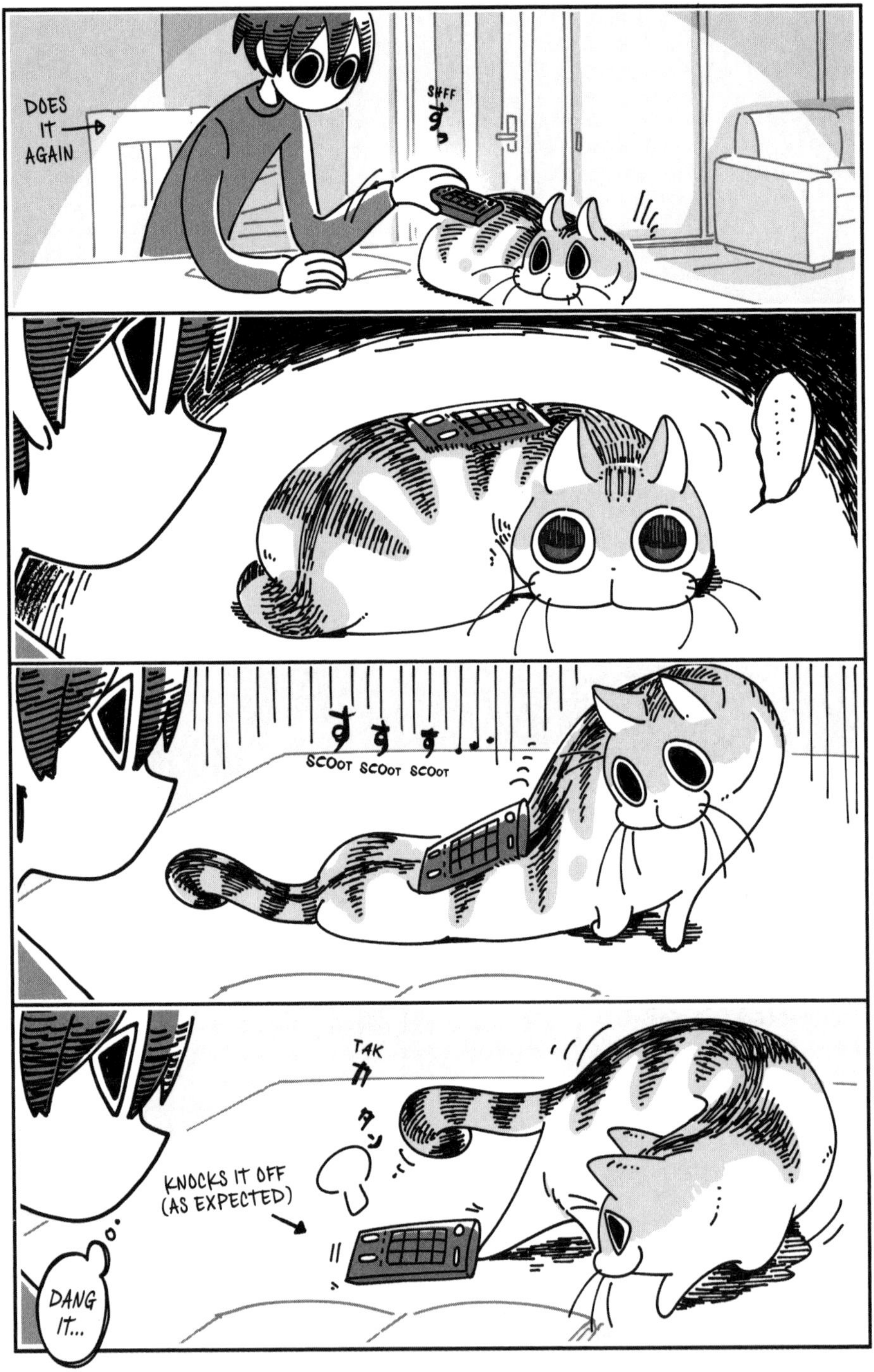
SHFF
すっ
DOES IT AGAIN
すすす…
SCOOT SCOOT SCOOT
TAK
カタン
KNOCKS IT OFF (AS EXPECTED)
DANG IT...

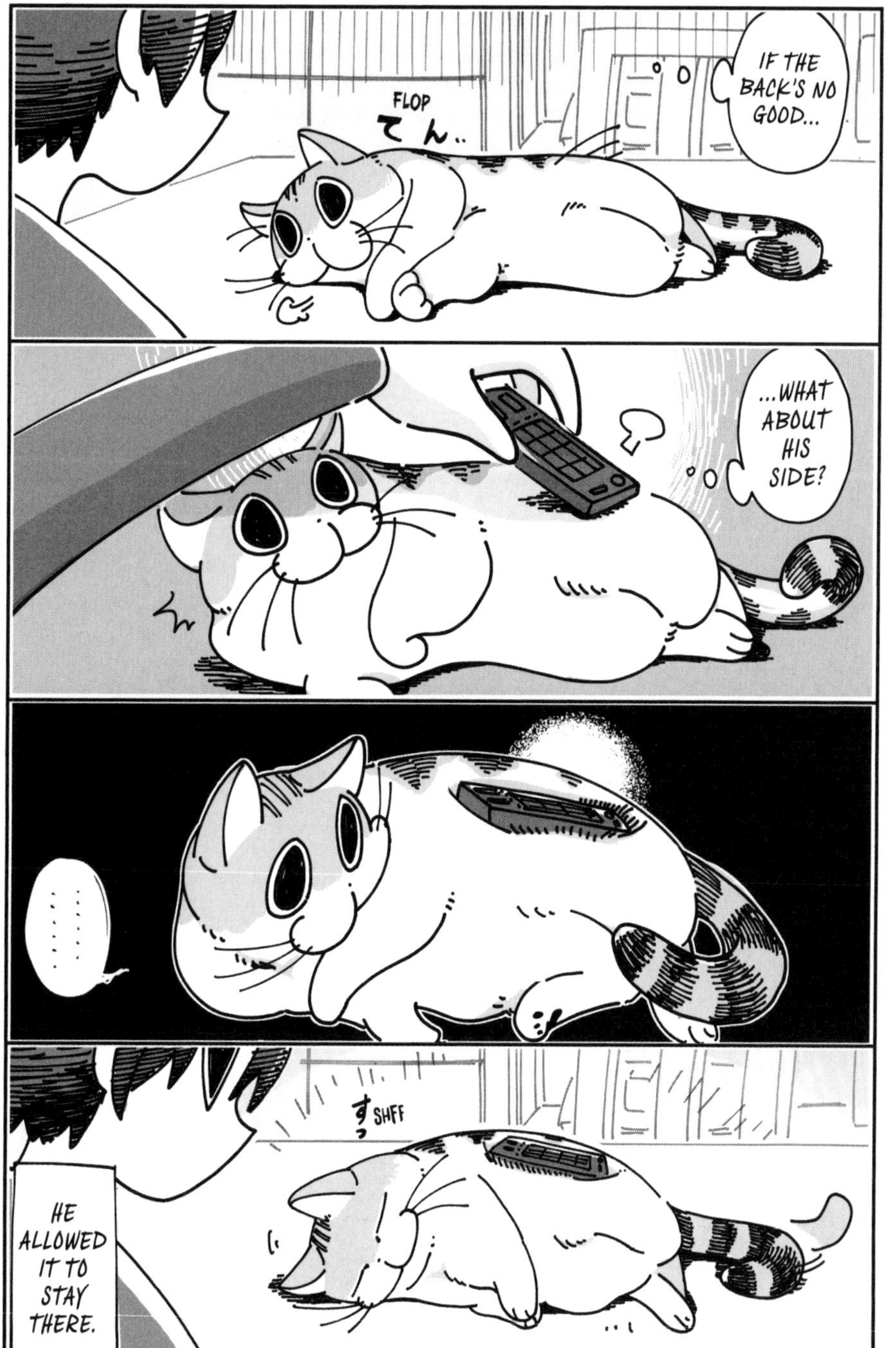
IF THE BACK'S NO GOOD...
FLOP
てん..
...WHAT ABOUT HIS SIDE?
......
HE ALLOWED IT TO STAY THERE.
すっ SHFF

A Cat Won't Move

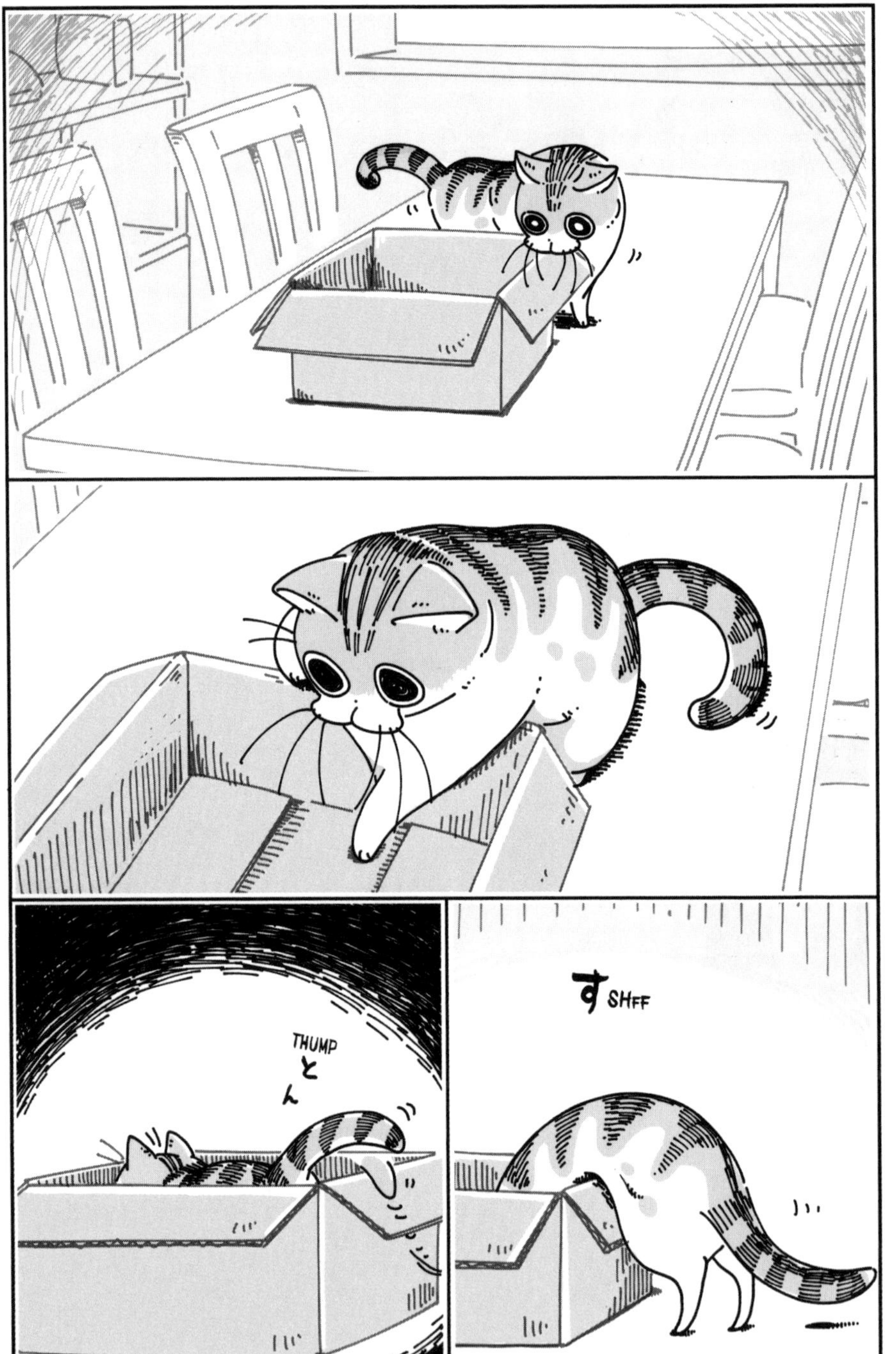
す SHFF
THUMP
とん

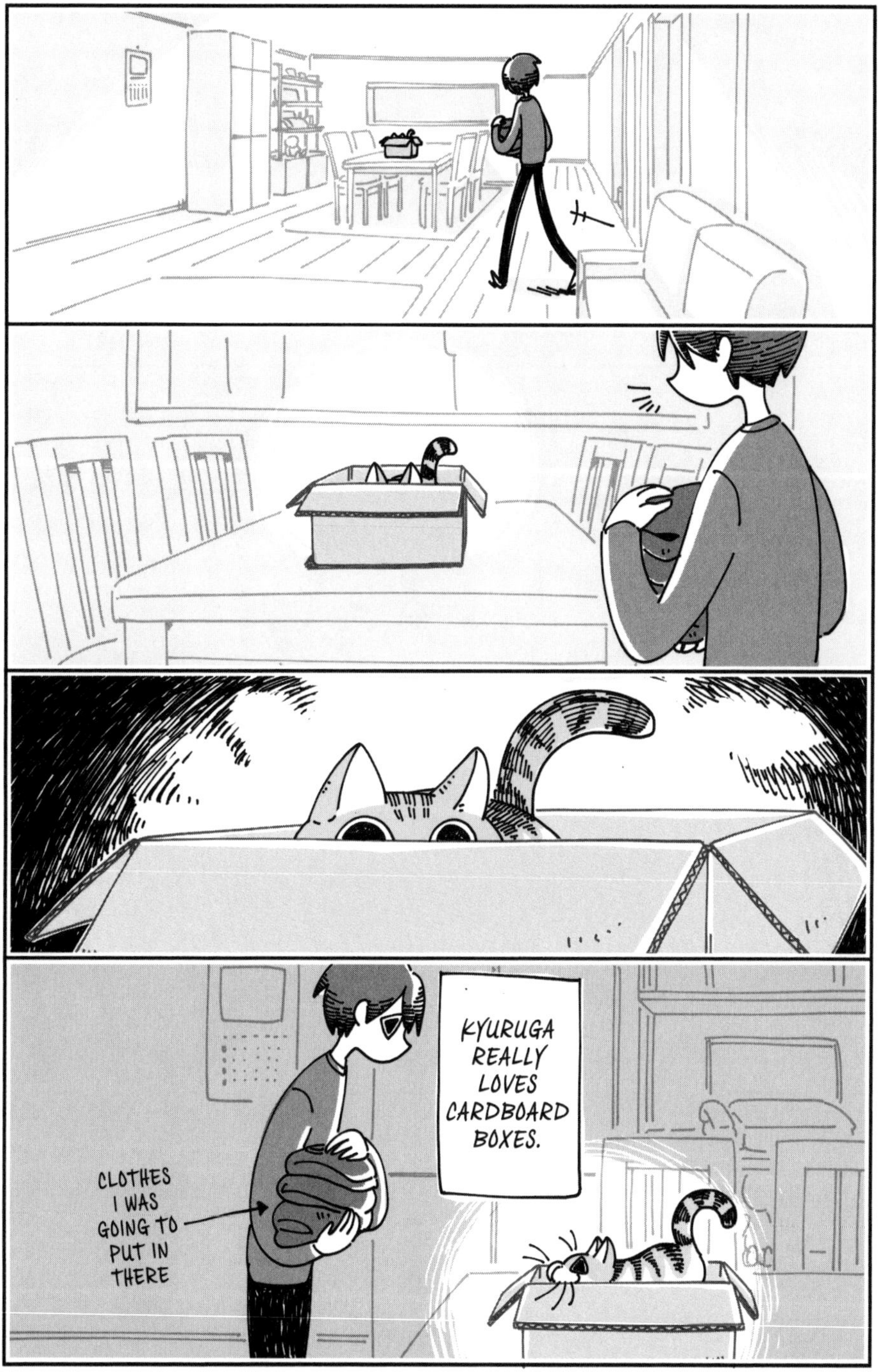
KYURUGA REALLY LOVES CARDBOARD BOXES.
CLOTHES I WAS GOING TO PUT IN THERE

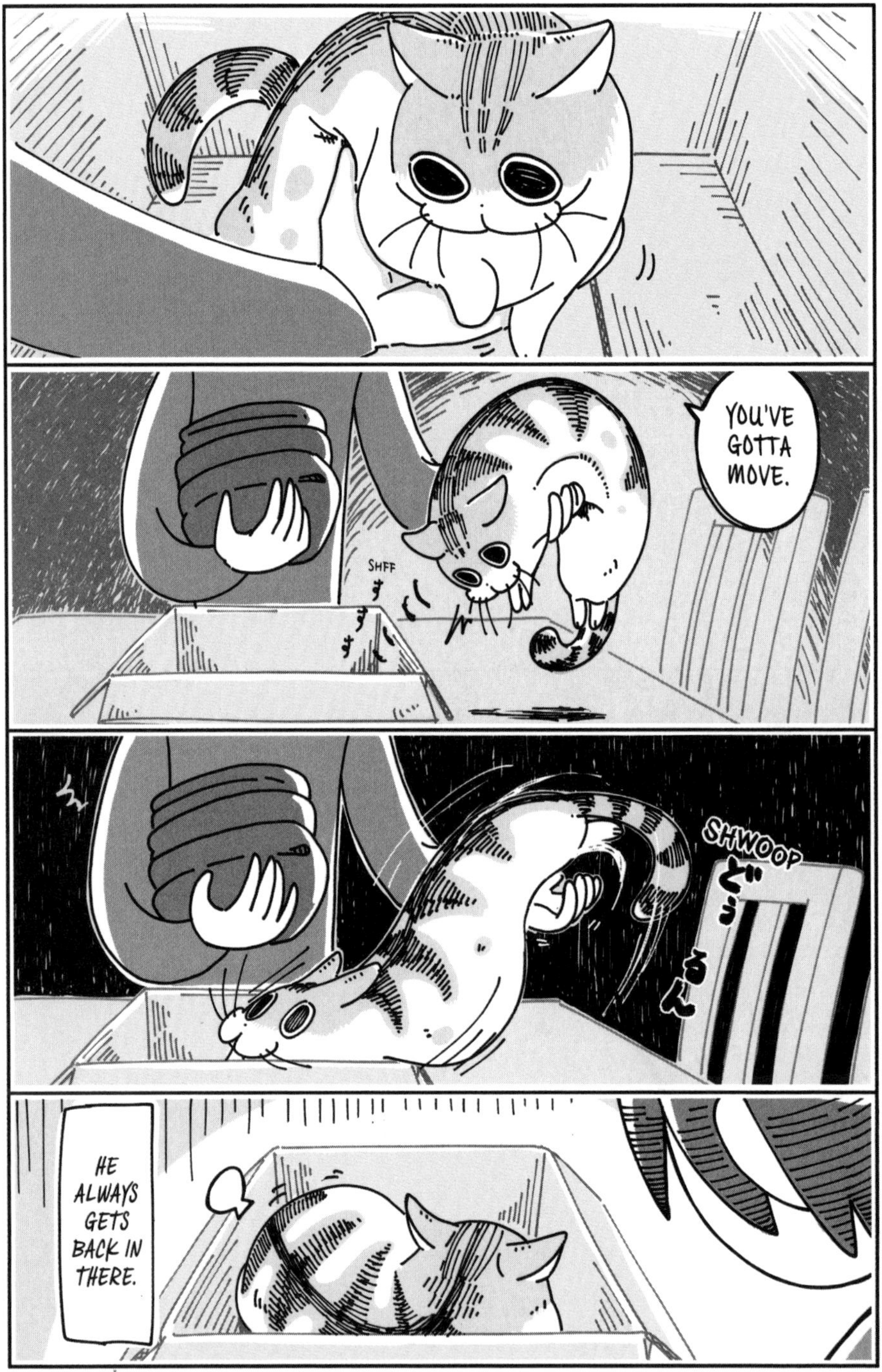
YOU'VE GOTTA MOVE.
SHFF
SHWOOP
HE ALWAYS GETS BACK IN THERE.

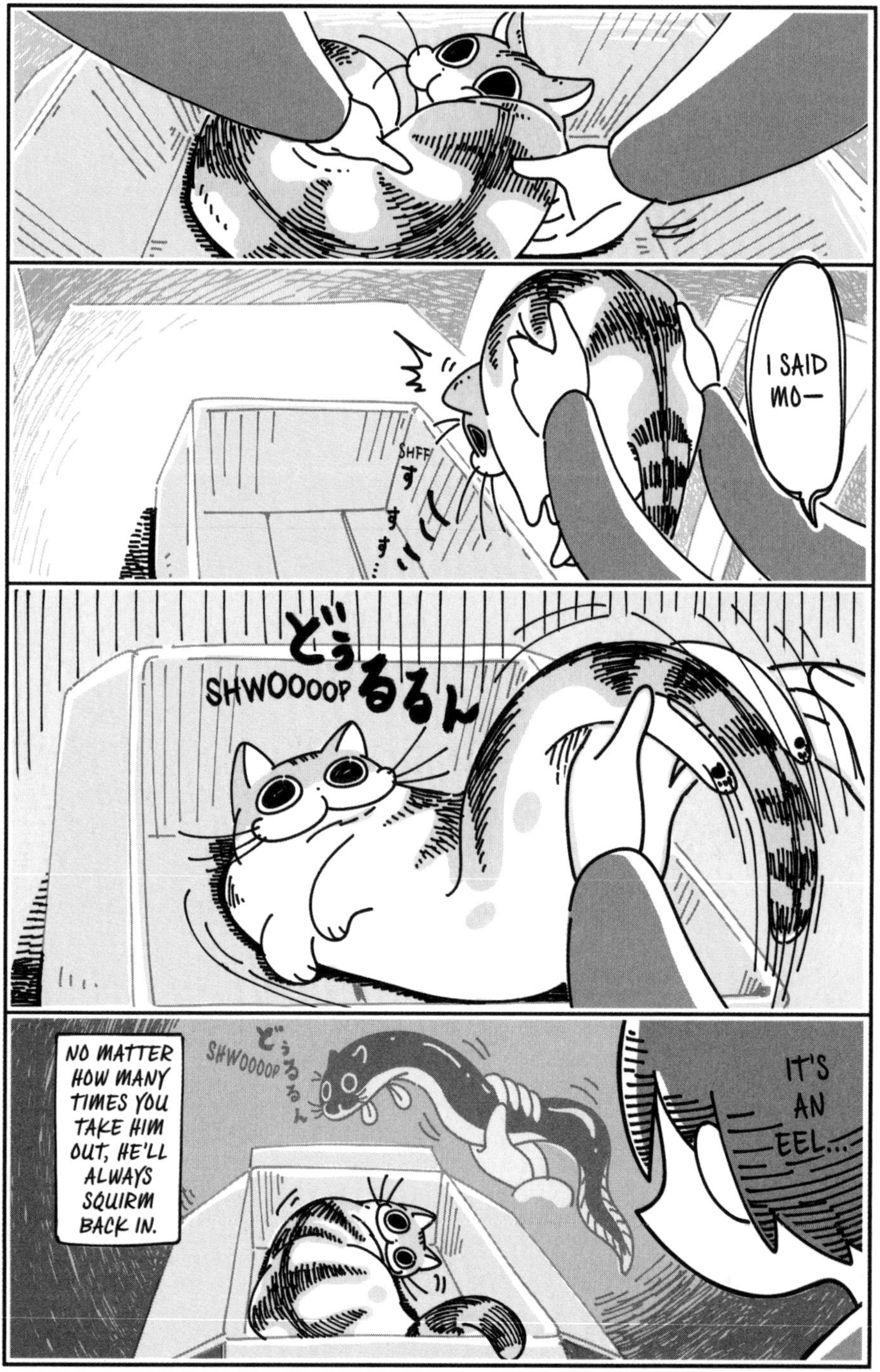
I SAID MO—
SHFF
すすす…
SHWOOOOP
どぅるるん
IT'S AN EEL...
NO MATTER HOW MANY TIMES YOU TAKE HIM OUT, HE'LL ALWAYS SQUIRM BACK IN.
SHWOOOOP
どぅるるん

Slapped by Cat Ears

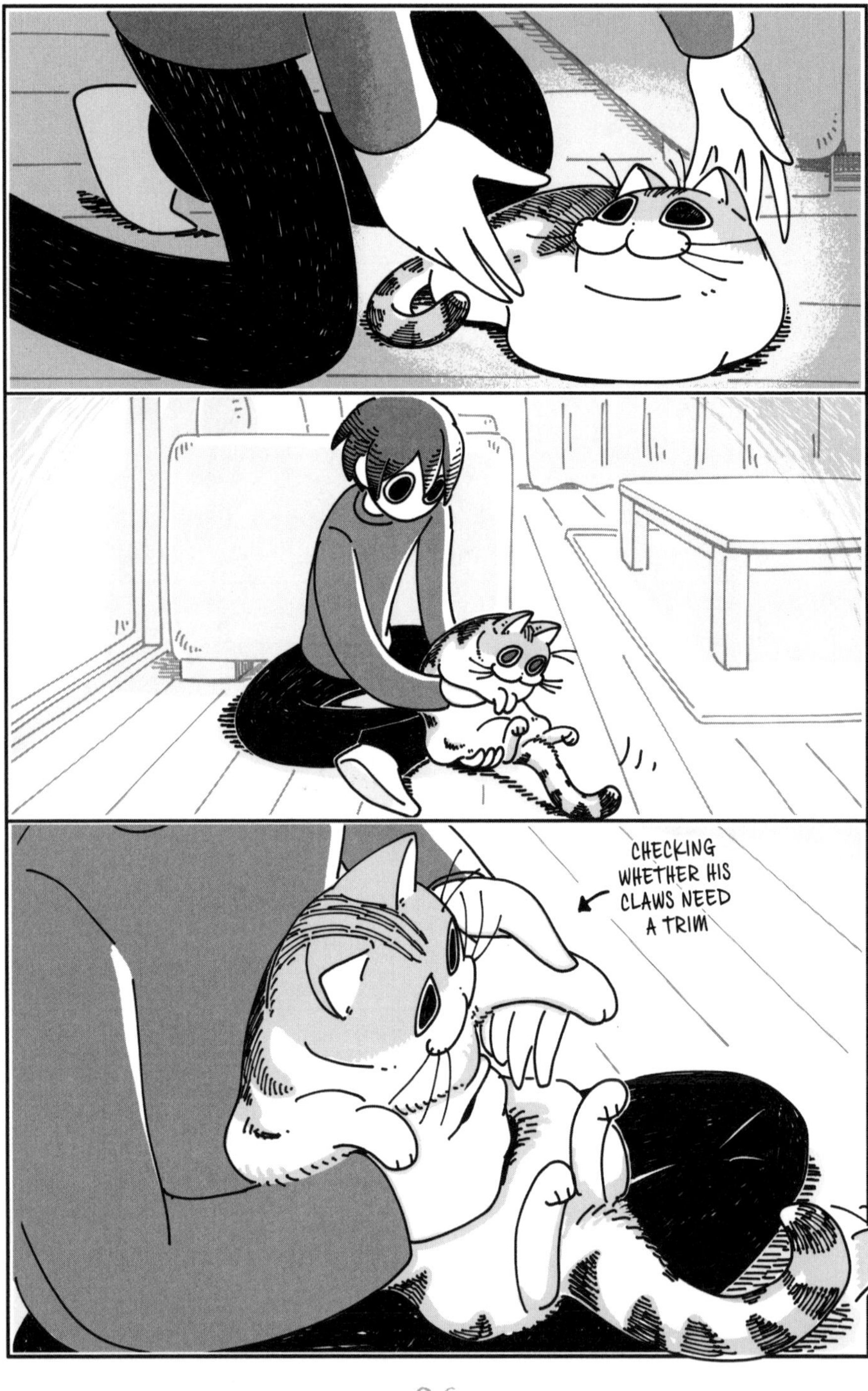
CHECKING WHETHER HIS CLAWS NEED A TRIM

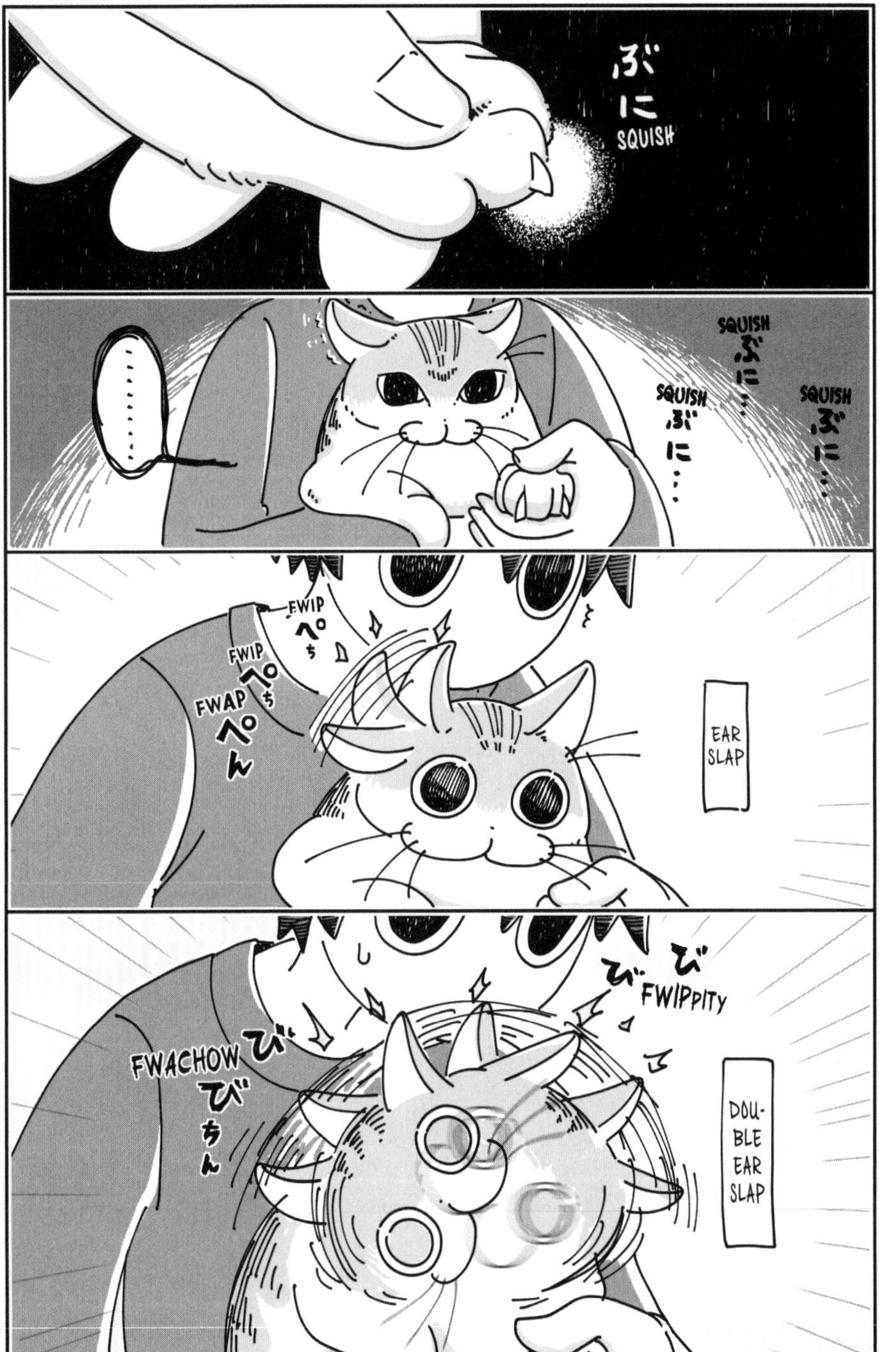

ぶに
SQUISH
SQUISH
ぶに…
SQUISH
ぶに…
SQUISH
ぶに…
……
EAR SLAP
FWIP
ぺち
FWIP
ぺち
FWAP
ぺん
DOUBLE EAR SLAP
びび
FWIPPITY
FWACHOW
びびちん

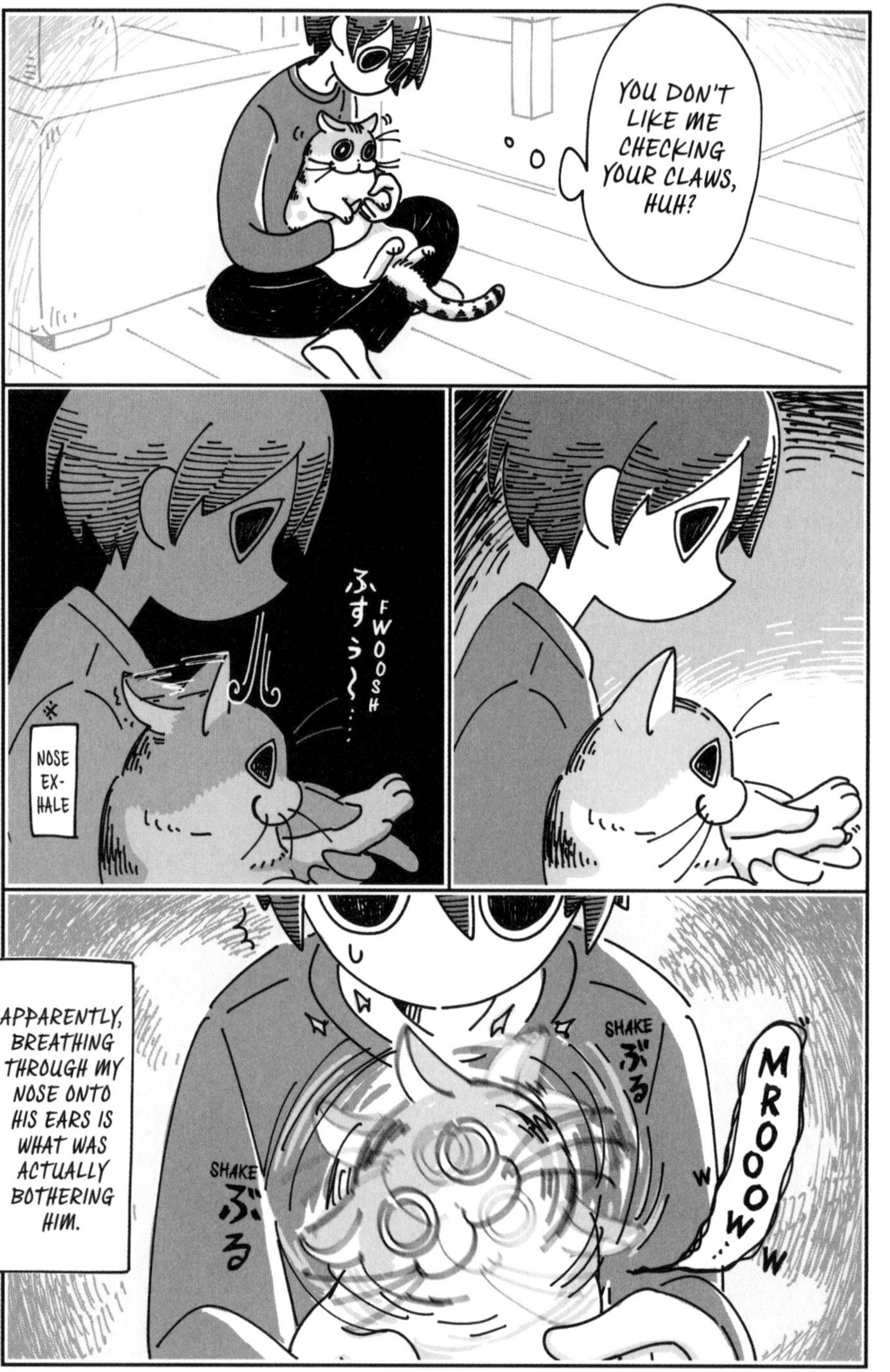
YOU DON'T LIKE ME CHECKING YOUR CLAWS, HUH?
ふすう〜…
FWOOSH
NOSE EX-HALE
SHAKE
ぶる
MROOOOW
SHAKE
ぶる
APPARENTLY, BREATHING THROUGH MY NOSE ONTO HIS EARS IS WHAT WAS ACTUALLY BOTHERING HIM.

Sleeping Cat

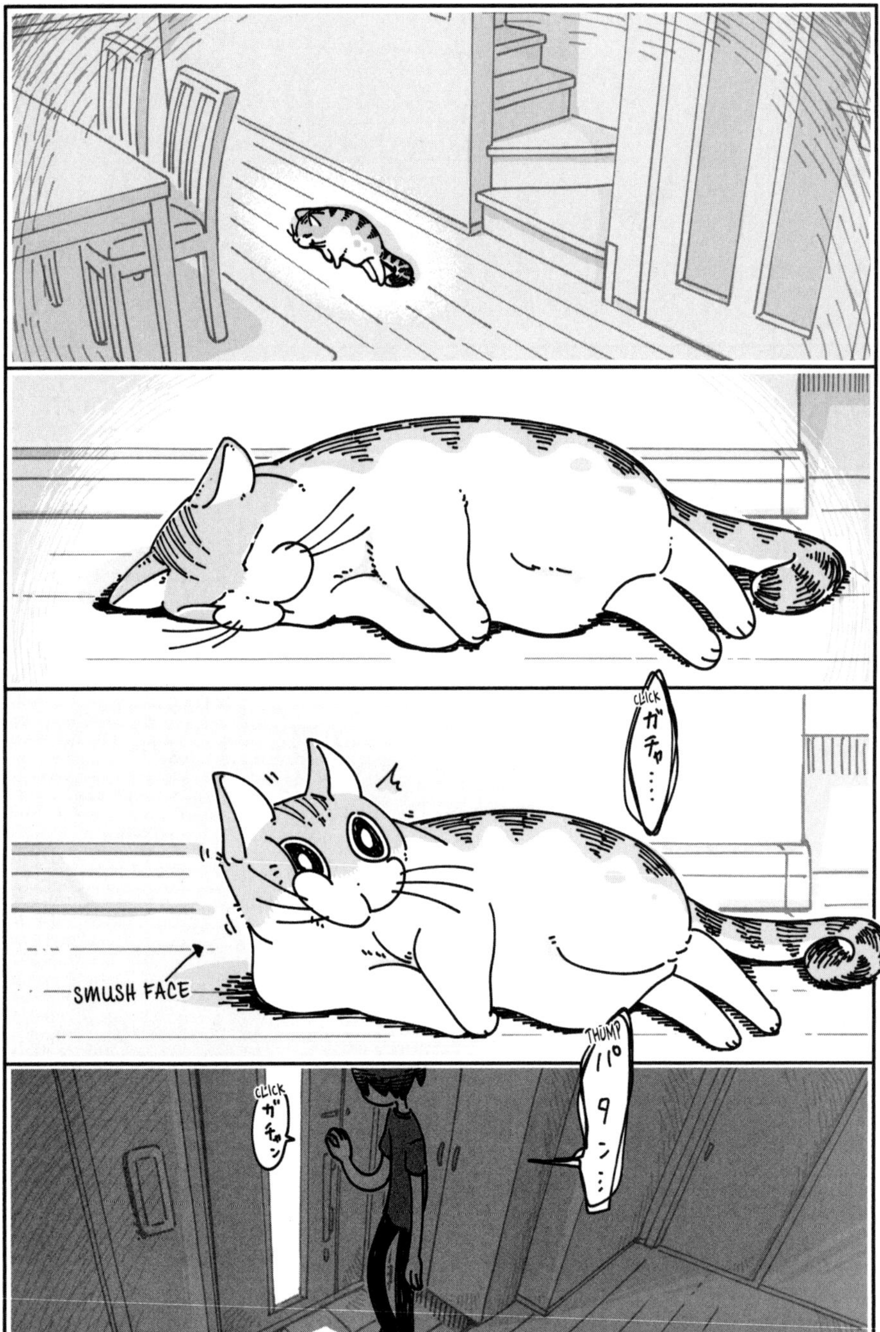
CLICK
ガチャ……
SMUSH FACE
THUMP
パタン……
CLICK
ガチャン

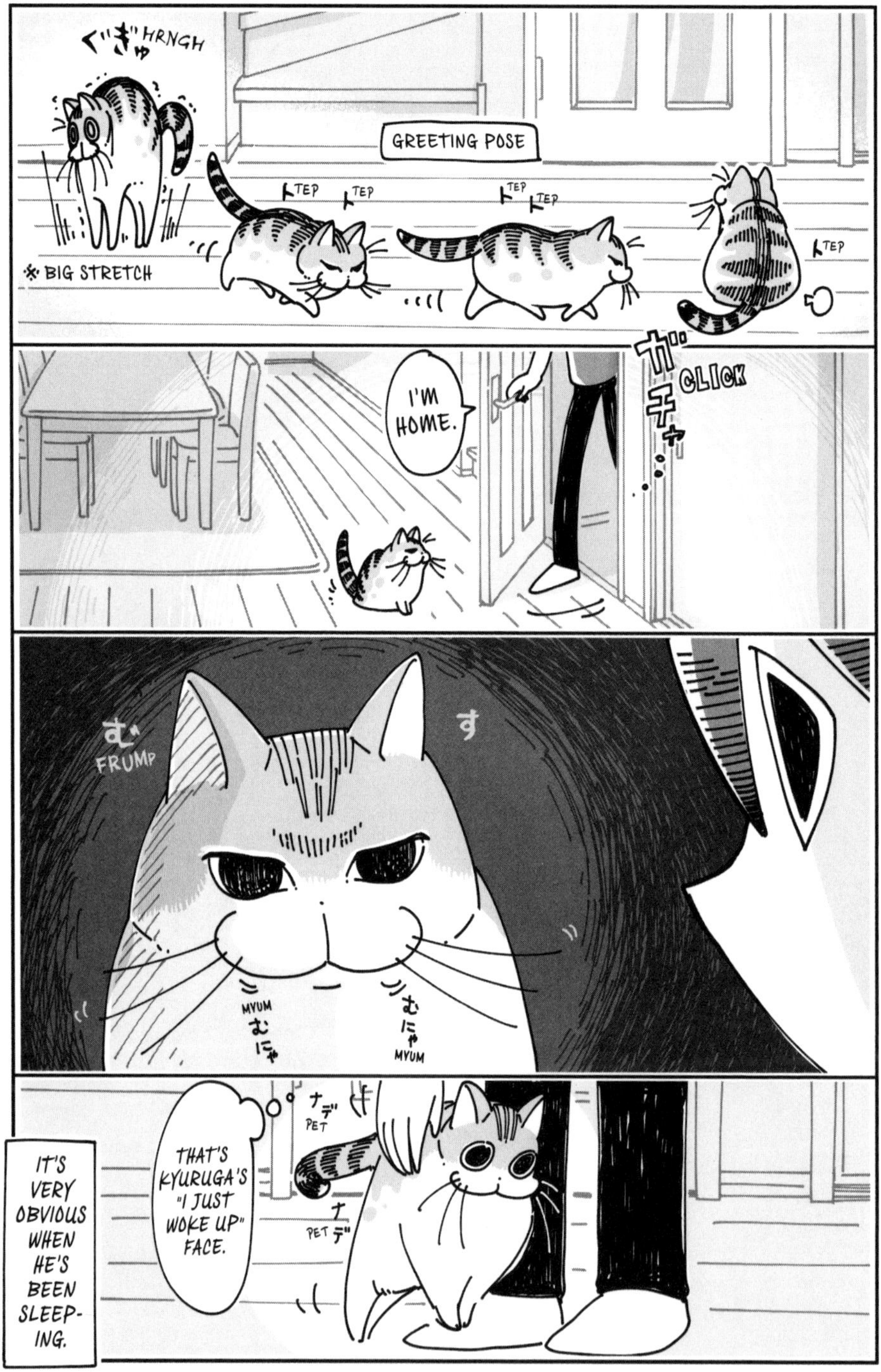
GREETING POSE
ト TEP
ト TEP ト TEP
ト TEP ト TEP
ぐぎゅ HRNGH
※ BIG STRETCH
ガチャ CLICK
I'M HOME.
す
むっ FRUMP
むにゃ MYUM
MYUM むにゃ
ナデ PET
PET ナデ
THAT'S KYURUGA'S "I JUST WOKE UP" FACE.
IT'S VERY OBVIOUS WHEN HE'S BEEN SLEEP-ING.

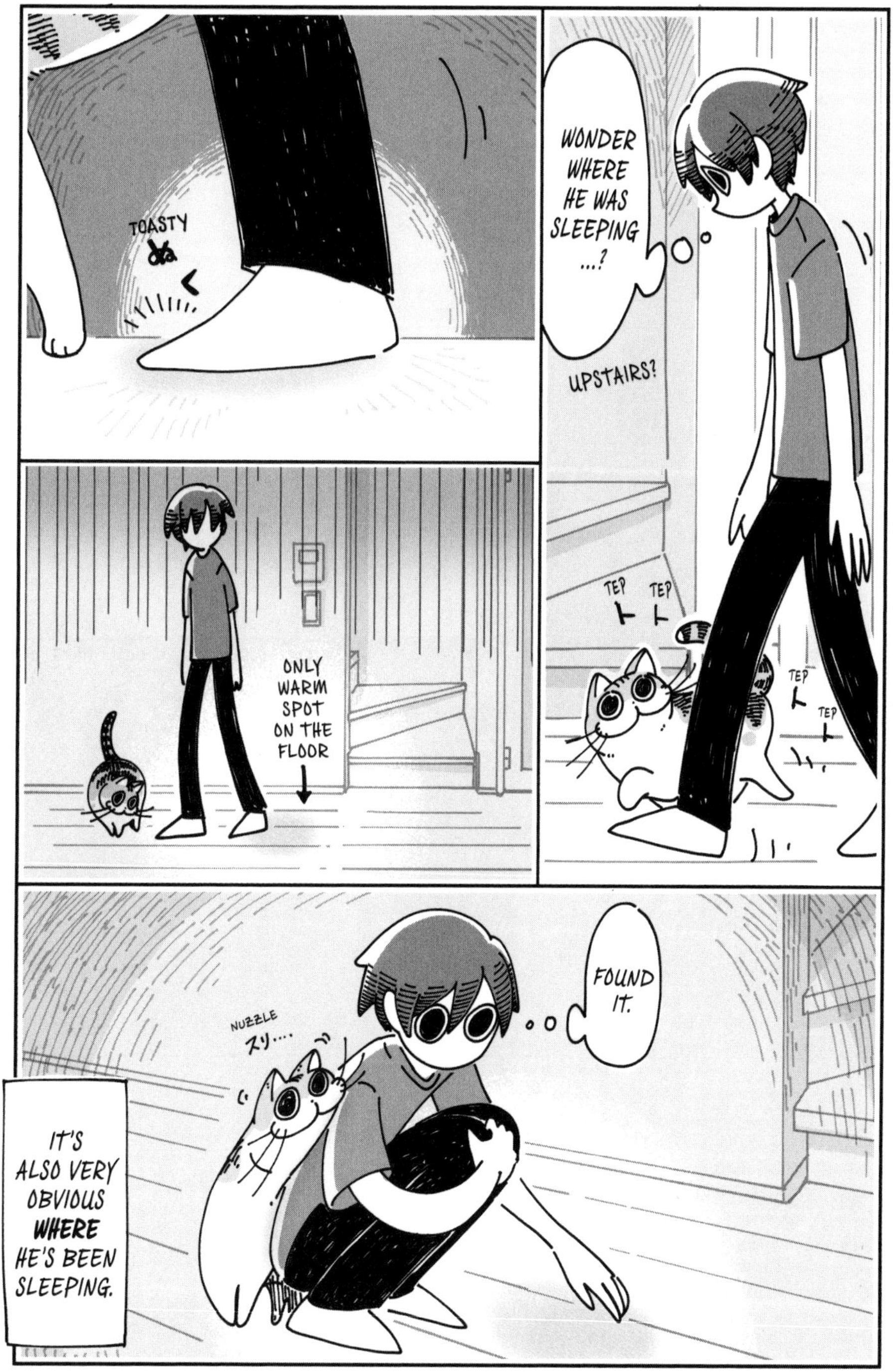
WONDER WHERE HE WAS SLEEPING ...?
UPSTAIRS?
TEP ト TEP ト
TEP ト
TEP ト
TOASTY ぬく
ONLY WARM SPOT ON THE FLOOR
FOUND IT.
NUZZLE スリ....
IT'S ALSO VERY OBVIOUS **WHERE** HE'S BEEN SLEEPING.

Kyuruga's Bath

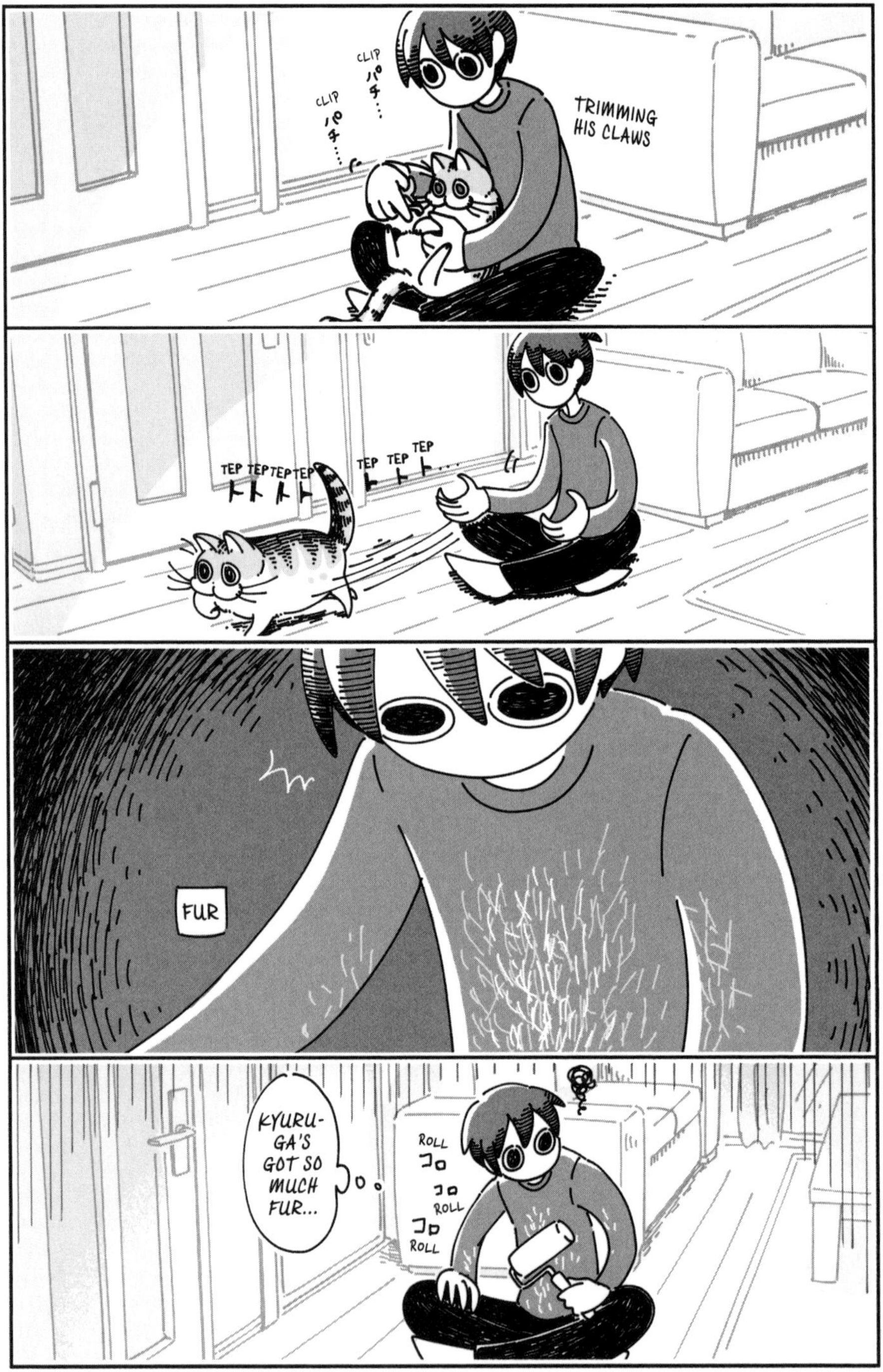
TRIMMING HIS CLAWS
CLIP パチ…
CLIP パチ…
TEP TEP TEP トトト…
TEP TEP TEP TEP トトトト
FUR
ROLL コロ
コロ ROLL
コロ ROLL
KYURU-GA'S GOT SO MUCH FUR...

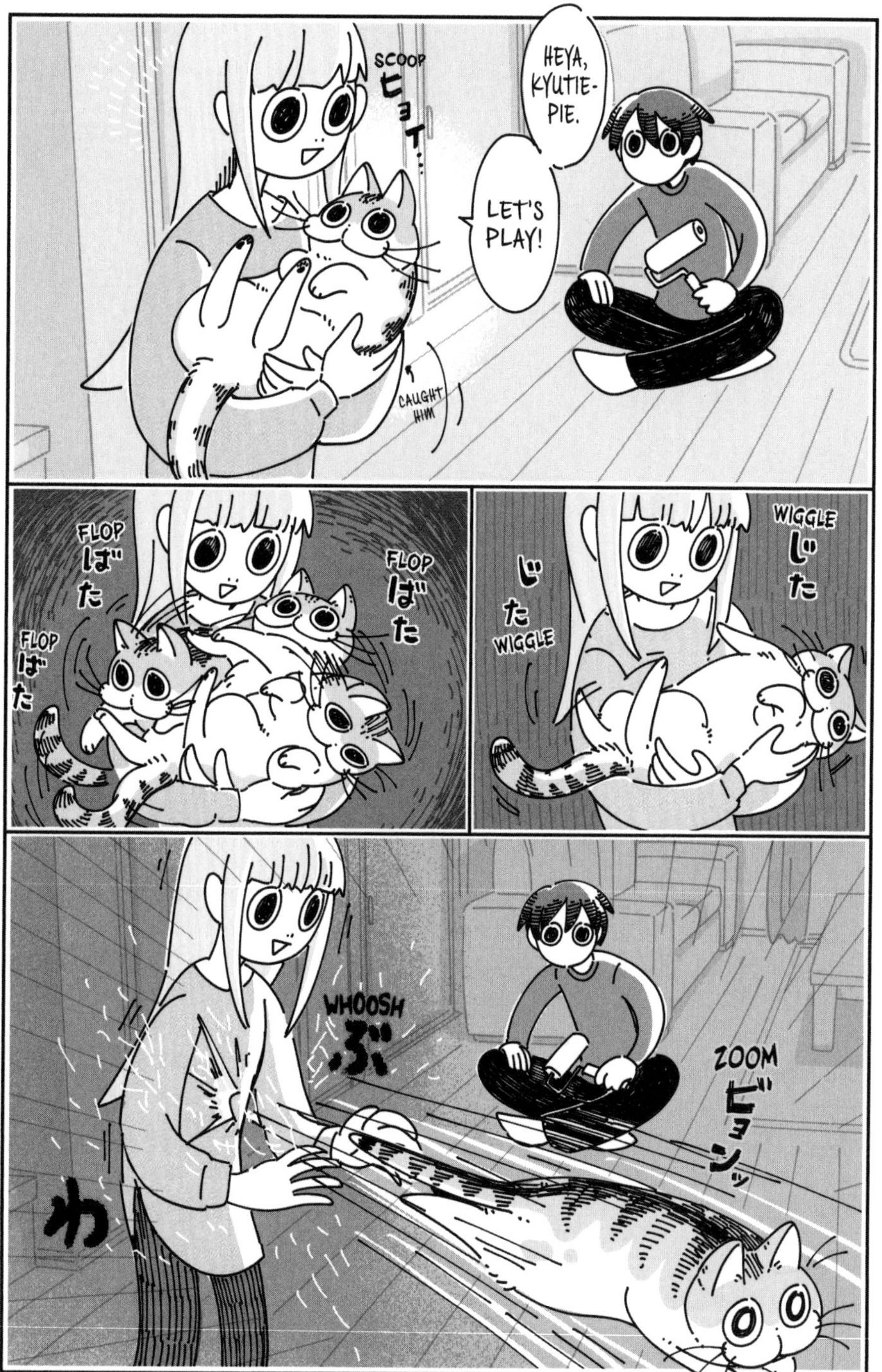
HEYA, KYUTIE-PIE.
LET'S PLAY!
SCOOP ヒョイ…
CAUGHT HIM
WIGGLE じた
じた WIGGLE
FLOP ばた
FLOP ばた
FLOP ばた
ZOOM ビョンッ
WHOOSH ぶ
わ

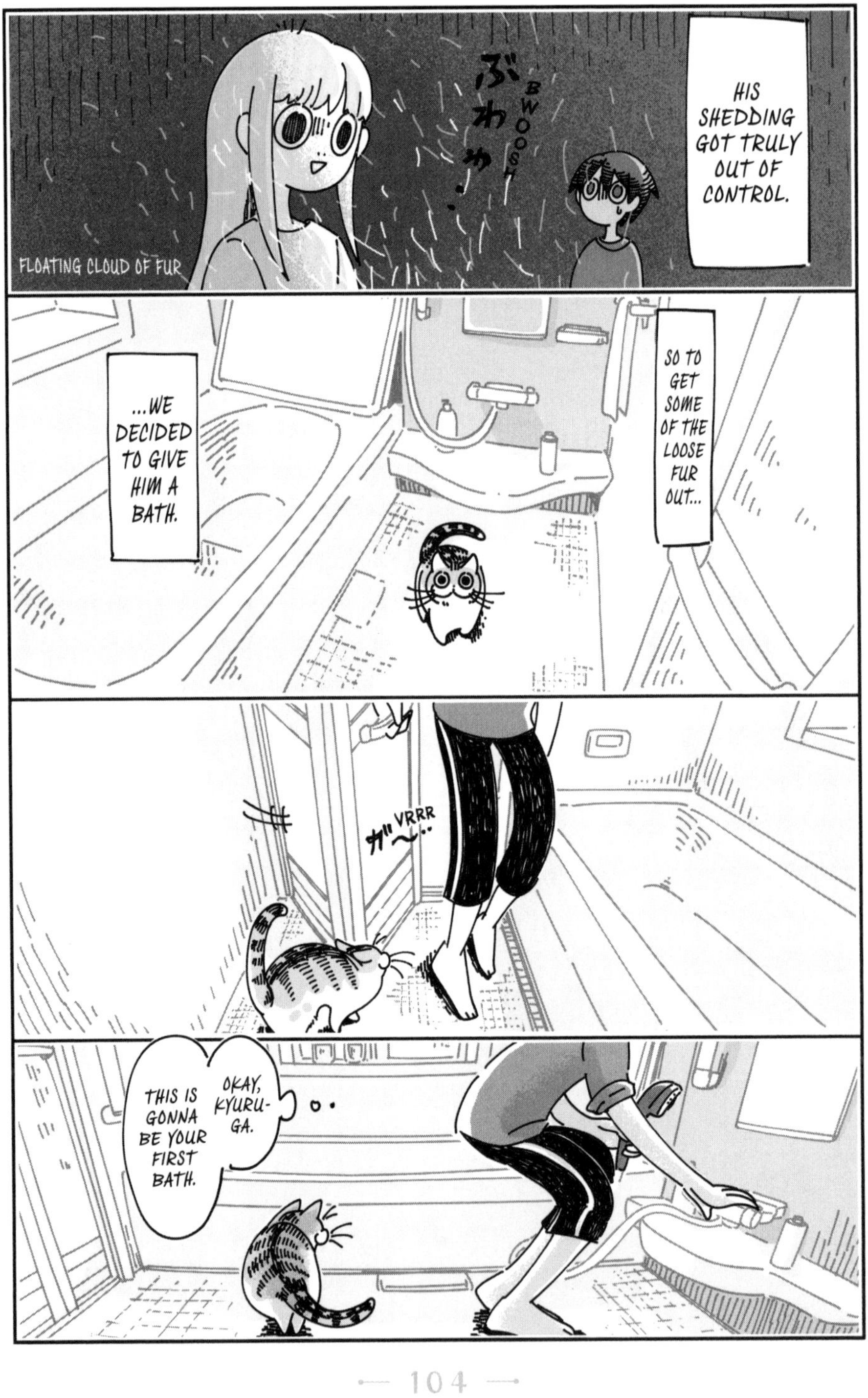
HIS SHEDDING GOT TRULY OUT OF CONTROL.
ぶわゎ・・
BWOOSH
FLOATING CLOUD OF FUR
SO TO GET SOME OF THE LOOSE FUR OUT...
...WE DECIDED TO GIVE HIM A BATH.
ガ〜・・
VRRR
OKAY, KYURU-GA.
THIS IS GONNA BE YOUR FIRST BATH.

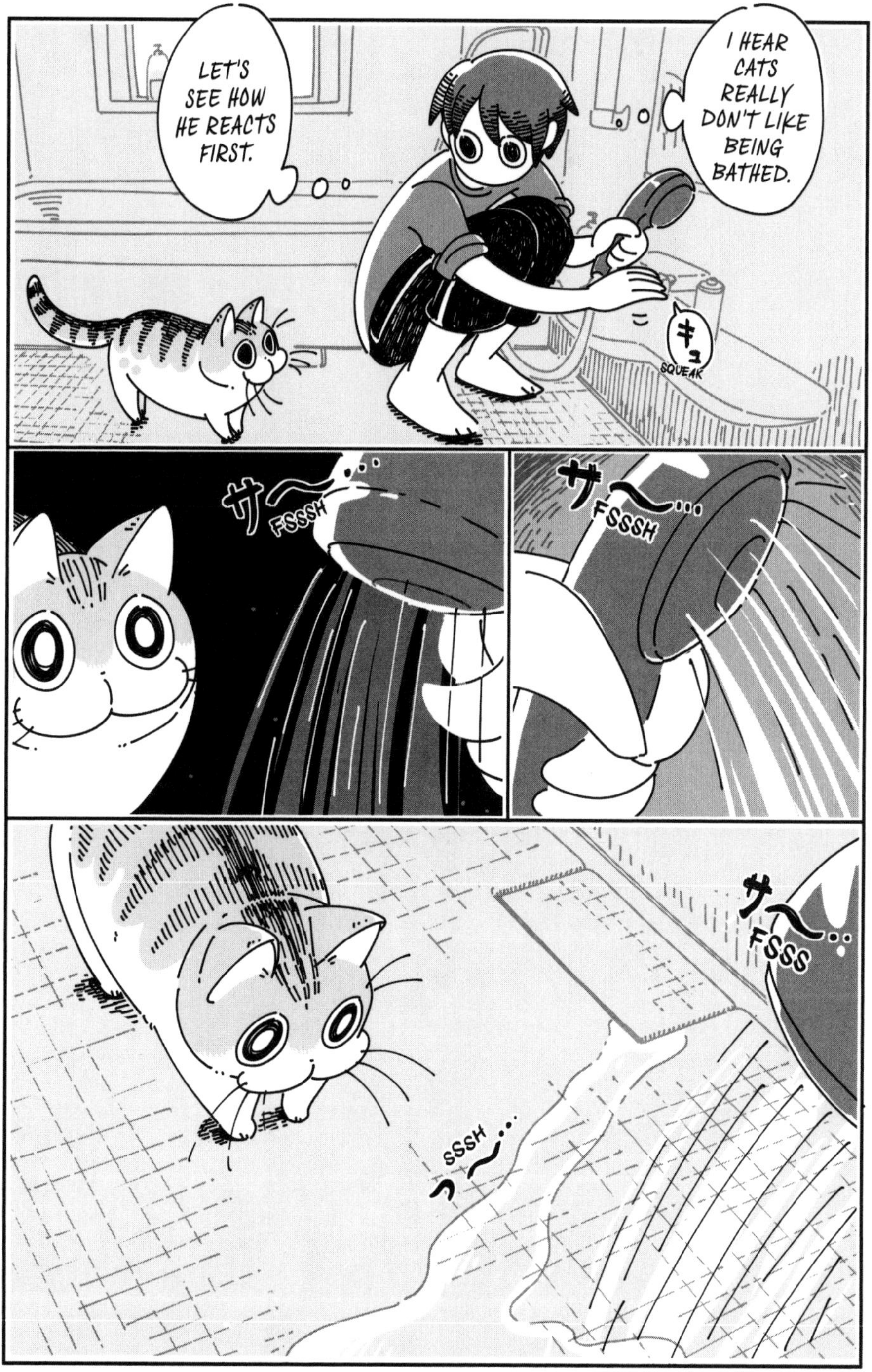
I HEAR CATS REALLY DON'T LIKE BEING BATHED.
LET'S SEE HOW HE REACTS FIRST.
キュ SQUEAK
サ〜… FSSSH
サ〜 FSSSH
サ〜… FSSS
つ〜… SSSH

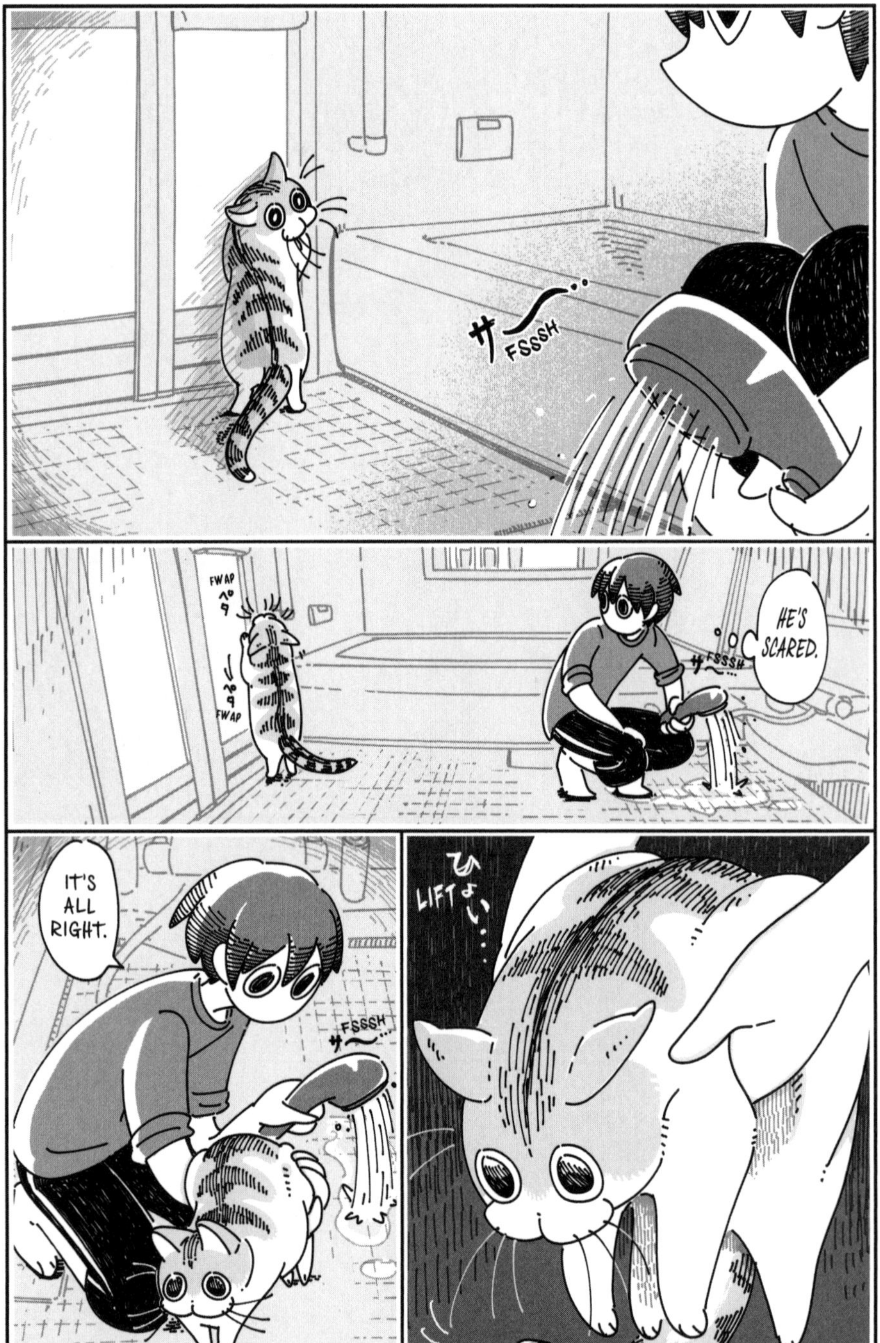
サ~ FSSSH
HE'S SCARED.
サ~ FSSSH
FWAP ペタ
ペタ FWAP
ひょい LIFT…
IT'S ALL RIGHT.
サ~ FSSSH

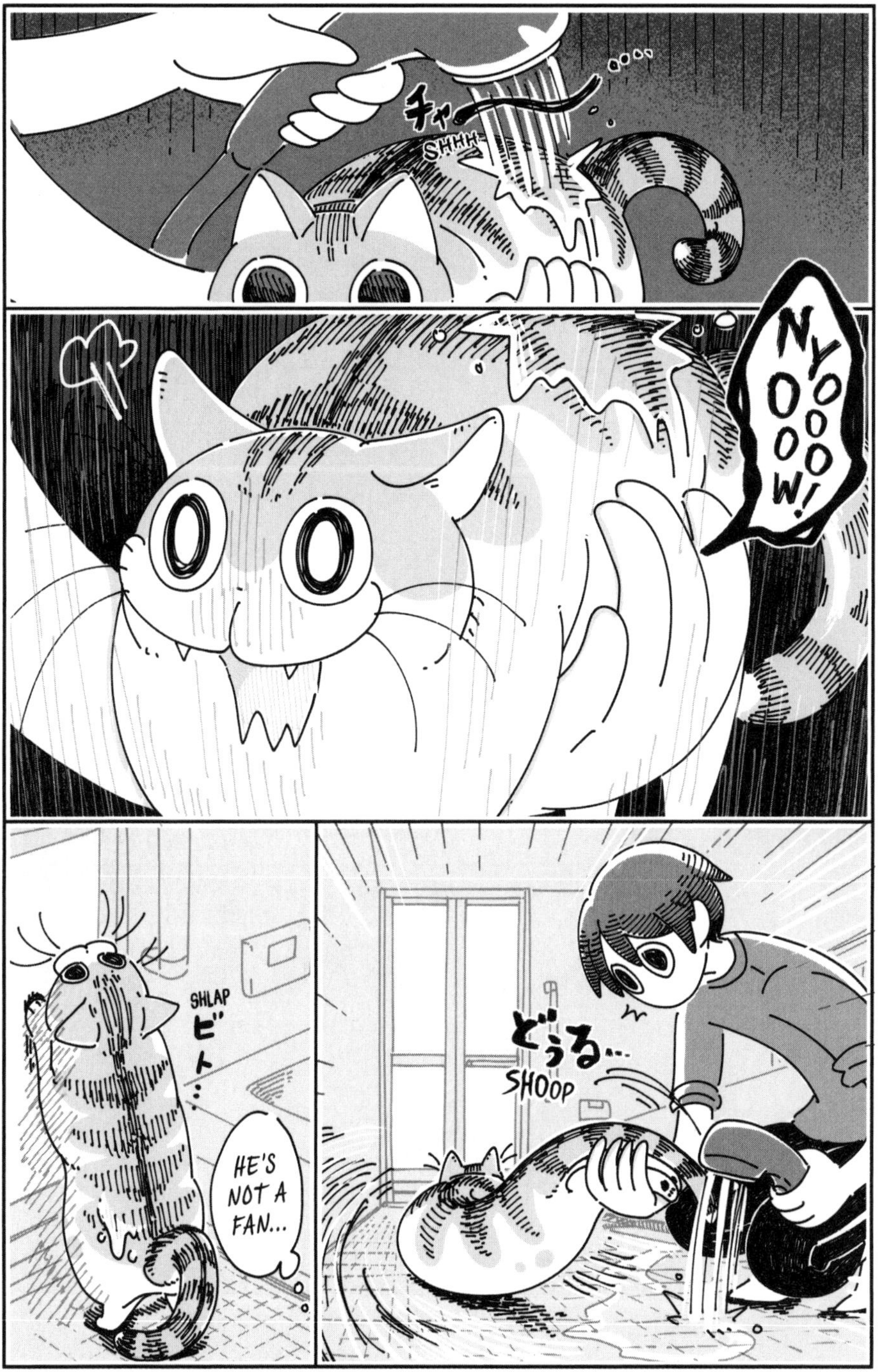
チャ
SHHH
NYOOOOOW!
どぅる…
SHOOP
ビん…
SHLAP
HE'S NOT A FAN...

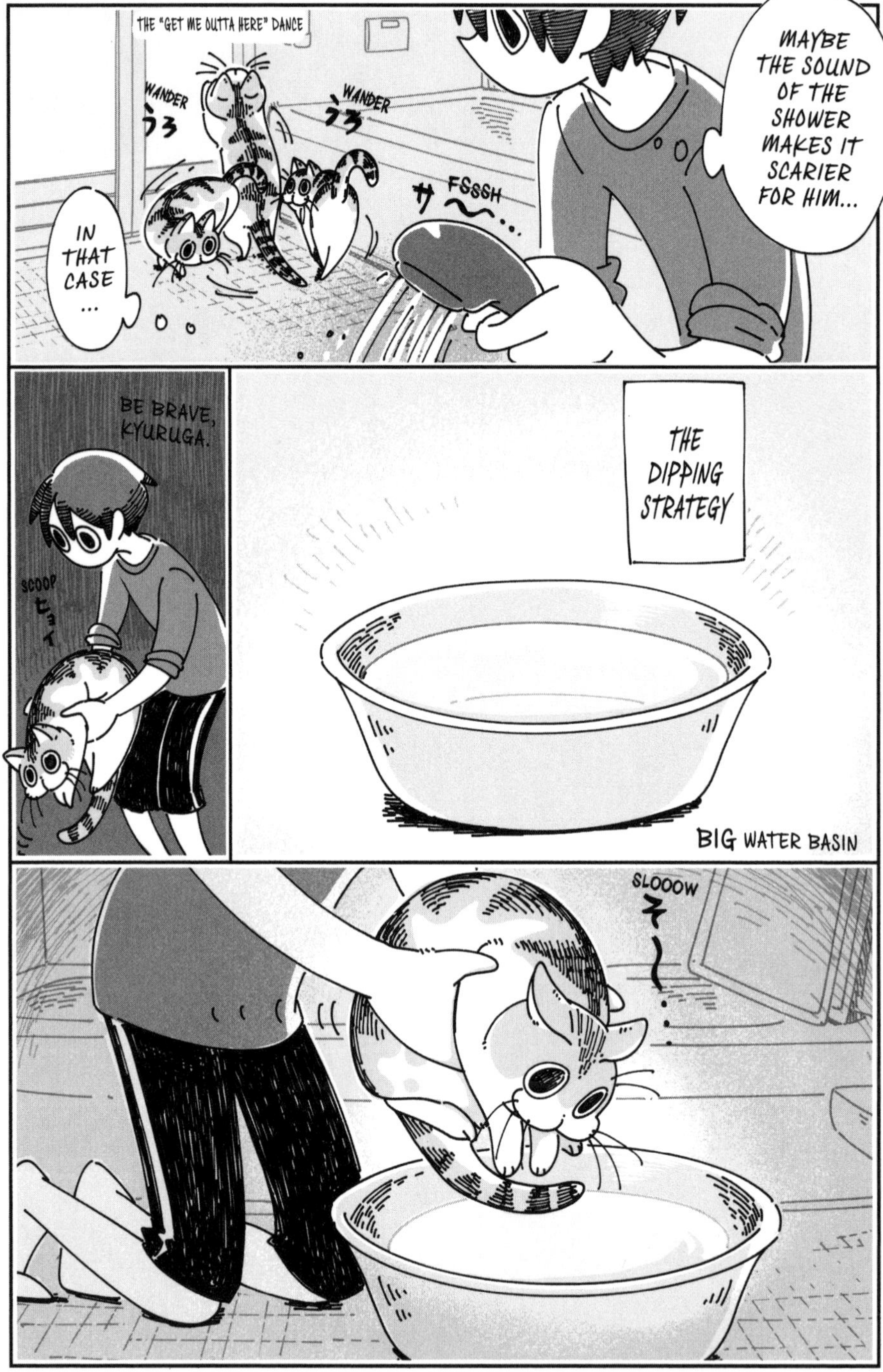
MAYBE THE SOUND OF THE SHOWER MAKES IT SCARIER FOR HIM...
THE "GET ME OUTTA HERE" DANCE
WANDER うろ
WANDER うろ
FSSSH サ〜...
IN THAT CASE...
THE DIPPING STRATEGY
BIG WATER BASIN
BE BRAVE, KYURUGA.
SCOOP ヒョイ
SLOOOW そ〜...

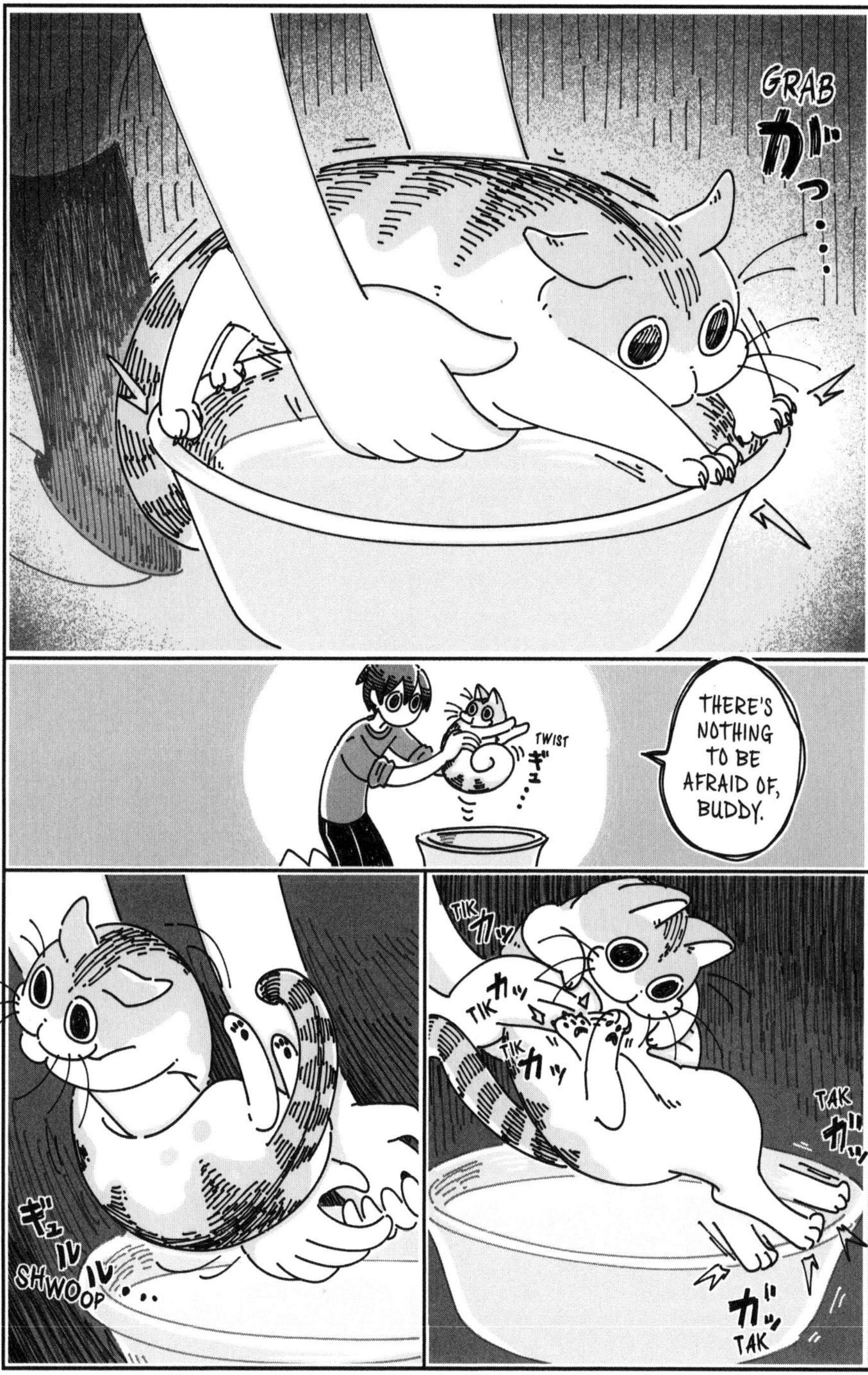
GRAB
がっ…
TWIST
ギュ…
THERE'S NOTHING TO BE AFRAID OF, BUDDY.
TIK
カッ
TIK
カッ
TIK
カッ
TAK
ガッ
ガッ
TAK
ギュルル…
SHWOOP

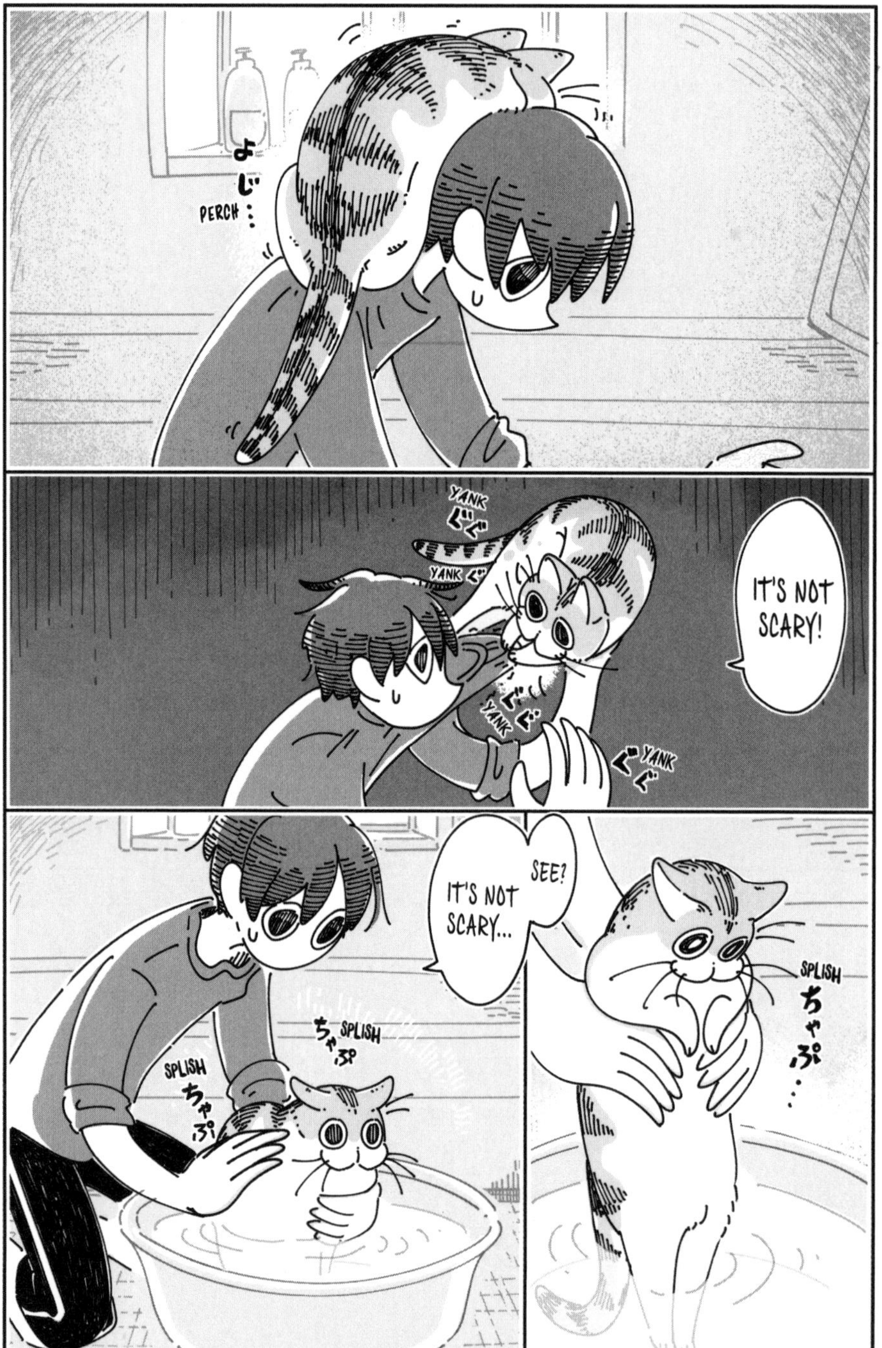
よじ
PERCH...
YANK
ぐぐ
YANK ぐ
IT'S NOT SCARY!
ぐぐ
YANK
ぐぐ
YANK
SEE?
IT'S NOT SCARY...
SPLISH
ちゃぷ...
SPLISH
ちゃぷ
SPLISH
ちゃぷ

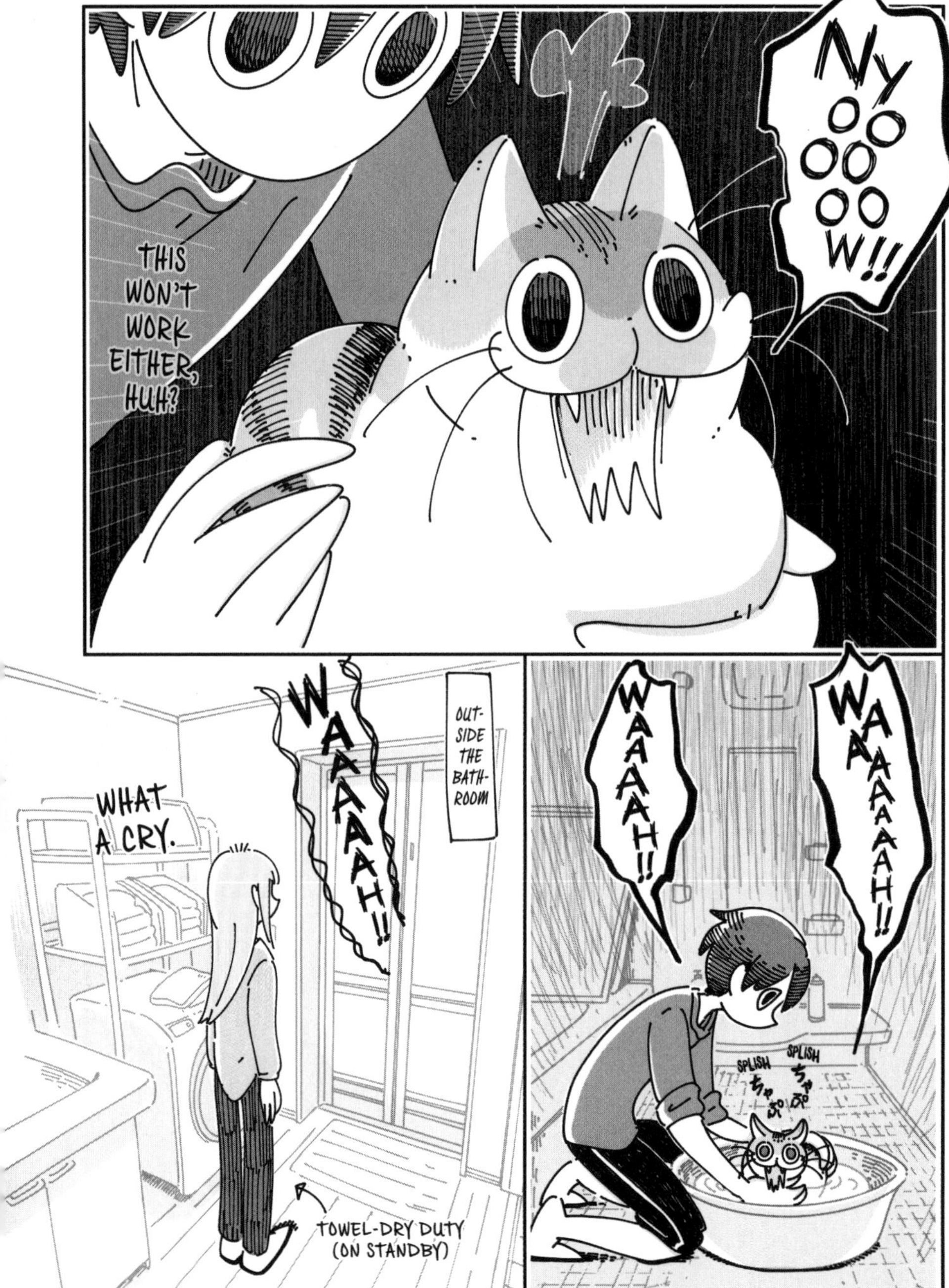
NYOOOOOOOOW!!
THIS WON'T WORK EITHER, HUH?
WAAAAAAAAH!!
WAAAAH!!
SPLISH
ちゃぷ
SPLISH
ちゃぷ
OUTSIDE THE BATHROOM
WAAAAAH!!
WHAT A CRY.
TOWEL-DRY DUTY (ON STANDBY)

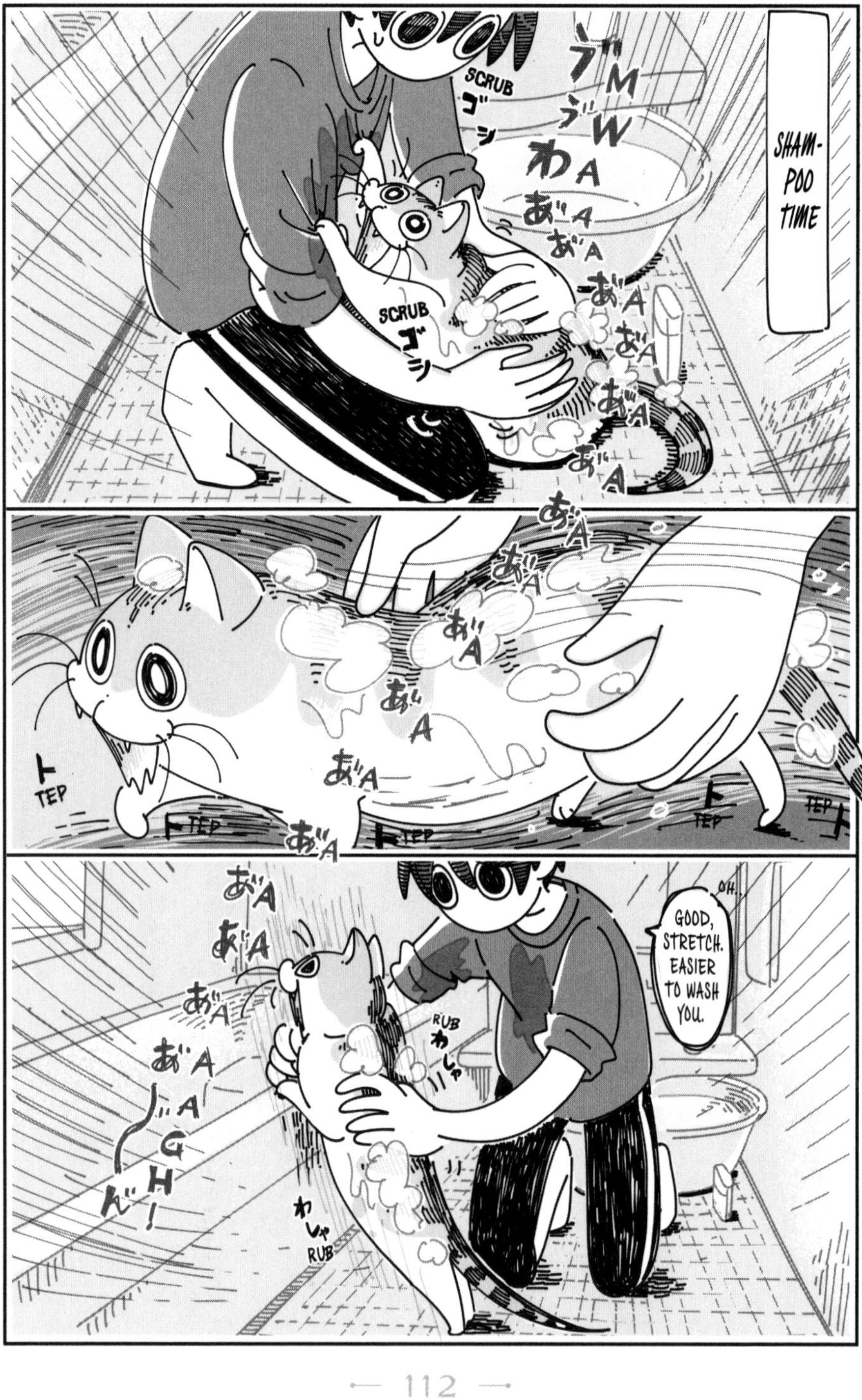
SHAM-POO TIME
SCRUB ゴシ
ブMW
わA
あ゛A
あ゛A
あ゛A
あ゛A
あ゛A
あ゛A
SCRUB ゴシ
あ゛A
あ゛A
あ゛A
あ゛A
あ゛A
あ゛A
あ゛A
ト TEP
ト TEP
ト TEP
ト TEP
ト TEP
OH..
GOOD, STRETCH. EASIER TO WASH YOU.
あ゛A
あ゛A
あ゛A
あ゛A
AGH! ん゛!
RUB わしゃ
わしゃ RUB

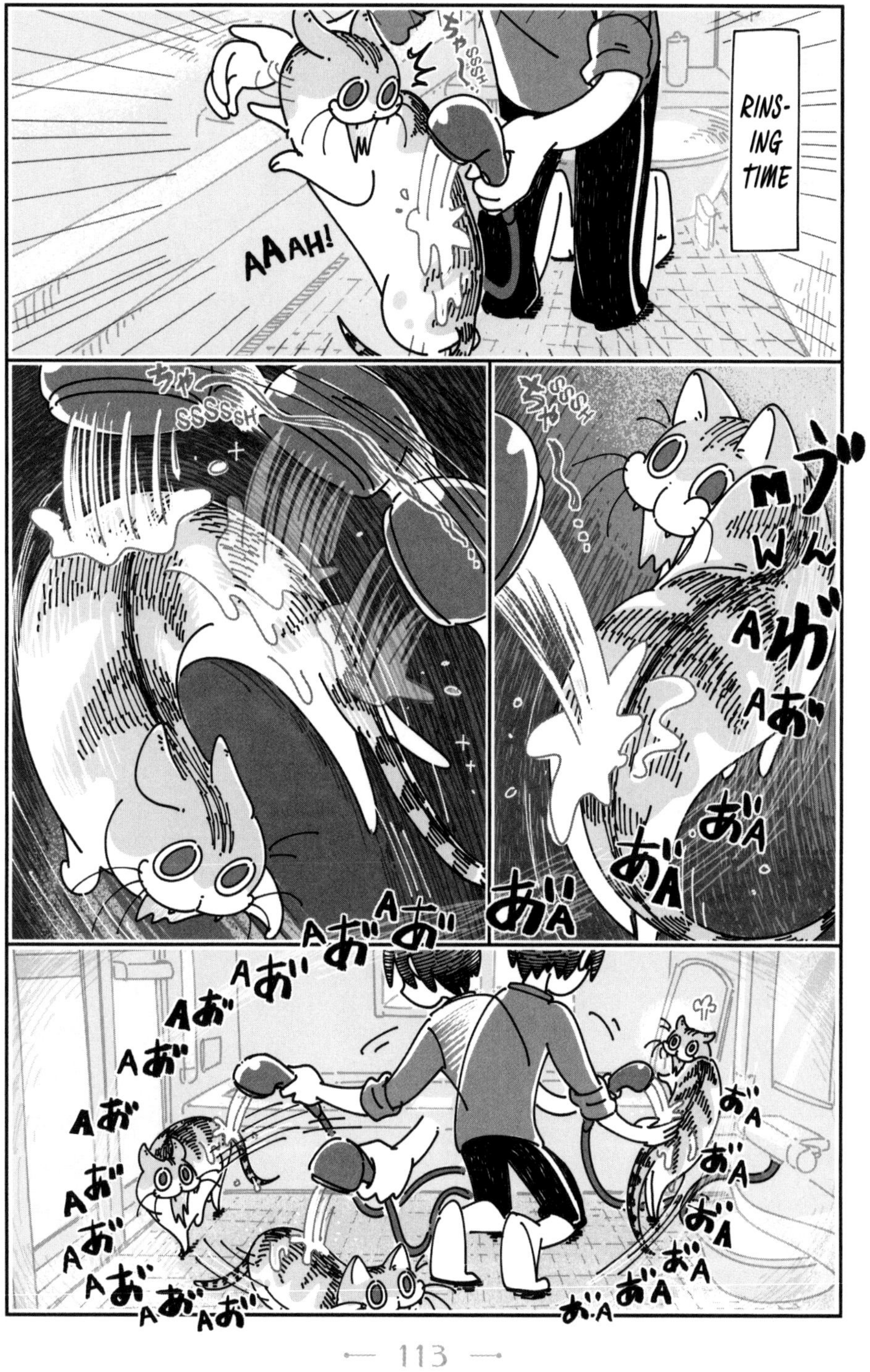
RINS-ING TIME
ちゃ～
SSSH
AAAH!
ちゃ～
SSSH
ぶんげあ
MWAA
あAあAあA
ちゃ～
SSSSSH
AあAあ
AあAあAあAあAあAあAあAあAあ
あAあAあAあAあAあA

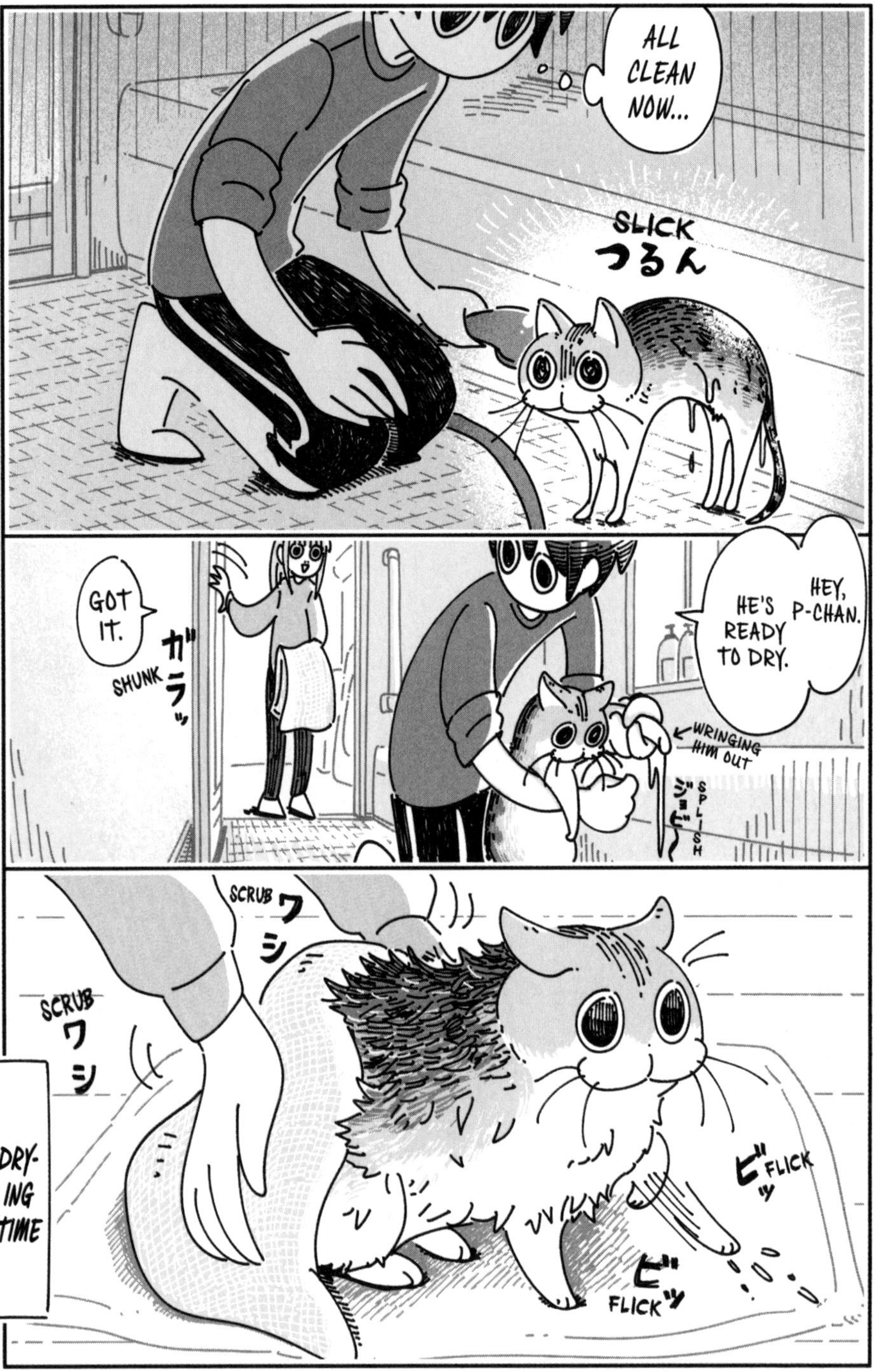
ALL CLEAN NOW...
SLICK
つるん
HEY, P-CHAN. HE'S READY TO DRY.
WRINGING HIM OUT
SPLISH
ジョビ
GOT IT.
SHUNK
ガラッ
SCRUB
ワシ
FLICK
ビッ
FLICK
ビッ
SCRUB
ワシ
DRY-ING TIME

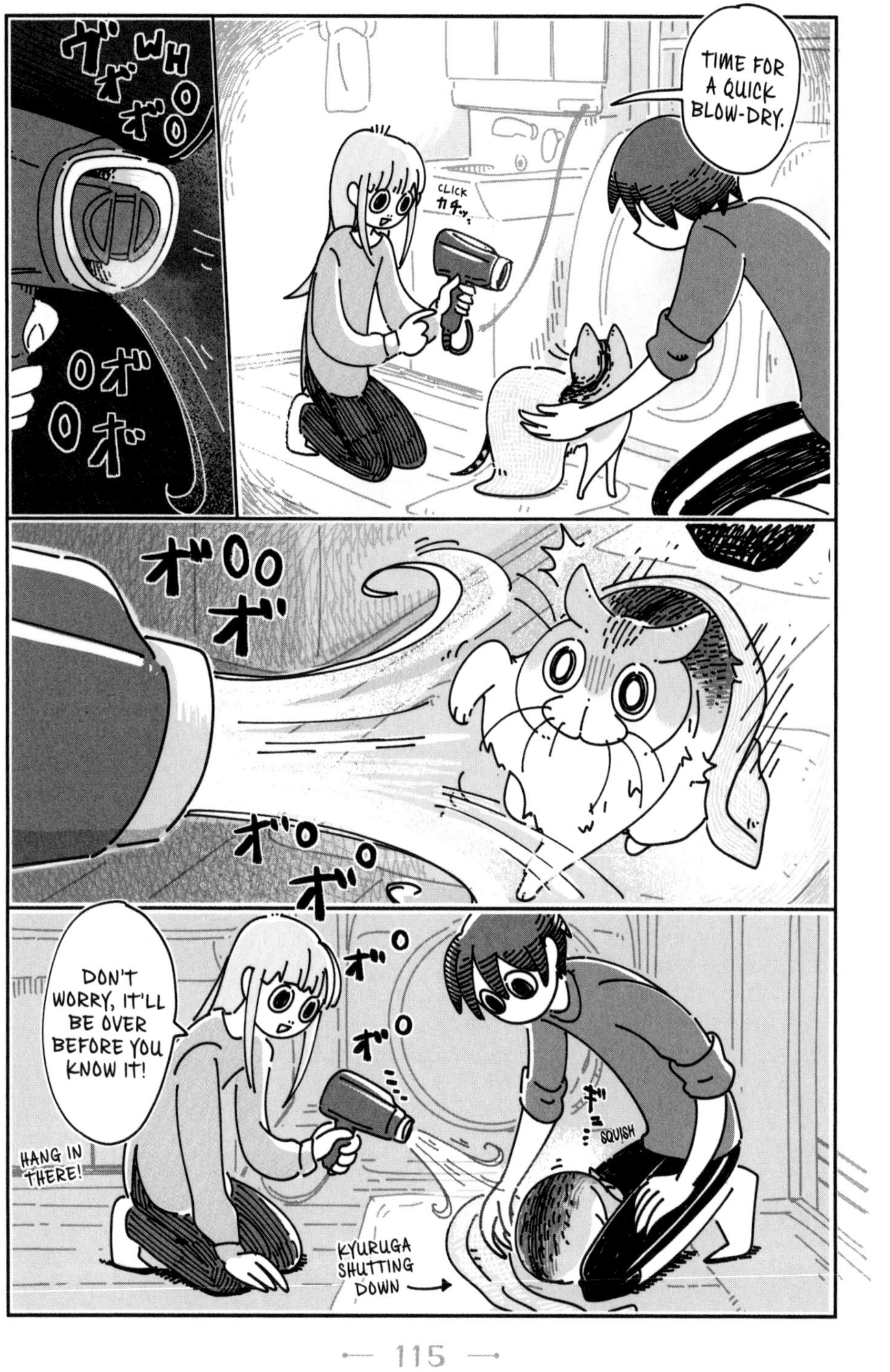
TIME FOR A QUICK BLOW-DRY.
CLICK
カチッ
WHOOO
ヴォオオ
オオ
オオ
オオオ
オオオ
ギュ
SQUISH
オオオ
DON'T WORRY, IT'LL BE OVER BEFORE YOU KNOW IT!
HANG IN THERE!
KYURUGA SHUTTING DOWN →

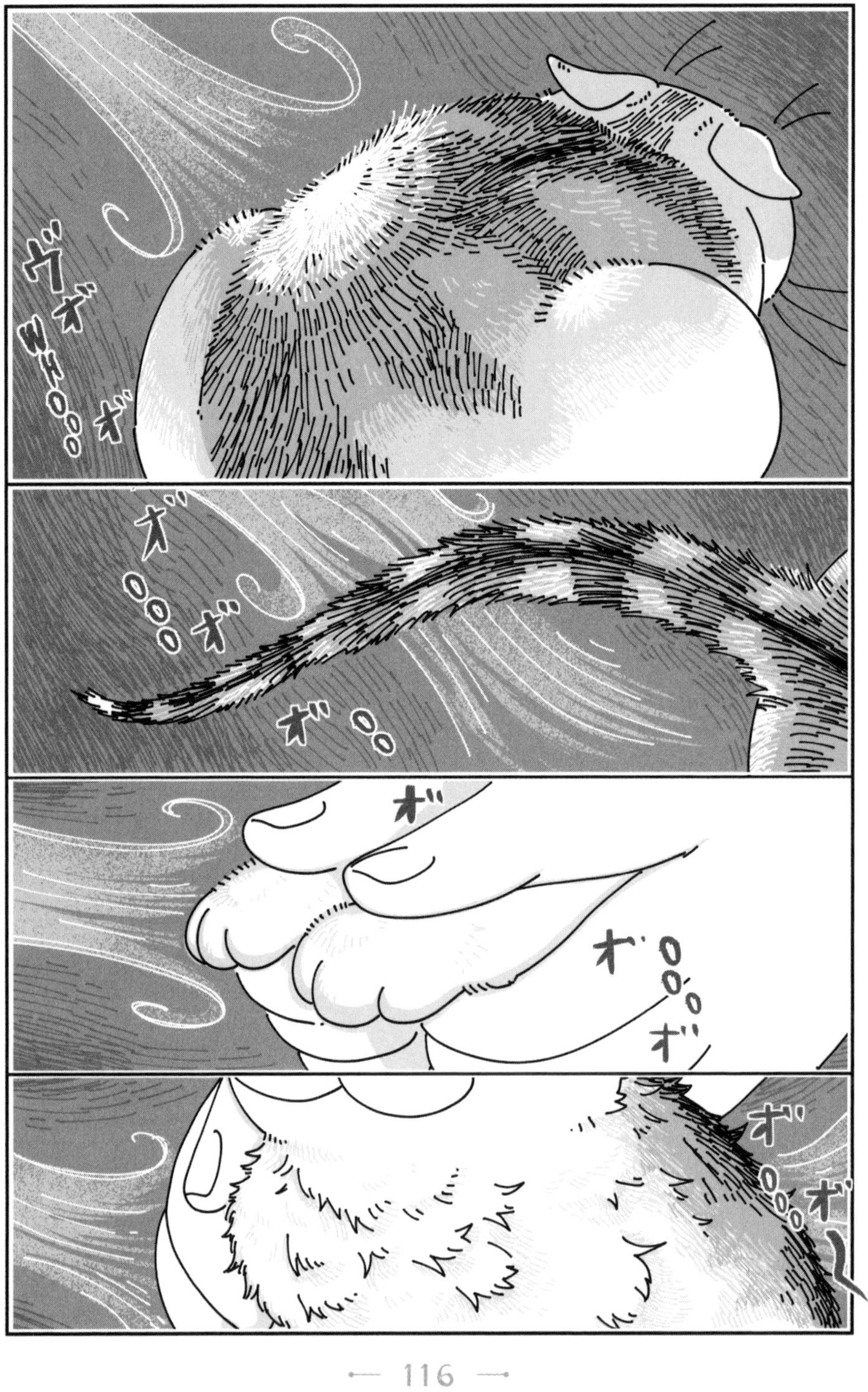
ヴオ゙
WHOOO
オ゙
オ゙
OOO
オ゙
オ゙
OO
オ゙
オ゙
OOO
オ゙
オ゙
OOO
オ゙〜

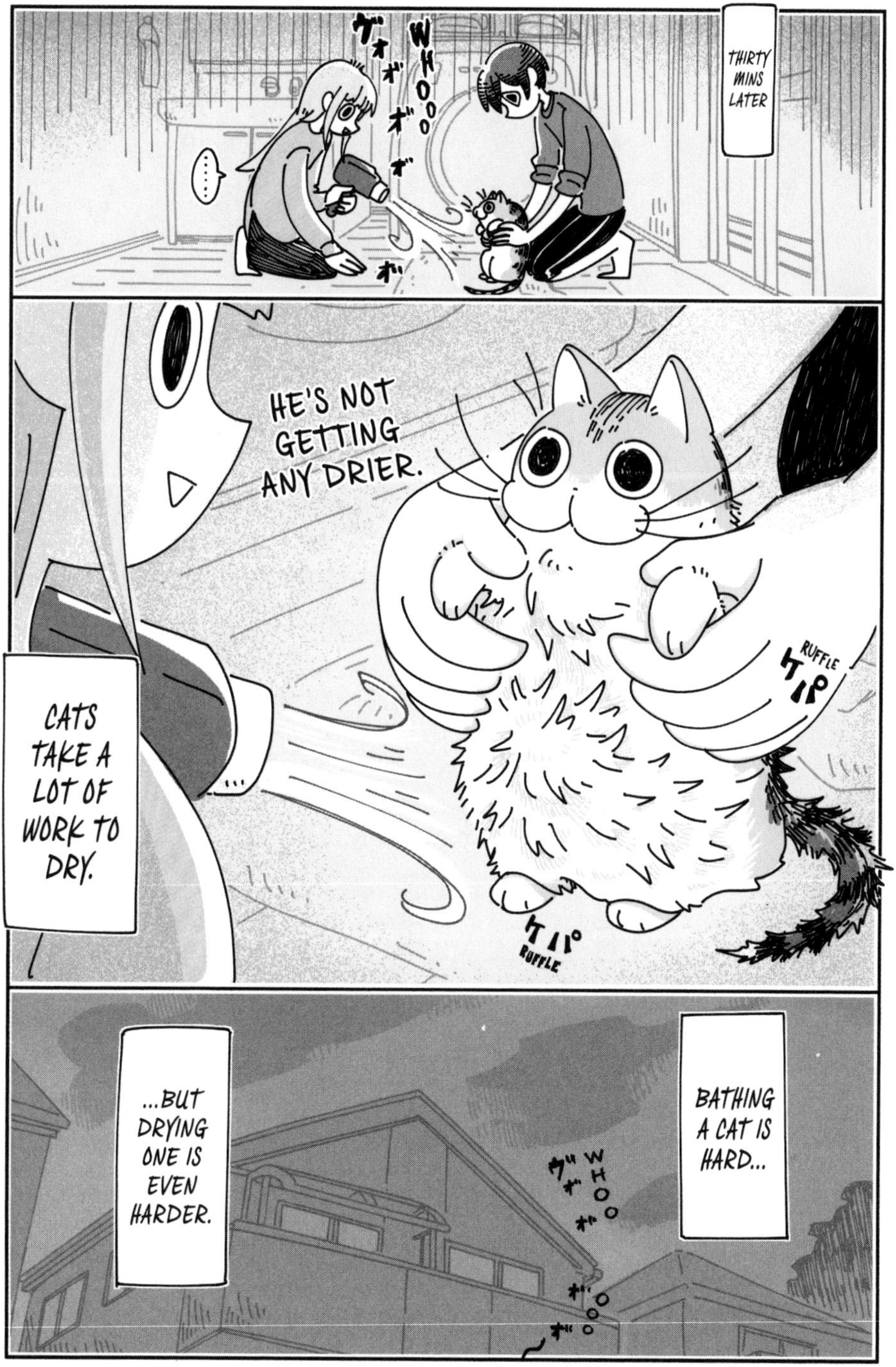
THIRTY MINS LATER
WHOOO
...
RUFFLE
HE'S NOT GETTING ANY DRIER.
CATS TAKE A LOT OF WORK TO DRY.
RUFFLE
BATHING A CAT IS HARD...
WHOOO
...BUT DRYING ONE IS EVEN HARDER.

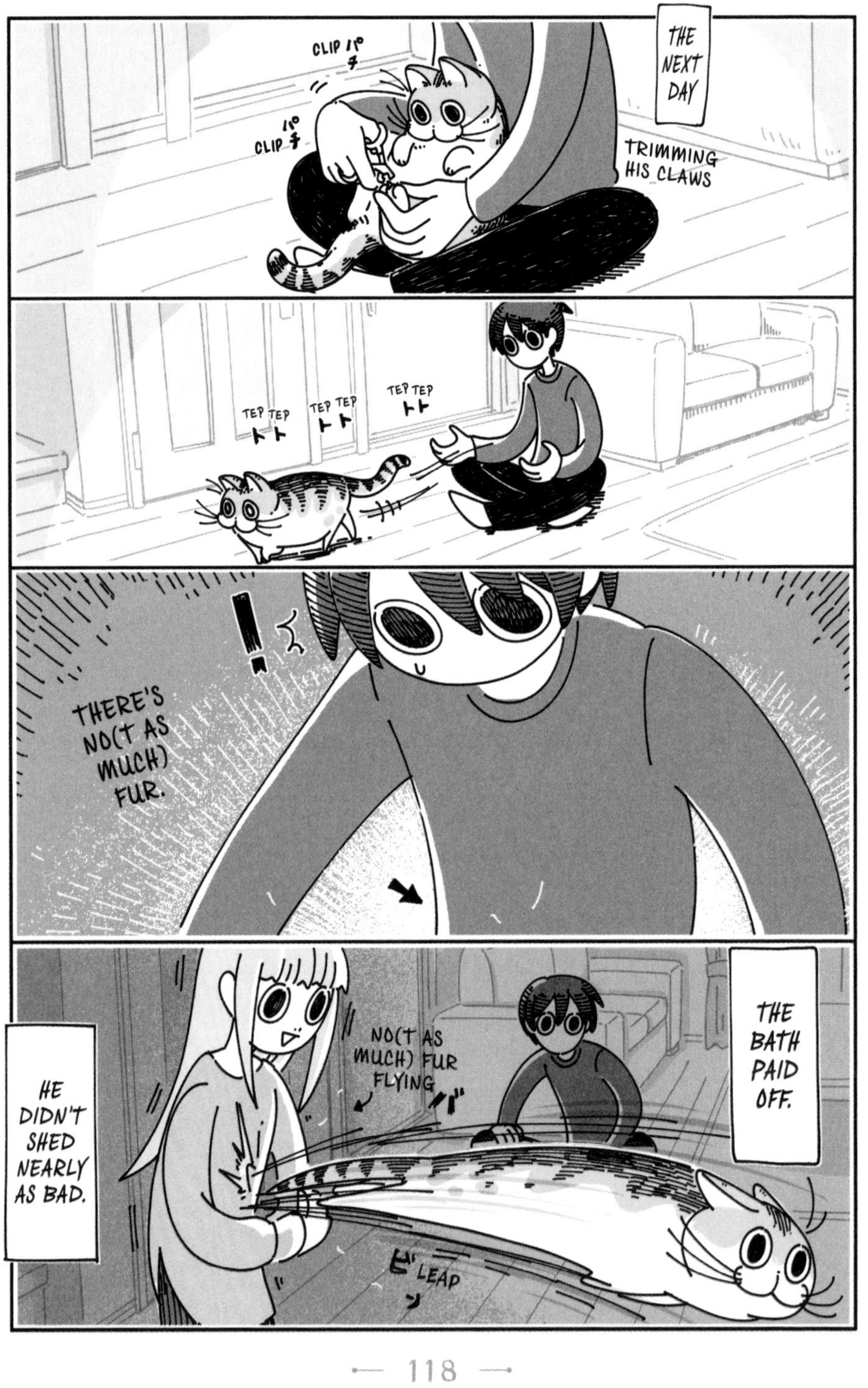
THE NEXT DAY
TRIMMING HIS CLAWS
CLIP パチ
CLIP パチ
TEP TEP トト
TEP TEP トト
TEP TEP トト
!
THERE'S NO(T AS MUCH) FUR.
THE BATH PAID OFF.
NO(T AS MUCH) FUR FLYING
ビッ LEAP
HE DIDN'T SHED NEARLY AS BAD.

Character Purrofiles

FUUTA-KUN
WORKING ADULT

SIBLINGS

P-CHAN
STUDENT.
FUUTA'S SISTER.

KYURUGA
LONG-LEGGED
MUNCHKIN

Sleeping with Kyuruga

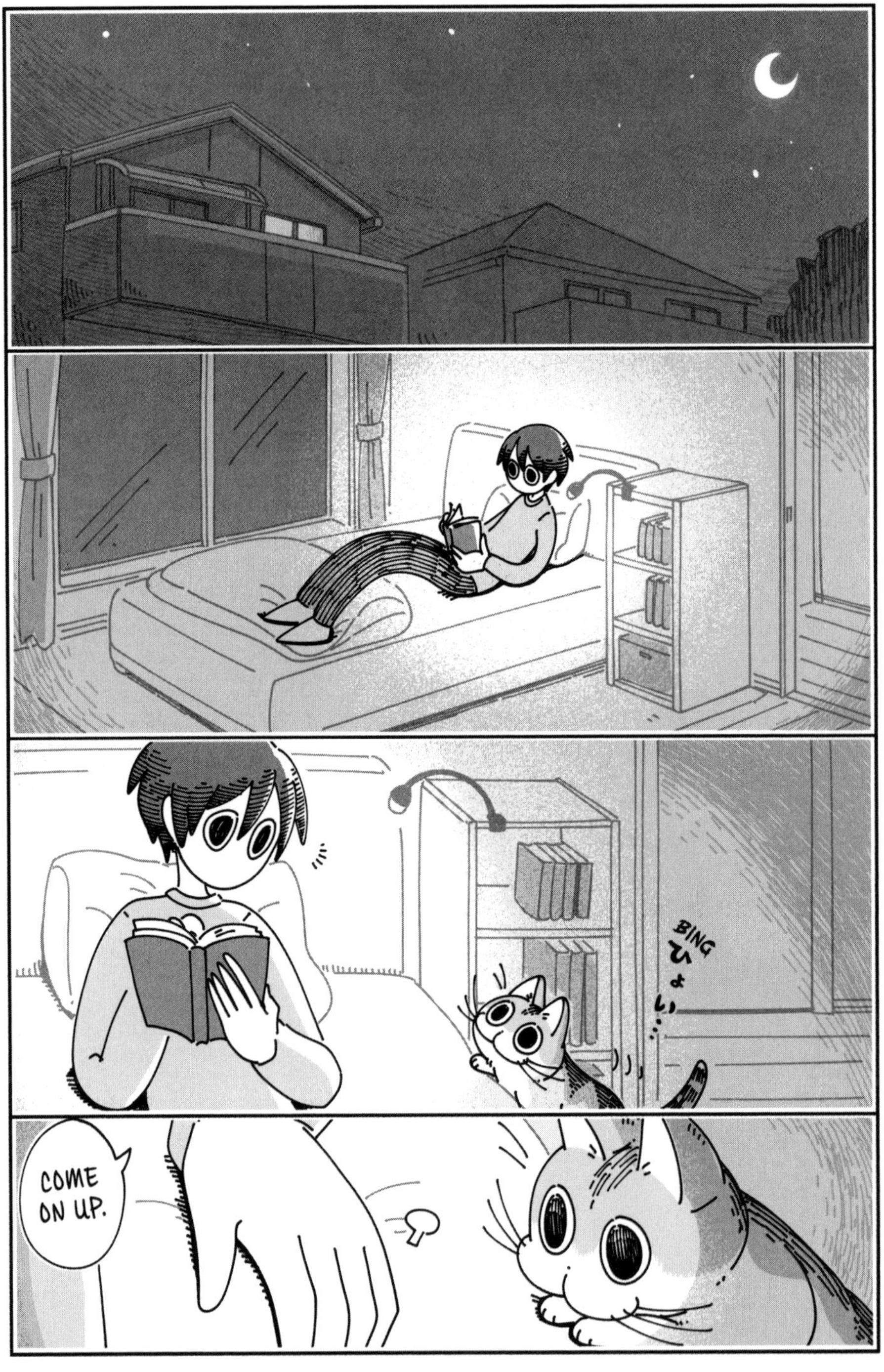
BING
ひょい
COME ON UP.

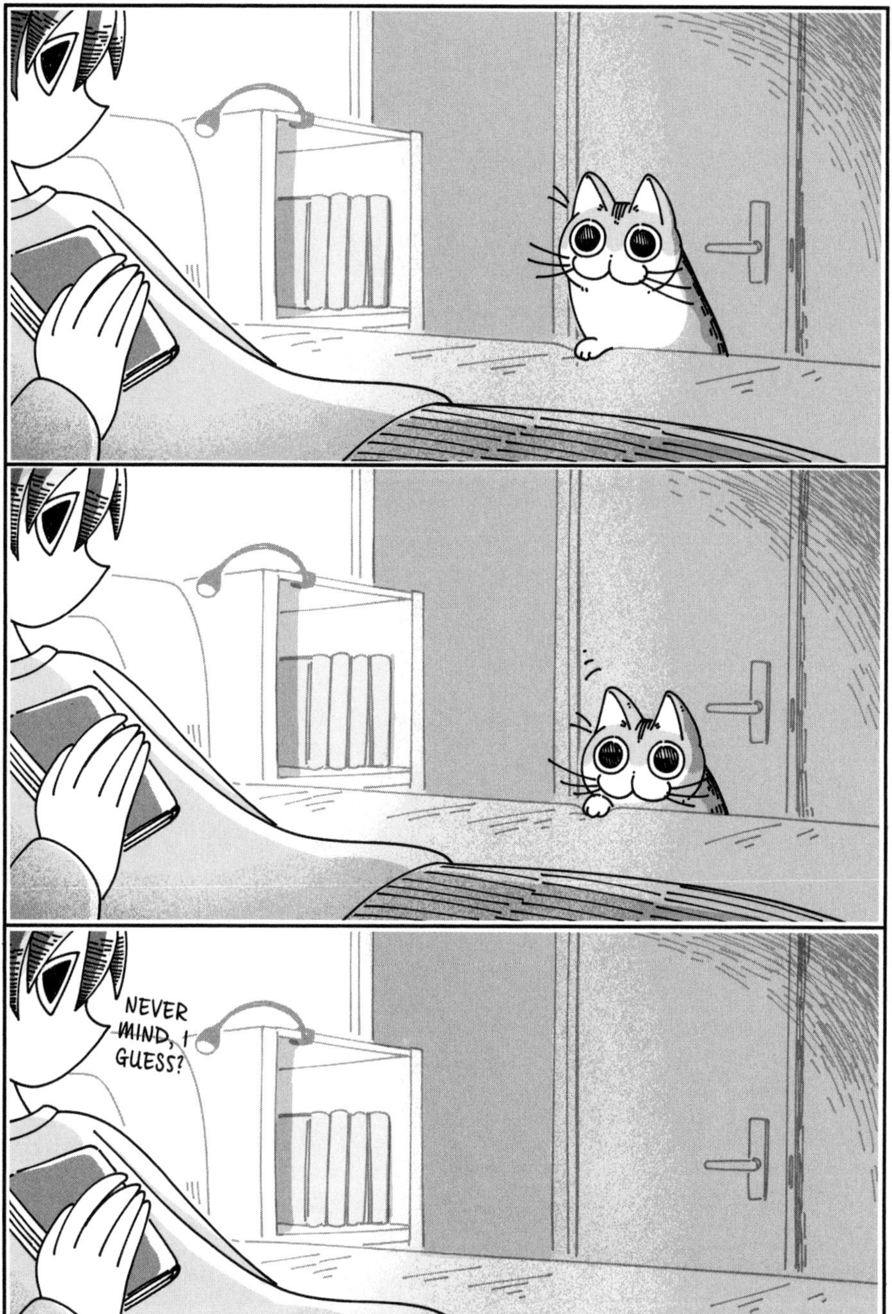
NEVER MIND, I GUESS?

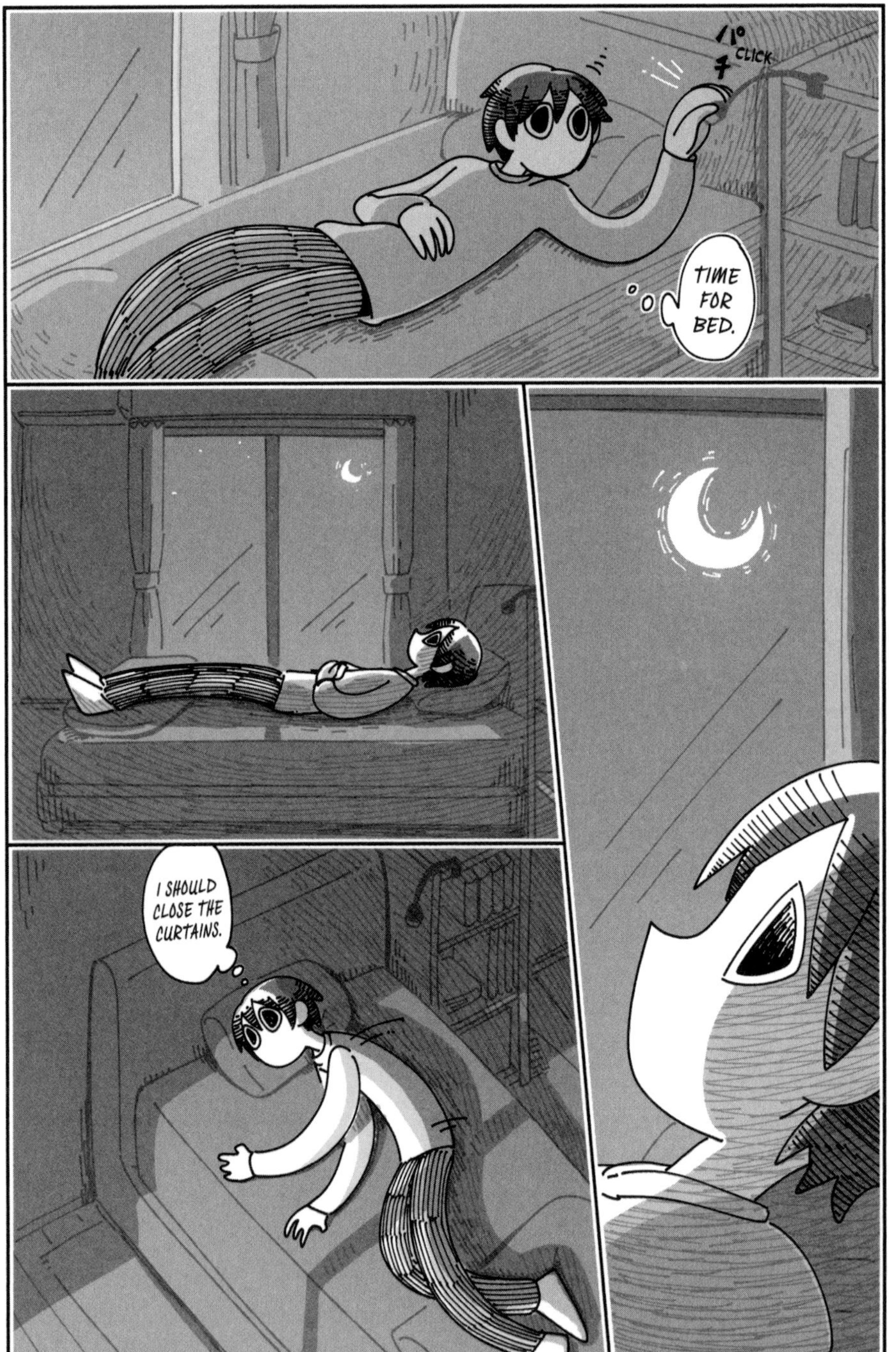
パチ
CLICK
TIME FOR BED.
I SHOULD CLOSE THE CURTAINS.

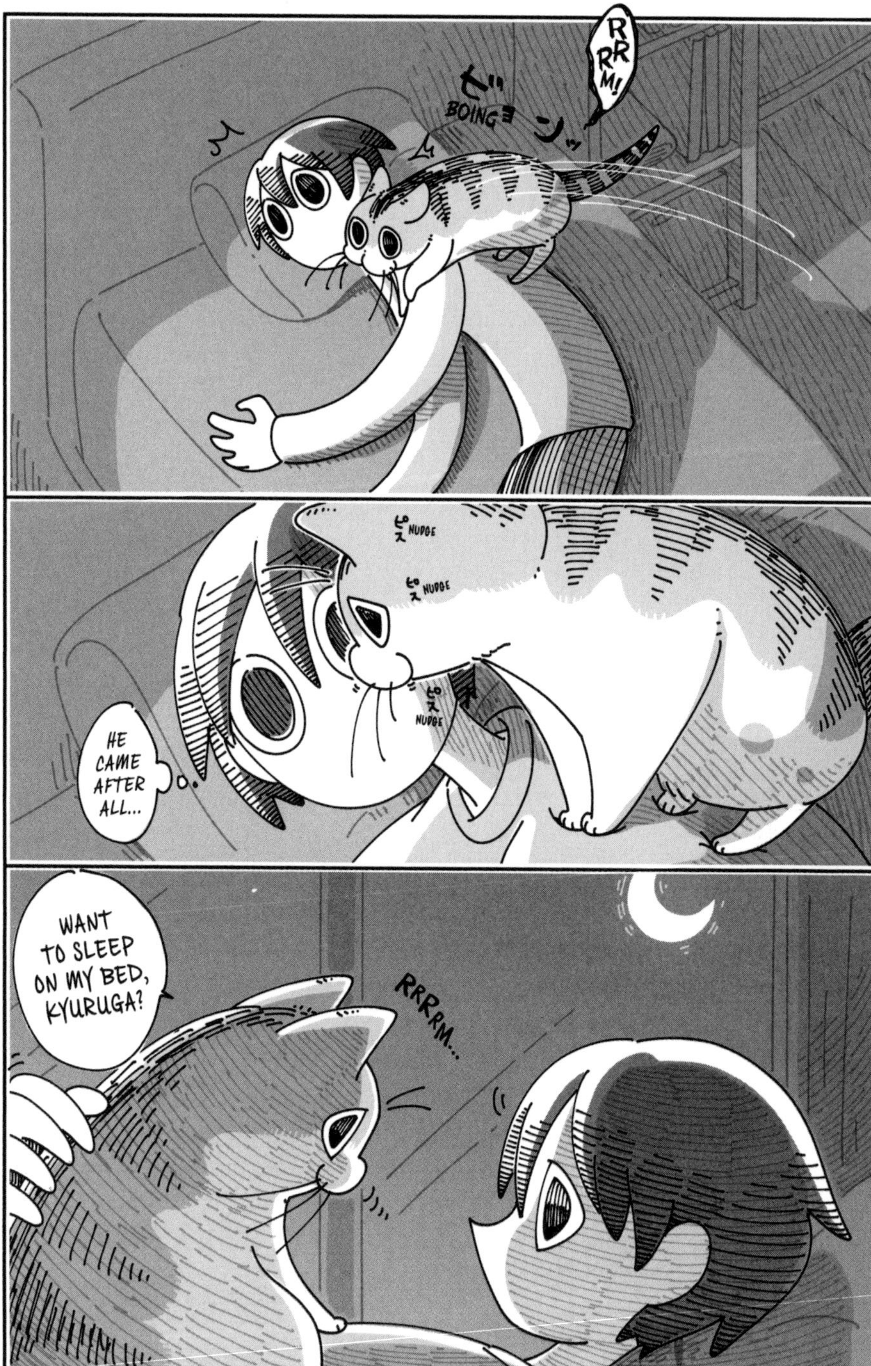
RRRM!
びょンッ
BOING
ピス NUDGE
ピス NUDGE
ピス NUDGE
HE CAME AFTER ALL...
WANT TO SLEEP ON MY BED, KYURUGA?
RRRRM...

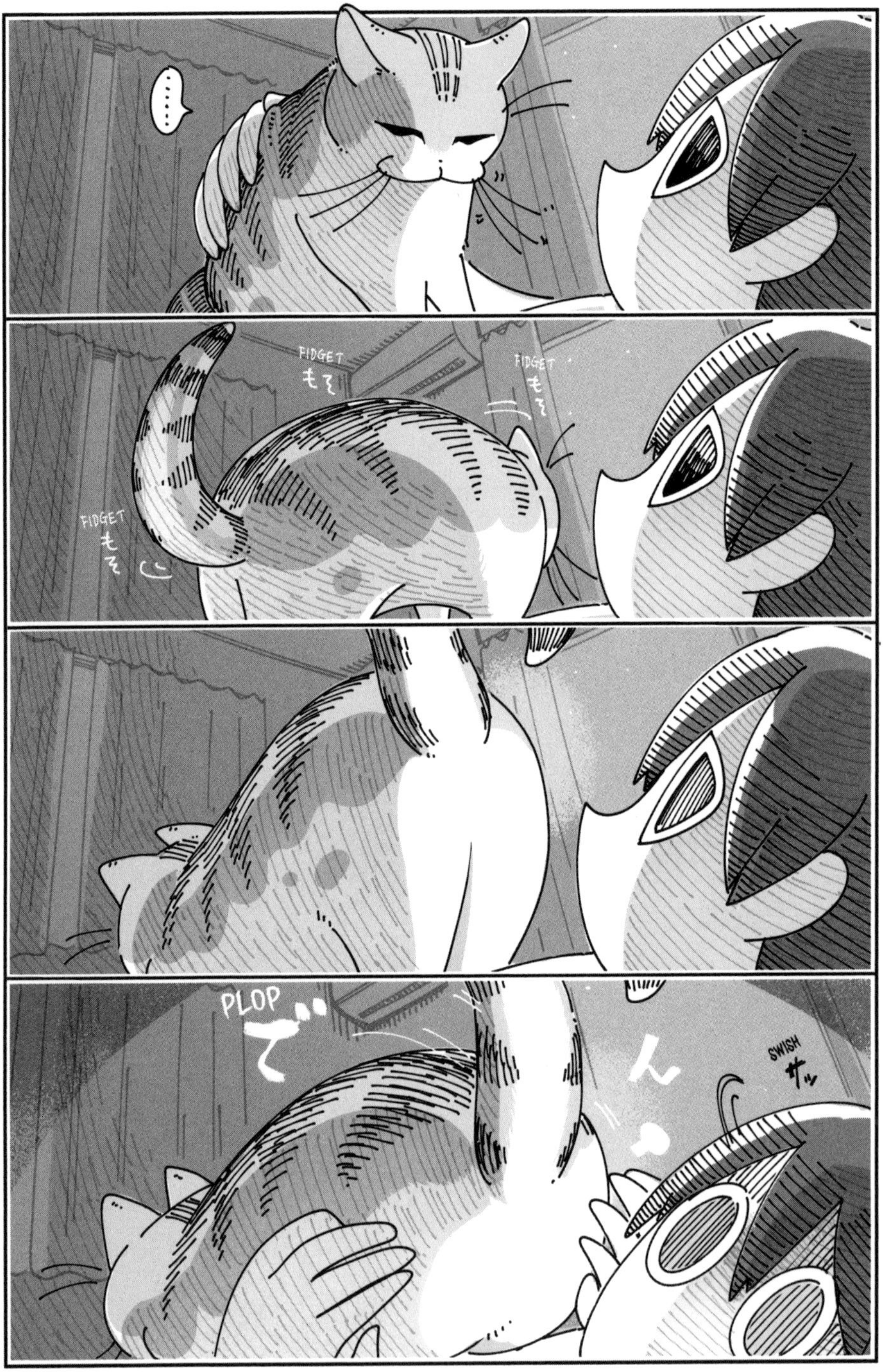
……
FIDGET もぞ
FIDGET もぞ
FIDGET もぞ
SWISH サッ
PLOP でん

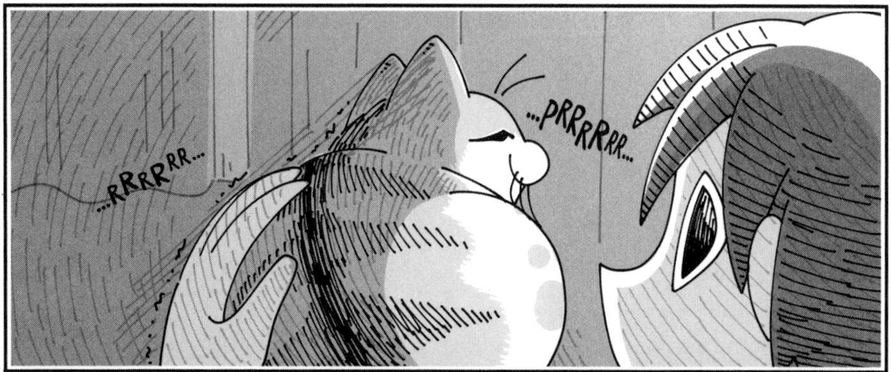
...PRRRRRR...
...RRRRRR...

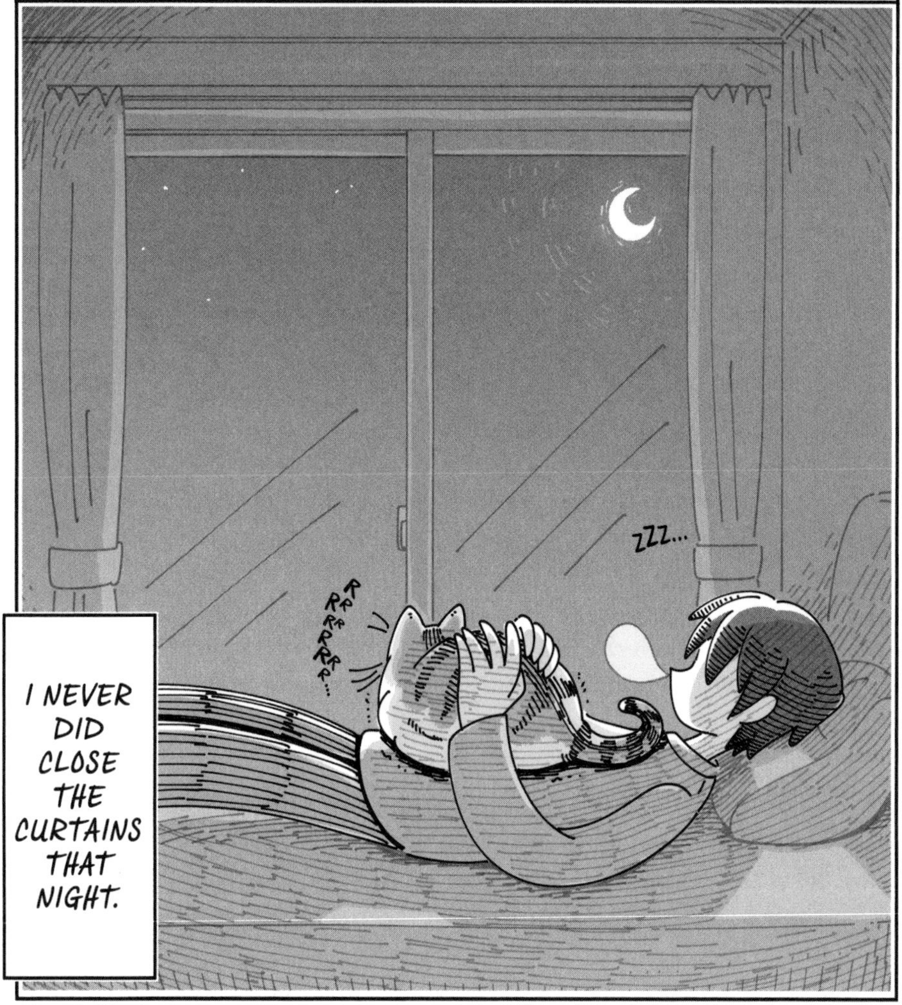
ZZZ...
RRRRRRRR...
I NEVER DID CLOSE THE CURTAINS THAT NIGHT.

Afterword

Hello. This is Kyuryu Z.
Thank you so much for reading my manga.

Never in my wildest dreams did I imagine that a manga I drew
would actually see print. I am truly grateful to all my readers
and everyone who helped get this published.

I started drawing about Kyuruga six years ago and posted
that first chapter on an illustration message board, which
ended up becoming the spark for an entire series. I posted
other chapters there from time to time for a couple of
years, but now I host them on my blog and Twitter.

Sometimes people ask me if this series is fiction or nonfiction.
Basically, it's a fictional manga based on real experiences.
I draw about things that actually happened, but none of the
characters are real people. They're sort of like simplified
projections of my family and me.

Kyuruga is also (very closely) modeled after my own cat.
The barcode-scan and gochujang incidents both really happened.

I've lived with animals at many different points in my life, and I find living with cats especially strange and enjoyable. Even after spending the last six or seven years with one, I still feel like I barely understand anything about them and get blown away by new discoveries on a regular basis. But even though many of his behaviors are still a mystery to me and I have no insight about what's going on inside his head, I love everything about him.

If reading this manga got you even a little bit curious about the sheer weirdness of cats, or made you want to hang out with one, or reminded you of your own, then that would just make my day.

Thank you for reading.
I'm going to keep searching for all sorts of wonderful new discoveries about cats.

Kyuryu Z

Nights with a Cat 1

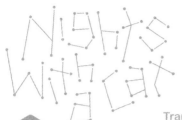

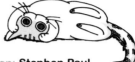

KYURYU Z

Translation: **Stephen Paul**

Lettering: **Lys Blakeslee**

YORU WA NEKO TO ISSHO Vol 1

First published in Japan in 2020 by KADOKAWA CORPORATION, Tokyo
English translation rights arranged with KADOKAWA CORPORATION, Tokyo through Tuttle-Mori Agency, Inc.

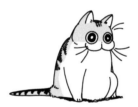

Yen Press
150 West 30th Street, 19th Floor
New York, NY 10001

Visit us at yenpress.com
facebook.com/yenpress
twitter.com/yenpress
yenpress.tumblr.com
instagram.com/yenpress

First Yen Press Edition: July 2022

Edited by Yen Press Editorial: Riley Pearsall, JuYoun Lee
Designed by Yen Press Design: Andy Swist

Yen Press is an imprint of Yen Press, LLC.
The Yen Press name and logo are trademarks of Yen Press, LLC.

The publisher is not responsible for websites (or their content) that are not owned by the publisher.

Library of Congress Control Number: 2022934326

ISBNs: 978-1-9753-4169-5 (paperback)
978-1-9753-4170-1 (ebook)

10 9 8 7 6 5 4 3 2 1

LSC-C

Printed in the United States of America

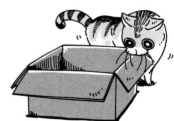